David Alex Jones

CONSTITUTION AVENUE

A Novel

Text Copyright 2024
David Alex Jones and
Apparently Normal Publishing

All Rights Reserved, including the right to reproduce this book, or portions thereof, in any form. No part of this text may be reproduced, transmitted, downloaded, decompiled, reverse engineered, or stored in or introduced into any information storage and retrieval system, in any form, or by any means, whether electronic or mechanical, without the express written permission of the author. The scanning, uploading, and distribution of this book via the Internet or via any other means without the permission of the publisher is illegal and punishable by law. Please purchase only authorized electronic editions and do not participate in, or encourage, electronic piracy of copyrighted materials.

Cover Art by SelfPub Book Covers
Published by:
Apparently Normal Publishing
Waterloo, Ontario, Canada

ISBN (Paperback Edition): 978-1-7388205-3-5
Version 2025.04.15

ALSO BY DAVID ALEX JONES

The Survivor Trilogy

Walls (Book One)
Faces (Book Two)
Spirits (Book Three)
Angela's Eyes (Prequel)

The Survivor Trilogy (eBook Collection)

Standalone

The Night Class

Watch for more at DavidAlexJones.com.

LAND ACKNOWLEDGEMENT

This book was written in Southwestern Ontario, Canada, on land located within the Haldimand Tract, land that was granted to the Haudenosaunee of the Six Nations of the Grand River, and is within the shared traditional territory of the Neutral, Anishinaabe, and Haudenosaunee peoples.

FOREWORD

Constitution Avenue is a work of fiction. Any references to real-life characters, documents, locations, and events are made only to provide historical or political context, and are used fictitiously. The remaining characters and events in this book, like any other work of fiction, are drawn from a multitude of life experiences. Those characters are a composite of tiny snippets of physical or psychological characteristics drawn from a lifetime of interactions with a multitude of people. Thus, any significant resemblance of the fictional characters in this story to real-life persons, dead or alive, is purely coincidental.

In addition, every effort has been made to make characters of different races, portrayed in this story, realistic enough to make the story believable. However, in no way does the author claim to be an authentic voice for people of those races.

ACKNOWLEDGEMENTS

During the long process of researching and writing *Constitution Avenue*, there are always many people whose contributions help to grow an idea into a story. In this case, I would like to thank the large number of friends who sent a very clear message as to which art I should use on the book's cover. A huge vote of thanks also goes out to Alexa Dupuis-Bissonnette, who edited a large chunk of the manuscript and helped me to eliminate quite a few bad writing habits that I had picked up along the way. Most of all, a huge thank you goes out to my loving wife, Peggy, for her ongoing patience and support during the research, writing, and editing process.

Last, but certainly not least, a huge vote of thanks goes to you, the reader, for reading *Constitution Avenue*. Independent authors, like myself, depend on your reviews and your word-of-mouth recommendations of our books to others. So, thank you for purchasing this book and for recommending it to your friends, neighbours, colleagues, and even your book club and your local library. And finally, thank you for taking a few minutes at the end of this book to review it, and to tell potential readers what you liked best about this story.

TABLE OF CONTENTS

ALSO BY DAVID ALEX JONES	ii
LAND ACKNOWLEDGEMENT	iii
FOREWORD	iv
ACKNOWLEDGEMENTS	v
TABLE OF CONTENTS	vi
PROLOGUE	1
A TEA PARTY	2
A SERENDIPITOUS MEETING	7
THE GREAT COMPROMISE	12
CHAPTER 1—A FISH CALLED RACHEL	19
CHAPTER 2—FREEDOM OF SPEECH	32
CHAPTER 3—CAMP DAVID	45
CHAPTER 4—AND I'M TAYLOR SWIFT	55
CHAPTER 5—CRANBERRY FLATS	73
CHAPTER 6—REUNION	85
CHAPTER 7—ULTIMATUM	111
CHAPTER 8—VODKA SHOTS	124
CHAPTER 9—ISLANDS IN THE STREAM	149
CHAPTER 10—Q-SORT	169
CHAPTER 11—THE SHADOW	185

CHAPTER 12—SPIES IN THE NIGHT	209
CHAPTER 13—BREAKDOWN	226
CHAPTER 14—NOTHIN' BUT THE TAIL LIGHTS	255
CHAPTER 15—CHANGING TIDE	277
CHAPTER 16—COME TOGETHER	289
CHAPTER 17—BUSINESS AS USUAL	296
CHAPTER 18—NEW BEGINNING	318
CHAPTER 19—GEORGIAN BAY	325
EPILOGUE—COMPLICATED SHADOWS	331
ABOUT THE AUTHOR	335
DON'T MISS OUT	336
SNEAK PEEK	337
ALSO BY DAVID ALEX JONES	338

PROLOGUE

DAVID ALEX JONES

A TEA PARTY

Boston, Massachusetts
December 13, 1773

THE TEMPERATURE dropped quickly as dusk fell over a cloudless Boston in late autumn. An orange glow painted the western sky as the sun crept relentlessly towards the horizon, the eastern sky foreshadowing the deepening blue to come. Thousands of citizens of Boston made their way to the Old South Meeting House, once a house of worship, near the city's Liberty Tree. Mixed into the crowd were merchants, traders, British Loyalists, and religious affiliates. Most easily spotted, however, were the Sons of Liberty, a clandestine and often violent group of radicals, whose campaign for colonial representation in English parliament often led to clashes with the Loyalists. Many of the Sons were dressed that evening like Mohawk warriors, their grim, angry faces disguised by traditional face paints.

Twenty-four hours prior, word spread through the city of an impending town hall meeting and, right on time, a ragtag crowd swelled in front of a makeshift, raised platform in front of the Meeting House. Before long, the mob extended from the Meeting House to the outer edges of the Common. And, as the temperature dropped to just below freezing, a cloud of condensate and frozen breath rose up from the crowd and into the calm night air.

A man emerged from the Meeting house, attired in a fashionable blue waistcoat and britches, white knee-high stockings, polished black buckle shoes, and a powdered wig. Looking out at the bobbing sea of ubiquitous tricorn hats, Samuel Adams made his way to the platform, carrying a large leather megaphone. The crowd of commoners began to acknowledge him with a conflicting mixture of cheers and jeers, so that, unassisted, Adams' voice could not be heard over the din.

"Ahemmm," Adams began, shouting into the giant cone. "Welcome. I express my gratitude to each and every one of you for your attendance."

Unbothered by Adams' attempts to capture the crowd's attention, a significant racket still rolled in from the outer edges of the crowd.

"Order!" Adams shouted. "Order, good citizens of Boston!"

Adams waited for several seconds, then raised the megaphone again.

"Silence, please. I beg for your indulgence."

Signalling for quiet from the crowd, the din finally receded enough for Adams to begin his address.

"Fellow citizens! We are gathered here today, near our Liberty Tree, to share our collective vexation over the actions of His Majesty, King George, and his parliament!"

A large cheer of agreement arose from the majority, interrupted by scattered shouts of "Long live the King" from Loyalists, which were then met with their own taunts from the rest of the gathering.

"I also share your disesteem at the idleness of Governor Hutchinson," Adams continued.

The vast majority of the crowd cheered their agreement.

"Where other cities in our colonies have been able to convince their governors to either abandon their positions and flee to England, to prohibit East India Company ships from unloading their tea shipments, or to dispatch those ships back to England, Governor Hutchinson has steadfastly and repeatedly rejected our pleas," Adams added.

Above the sound of resounding agreement, a single voice boomed from a member of the Sons of Liberty.

"Tar and feather the bastard, I say!"

A huge cheer erupted from the crowd in response, then other members of the clandestine organization began to chant over the crowd noise.

"No taxation without representation! No taxation without representation!"

Adams raised his arms to quell the mob before relying on the megaphone once again.

"I give ear to you!" Adams added. "It is only right that we should have a voice in decisions about our colony. Tell me, what other things grieve you?"

He looked down into the crowd for people who were willing to speak.

"Why can we not establish our own tea trade with China?" shouted a voice near the platform. "What right does the King have to interfere? Why should English Lords get fat from our commerce while we starve?"

The crowd cheered and applauded the voice. Adams pointed to another person in the crowd.

"If they do this to the tea trade, what is to stop them from stealing the remainder of our commerce?" another voice shouted.

"Our King knows best!" shouted a Loyalist voice. "Everything we have in our colony, we have because of King George. We owe him our fealty. God save the King!"

Angry members of the mob responded by jeering and throwing rotten vegetables at the Loyalist.

"Order!" Adams shouted into his megaphone. He signalled the increasingly unruly mob to silence them again. "Lend him your ear. Judge him not, simply because you cross swords with him."

Adams spotted a man in the crowd wearing Puritan attire.

"You, sir. What do you have to say?"

"Taking away our rights to earn a living and to feed ourselves is only the beginning! When will they persecute us and take away our religious freedom as they did in England? When will they deny us our right to gather as we are tonight?"

Loud, extended applause and cheers erupted in response to the Puritan's concerns. Adams waited for a few moments for the crowd noise to abate. While he waited, he caught some movement coming from his right. A small horse-drawn carriage, transporting his personal messenger, moved quickly up a side-street towards the crowd. With a wave of his arms, Adams commanded quiet, then he raised his megaphone.

"I have dispatched an emissary to make one final plea to the Governor. He is returning to us now! Let us hear what he has to say."

As Adams' messenger jumped from the carriage and ran to the stage, competing chants of "Long live the King" and "No taxation without representation" fuelled the mob. The messenger whispered in Adams' ear, and Adams' face fell. He turned to the gathering and an expectant hush descended over the masses.

"I fear the news is not good," Adams began. "The Governor will not see reason and will not relent. He has ordered that *The Dartmouth, The Eleanor,* and *The Beaver* should be unloaded immediately, and he will be summoning troops to oversee the unloading."

Chaos erupted. The competing chants of "No taxation without representation" and "Long live the King" grew louder, and localized skirmishes broke out within the crowd. Adams tried in vain to regain their attention.

"Order, good citizens! ... Order ... Order, please. I beg of you!" he shouted. But he was overpowered by a new chant.

"The King shall pay! Take the tea!"

Almost immediately, another voice chimed in.

"To the wharf! ... Take the tea!"

The chant to take the tea grew exponentially in volume. Suddenly, the leader of the "to the wharf" chant broke from the main crowd, along with a handful of supporters. As they continued their chant, they were joined by a large number of the Sons of Liberty, disguised as Mohawk warriors. The breakaway mob continued to grow until there were nearly a hundred men. Carrying lanterns and torches, they marched towards Griffin's Wharf, where *The Dartmouth, The Eleanor,* and *The Beaver* were docked: so far, only protected by a few guards. Adams could only watch helplessly from the podium.

Finally, Adams motioned to the messenger and they hurried to their carriage.

"This meeting can do nothing further to save the country," he said to the messenger.

Their carriage followed the mass of bobbing tricorn hats, painted faces, torches, and lanterns, as the angry mob swept through the streets towards the harbour in front of them, rapidly approaching the three tea-laden ships. Adams continued to watch helplessly as the mob reached the harbour, where the protesters broke into three groups, quickly overwhelming each ship's poorly-outfitted guards before storming onto the three vessels. Within moments, Adams saw bales of tea flying overboard into the harbour.

He turned to his messenger, his weary face displaying a look of shock and disappointment.

"Remember this day well, my friend. We will pay dearly for what is happening before us. These actions will not go without retribution!"

A SERENDIPITOUS MEETING

London, England
October, 1774

BEN FRANKLIN shivered, then he paused to adjust his black tricorn hat and tighten his heavy overcoat to protect his aging body from London's cold, damp October air. He covered his face with a handkerchief in a fruitless attempt to filter out the grey pall suspended over Leicester Square. Finally, with his destination only a hundred yards ahead, he resumed walking and picked up his pace. As he crossed the street, his walking stick clicked a steady rhythm on the cobblestones.

Once across the street, Ben approached a building with a ladies' dress shop on the main floor. Bypassing the shop's main entrance, he entered a less conspicuous doorway a few paces to the right. Then, using his walking stick for support, he ascended a worn wooden staircase, following in the footsteps of many before him. As he neared the top, his breathing deepened and Ben felt his sixty-nine-year-old heart beating faster in his chest. Finally, he reached the second floor, where he paused to catch his breath. He looked at the numbers on the door of each flat, then walked down the hallway to his left. Still breathing heavily, Ben tapped on a door with his walking stick.

"Coming!" shouted a voice from within the flat.

The door opened with some effort, revealing a carefully groomed elderly gentleman, wearing a blue silk waistcoat, britches, and white stockings. A white powdered wig sat precisely on his head. The buckle on his polished black shoes sparkled. George Edward Scott's face lit up with surprise and joy.

"If it isn't Benjamin Franklin! How good to see you, old friend."

George opened the door wider with one hand, then he shook Ben's hand enthusiastically with the other.

"Wonderful to see you as well, George. How have you been keeping?"

George shrugged his shoulders.

"As well as any old man, I imagine," he said. "I have my good days and bad. Do come in old chap."

As Ben entered the flat, George hung his overcoat and walking stick on the coat tree by the door.

"Can I fetch you something? Tea? A nip of brandy, perhaps?"

"Tea will suffice nicely," Ben replied. He turned around and was surprised to see another man in George's sitting room, already seated in a chair to the right of the fireplace. Unlike George—who was relatively well off, and was well-connected in many different science and art circles, as well as with King George III—this man's clothes were rumpled, threadbare, and far from clean. His shoes were scuffed and seams were beginning to come apart.

"Oh, my! Excuse my manners," George said suddenly. "This is my friend, Mr. Thomas Paine. Thomas, meet my good friend from the Pennsylvania colony, Mr. Benjamin Franklin."

Ben walked across the room and shook hands with Thomas, who had stood to greet him.

"A pleasure to meet you, Mr. Franklin," Thomas said. "I have heard nothing but good things about you."

"You are too kind," Ben replied.

"Have a seat, gentlemen, while I fix some more tea," George said.

Ben sat in a love seat, to the left of the fireplace.

"So, what brings you to London, Mr. Franklin?" Thomas began. "Rumour has it that you have come to meet with the King."

"Word does get around quickly," Ben answered. "Yes, it is no secret that relations between the Colonies and His Highness are most precarious since the uprising in Boston last December. I have been sent to express our grievances to His Highness about his unjust and brutal retaliation to that event."

George returned and set a teacup on a small table beside Ben.

"Ah, yes," Thomas said, nodding his head in acknowledgment. "The Intolerable Acts, prohibiting merchant ships from entering Boston and ending self-government in New England, if I am not mistaken. An unacceptable and inhumane travesty, I maintain. Our monarchy and the aristocracy serve only themselves. They are completely blind to the needs of the common people. I am in complete and utter agreement with the people of the Colonies. They should not be required to pay taxes to support the monarchy and the aristocracy when they receive no benefit whatsoever from those taxes and have no representation in the English parliament!"

"You are well-informed," Ben answered, impressed by the other man's grasp of the current situation in the Colonies, but curious about his circumstances. "Have you lived in London for long?"

"No, I relocated here recently from Lewes, in Sussex," Thomas replied. "I was recently widowed, and my tobacco shop failed soon after. More recently, I could no longer support myself on the meagre wages I earned as an excise collector. Hence, like you, I am seeking justice from His Majesty after unjustly losing my new livelihood as a collector."

George returned, poured steaming tea into Ben's teacup, and then he turned to Thomas.

"Shall I warm up yours?"

"Yes, thank you," Thomas answered, nodding politely.

As George poured Thomas' tea, Ben took a sip of his and then sighed.

"Ahhh, how refreshing it is to taste English tea again."

Thomas took a sip from his replenished cup, set it down, and paused for a moment before continuing his story for Ben's benefit.

"Now where was I ... Oh, yes, I was printing leaflets and organizing my fellow collectors to demand fair compensation for our services from a parliament and a king that do not, in any way, represent or listen to their subjects. I have to thank my good friend, Mr. Scott, for taking me in after I fell on such hard times. Had he not come to my rescue, I would be sitting today in debtor's prison instead of this room. George and I are hoping that he can rely on his amity with the King, and on his connections as an Excise Commissioner, to persuade His Majesty to grant me an audience."

George turned his attention to Ben, who had just taken a sip of tea, and was listening patiently.

"In addition to losing his wife and unborn child, as well as his shop, Thomas was forced to sell all of his belongings," George added. "I could not live with myself if I did not try to help him. He makes a sound argument for higher compensation, and he is most eloquent in his writings. The increase that he and his colleagues seek is a mere pittance compared to total excise revenues."

"I am most sorry for your devastating losses," Ben replied, feeling genuine sympathy for Thomas and his situation. "However, I must say that I admire your resolve to overcome them, and your commitment to your cause, Mr. Paine. I wish you luck, as I fear that both you and I will need it in our endeavours with His Majesty."

"You are too kind," Thomas replied.

Ben paused for a moment, his mind busy while he took another sip of tea.

"Mr. Paine, would you be at all interested in returning to Philadelphia with me, to work at my newspaper."

A look of complete surprise crossed Thomas Paine's face.

"I am flattered, Mr. Franklin. But why me?"

"Why you?" Ben repeated. "My good man, during these uncertain times, the Colonies could most definitely benefit from a man with your political insight, your writing and organizational skills, and your commitment to the causes of justice and freedom from tyranny. We would be honoured to have you!"

Ben consulted a timepiece he pulled from his waistcoat pocket, noted the time, then he paused again to think before returning the watch. He looked at his friend, George.

"Do you have some paper and a quill that I could borrow?"

"Certainly," George answered. He rose from his chair and walked to a small desk, then returned with a quill, a bottle of ink, and a blank sheet of paper. He placed them on the table beside Ben.

"Thank you," Ben said. He set to work, writing a note on the paper. When he was finished, he lifted the paper and blew on it before handing it to Thomas.

"I must take leave soon for my audience with the King. Please consider my offer. I leave for Philadelphia in two days. If you wish to accompany me, leave word at this inn by tonight, and I will make the necessary travel arrangements."

Thomas's face flushed with a combination of embarrassment and joy.

"You flatter me yet again, Mr. Franklin," Thomas said. "I am not deserving of such charity."

"Nonsense, Mr. Paine," Ben replied. "You underestimate yourself and the contribution you could make towards improving the most basic rights of mankind. I look forward to your reply, and I hope we will be able to work together in the near future."

DAVID ALEX JONES

THE GREAT COMPROMISE

Philadelphia, Pennsylvania
September, 1787

BOTH THE horse-drawn and pedestrian traffic on Philadelphia's streets were heavy as Thomas Paine weaved his way up York Street towards Germantown and the Rising Sun Tavern. Dusk was settling over the city early due to a heavily overcast sky, but the air was crisp and clean after a recent rain shower. As he passed a shop window, Thomas caught a glimpse of his reflection. He retraced his steps and paused in front of his likeness, admiring the new suit, hat, and the shiny buckled shoes he had recently purchased for this journey from New Jersey to Philadelphia.

Thomas' mind drifted back in time. He remarked to himself that his new wardrobe was a far cry from the threadbare rags he wore upon his arrival in Philadelphia thirteen years earlier. What a change in fortune he had experienced after his unexpected and fortuitous meeting with Ben Franklin in London in 1774.

Satisfied with his reflection, Thomas walked the last block towards the tavern. Although he had not been chosen as a delegate to the Convention, he was still close to his colleagues, who continued to value his opinions on politics. As he gripped the handle and flung open the tavern's sturdy wooden door, an overwhelming jumble of aromas of sweat, stale beer, roasted meat, and tobacco smoke, combined with the ear-splitting clamour of raucous patrons, slammed into him like a sensory tidal wave. He entered the packed tavern, paused, and did his best to scan through the smoke, looking for his friends. Finally, he saw the familiar profile of Ben Franklin, and he began wading through the sea of humanity towards him. As he came closer, Thomas recognized George Washington, James Madison, and Alexander Hamilton, who were also seated around the table. Franklin looked up and, seeing Thomas approaching, waved his friend towards an empty seat.

"Thomas," he shouted. "So delighted that you could come to Philadelphia to share in our little celebration before you leave for Paris! We managed to save a spot for you. Take a seat and help yourself to some sustenance. There is plenty to go around."

At that moment, Franklin spotted a barmaid scurrying towards them and he waved to her.

"Another round, lass. And a pint for our friend as well!" he hollered, over the roar of the crowd.

The barmaid, a slim young woman with black hair and an olive-brown complexion, nodded and scurried away towards the bar.

"I came directly after receiving word that an agreement had been reached," Thomas shouted. "I wish to congratulate you on your great achievement!"

He reached towards the middle of the table and loaded some roast chicken, fresh corn, and roasted root vegetables onto a plate.

"Today is a momentous occasion, to be sure," Washington replied. "But this is only the beginning. An even larger battle awaits us in the coming months. Our old foe, Patrick Henry, already sows the seeds of fear in businessmen and the poor alike in Virginia, preaching that the Constitution will rob them of their liberty!"

"Mr. Washington is correct," Madison said. "We must not underestimate the resolve of our adversaries. They will stop at nothing to prevent us from ratifying this new Constitution."

A reserved smile crossed Thomas' face as he took in the mixed news.

"No more suspense, my friends. Tell me more about the final agreement!"

"Thankfully, we were successful in reaching a great compromise, proposed by Mr. Sherman from Connecticut," Hamilton answered. "There will be two legislative houses in Congress, a lower House of

Representatives elected by the people, based on population to please the larger states. But there will also be an upper Senate, with two Senators elected from each state, to please the smaller states."

"And there shall be three branches of federal government," Washington added. "The legislative branch that Mr. Hamilton mentioned, plus an executive branch and a judicial branch."

"Many delegates had been lobbying for an executive with two or three officers," Madison said. "But, in the end, we succeeded in convincing them of the need for a strong central leader, a President who will have the power to veto Congress, if necessary. He will also be the one who selects justices for the judicial branch."

Thomas' eyes narrowed and wrinkles of concern appeared on his face as he processed what he had just heard.

"A single leader?" he asked. "With that much power?"

James Madison shot a cool, rather indignant glance in Thomas' direction.

"We would rather have had a Senate with the power to veto the lower house, *and* also to veto legislation from within the states. But, they were steadfast in their rejection of that idea. They claimed that it would infringe on the sovereignty of the states!" he scoffed. "As if they were ever sovereign under the British, or under our current Articles of Confederation, for that matter!"

"The good news," Hamilton said, "is that the new federal government will have the power to coin its own money, to levy taxes within each state, and to negotiate treaties with other nations on behalf of the states."

"That *is* good news!" Thomas replied. "I know that my dear friend, Mr. Jefferson, will be happy to know that a compromise was reached. He agrees that each branch of government should be able to keep the others in check, and I believe he agrees that it is essential for the federal government to be able to levy taxes and make treaties."

The barmaid returned to their table, balancing a large tray with five pints of ale, which she distributed around the table. She looked on as Thomas grasped his mug and took a long gulp of refreshing ale.

"A great compromise?" she shouted over the din. "May I ask the nature of this great compromise you gentlemen celebrate? Does this have to do with the Convention?"

Looks of surprise swept across the five men's faces.

"It does, indeed," Washington replied. "What do you know of the Convention?"

"Only that compromise can be a double-edge sword," she replied. "While it often appeases all parties, there are times when it pleases no one. And if that be the case, I fear that our current divisions could rear their ugly heads in the future.

She paused to survey the dumbfounded faces around the table, and then laughed aloud.

"But, what can a woman know of such things? I am just your humble server!"

"Perhaps," Thomas mused. "But you are wise to ask such questions."

"What is your name, and from where do you hail," Franklin inquired.

The young woman laughed again.

"You may call me Cass," she replied. "I hail from Upper Canada."

"A most unique name, to be sure. And what brings you so far from home?" Washington asked.

"There is little room in Canada for any person who has views that contradict the Loyalists'," Cass answered. "I travelled to Philadelphia to taste what true freedom is like."

"And what is your opinion? Does it meet with your approval?" Paine inquired.

"Yes, thus far I am most pleasantly surprised. But excuse me, I must return to my duties. Enjoy your celebration, gentlemen."

Cass turned and hurried to the bar, where she picked up another tray loaded with mugs of ale.

"An interesting young woman," Paine observed. "Now, where were we? ... Oh yes, the Constitution. What of a Bill of Rights? What rights does the new Constitution protect?"

"The delegates did not feel that such a document is needed at this time," Madison answered. "The issue of slavery is still too delicate a subject for a number of states. But we ensured that there are provisions for amending the Constitution and adding such rights in the future."

Thomas shook his head in disgust.

"Good God" he shouted. "I am dismayed, gentlemen! You have managed to place so much power in the hands of a President, and you have given so much power in the Senate to the states! How is having a powerful President any different from the King we so scorned, if that one man can override the voice of the people in the lower house? And yet, you grant no rights to the common citizen? Mr. Jefferson will be as outraged as myself at this travesty!"

"We have the judicial branch," Franklin interjected. "The judiciary can decide whether the President is acting outside the Constitution."

"And that is where your new Constitution is most flawed and vulnerable, gentlemen!" Thomas shouted. "Having a powerful President who appoints the judiciary makes it far too easy for a tyrant to corrupt the judicial branch into overriding the voice of the people. With this flaw, I fear that the freedom of the common people hangs by a thin thread!

Thomas took a hasty bite of chicken, then reached for his mug to help wash down the food. He wiped some froth and chicken from the corner of his mouth with a handkerchief that he pulled from his pocket. Then, he set down his mug firmly and looked each of the other men in the eye.

"Surely," he continued, "such a Constitution must express God's Will, that every man is born equal in value, with equal natural rights that extend for all time! What good is a Constitution without preserving every man's freedom of speech or freedom to worship God, each in his own way? What in this new Constitution distinguishes between each man's individual rights and the need for society to make laws to protect the rights of the many? Without this clear distinction, no man's property is secure and nothing is criminal. Each person may deem himself at liberty to act as he pleases, with no regard for his fellow man! How is this any improvement over the Articles of Confederation?"

"I fear that you over-react, my friend," Washington replied, his voice thoughtful and calm. "There was much disagreement about such a Bill of Rights, so the Convention thought it best to solidify the Constitution in its present form, while all parties are in agreement."

Washington looked around the table at his fellow colleagues who had attended the Convention. They nodded for him to continue.

"Rest assured, Thomas, that Mr. Madison has already made arrangements to begin consultations about a Bill of Rights, as soon as this Constitution is ratified."

Thomas took a deep breath and exhaled, pausing for a moment to think over Washington's comments.

"I hope you are right," he answered, finally. "We have already attempted one path of freedom, with our trifling and worthless Articles of Confederation. But, I fear that our prescient young barmaid may be correct! The compromises in this new Constitution, especially with no Bill of Rights and with a Senate that can overrule the will of the people in the lower House, creates the potential for a second road that could very well end in tyranny, loss of liberty, and another failure."

Thomas reached for his mug and took another long gulp of ale to soothe his dry throat.

"I agree with Mr. Jefferson," Thomas continued. "While I am sure that he would agree that your compromises and your new Constitution may suit our country now, while it is still young, and while there is room to grow, I am sure he would see it as being too easily corrupted over time, when our cities will surely grow and become more like the crowded cities of Europe. It will be necessary for your Constitution to evolve and change over time as the world changes.

Thomas paused one more time to look each of the other men in the eye.

"Surely, gentlemen," he continued, "there is a third road we can take: one that can protect liberty and freedom, where we ensure that the power rests where it belongs, in the hands of the people! But I fear that the compromises you have made in this Constitution will not take us down that road. Instead, I fear that it will eventually be doomed to chaos and failure, if it is not soon amended!"

CHAPTER 1—A FISH CALLED RACHEL

RACHEL WILLIAMS, now vested with the responsibility of being the leader of the free world, sat at the Resolute Desk scouring the latest security brief from the Pentagon's Chiefs of Staff. She finished reading the last paragraph when a door opened and her own Chief of Staff, Nicole Davies, entered the Oval Office. Rachel glanced at her watch.

"The Chinese Ambassador should be arriving in a few minutes, Ma'am," Nicole said. "You've had a chance to read the security brief on their increasing activities in the Taiwan Strait?"

Rachel laid the brief on her desk, leaned back in her chair, and sighed.

"I have," she replied. "I think it's just more of the same Chinese sabre rattling: nothing to be alarmed about."

"Most likely, Ma'am," Nicole answered. "What do the Chiefs of Staff think, if you don't mind me asking?"

"That's pretty much what they think," Rachel said.

"So, what are you going to say to the Ambassador? Anything short of condemning their actions will have your critics shouting from the hilltops that you're weak."

A loud knock on the door interrupted Nicole. Before she could reach the door to answer it, a Secret Service agent, dressed in a black suit and wearing an earpiece, let herself in. Nicole and Rachel both froze, confused by the sudden, unexpected entrance.

"Excuse the interruption, Madam President," the agent said. "But we've just caught wind of a significant security threat against the White House. We're going to have to evacuate you to Camp David immediately."

"What do you mean? I can't do that!" Rachel blurted. "The Chinese Ambassador will be here any minute …"

"I'm sorry, Ma'am," the agent interrupted. "I'm not at liberty to provide details. My orders are just to evacuate you immediately. Marine One will be here in less than five minutes. You can contact the Chinese Ambassador and receive a full briefing once you're safely in the air. I'd advise you to grab whatever is on your desk, because we have to leave right now."

Rachel froze momentarily, her mind spinning and trying to process the unexpected turn of events. Then, realizing the gravity of the situation, she and Nicole followed instructions by gathering up the documents on her desk and stuffing them hurriedly into two briefcases.

"This way, Madam President," the agent said, leading her and Nicole out of the office. They rushed through the White House's hallowed corridors to the rear entrance of the historic building, arriving just as Marine One touched down on the rear White House lawn. Moments later, when the aircraft's blades had slowed to a safe speed, the Secret Service agent placed her hand on Rachel's shoulder.

"Follow me, Madam President," she said.

Rachel and Nicole rushed across the perfectly manicured blades of grass, ducking down as they approached the aircraft. The agent helped Rachel up the stairs, and as Nicole entered the aircraft, the turbines' whine increased in pitch and the aircraft rocked from side to side. The agent escorted Rachel and Nicole to their seats and handed each of them a set of headphones.

"Fasten your seatbelts ladies," the agent said into her microphone.

The rocking of the aircraft and the whine of its turbines continued to increase, until Rachel finally felt the helicopter lift off the ground. It gained altitude swiftly, and she saw the White House lawn recede rapidly. High above Washington, they were now heading towards Maryland.

The Secret Service Agent tapped Nicole on the shoulder and plugged her headphones and headset into the aircraft's phone system.

Rachel watched as her assistant dialled the Chinese Embassy. After a long wait, Nicole had an animated conversation with somebody at the embassy, and then she ended the call. The agent reconnected her headphones and headset to the aircraft's communication system.

"We've rescheduled the Chinese Ambassador for eleven-hundred tomorrow at Camp David, Ma'am," Nicole said.

"You know I don't like that military clock stuff."

"Sorry, Ma'am," Rachel answered. "I meant 11 a.m."

Rachel nodded her acknowledgment, then she turned to the Secret Service Agent.

"So, what's happening? Why the evacuation?"

"We caught some online chatter late this morning about a secret far right convoy that was gathering in at least two locations inside D.C. The organizer appears to be associated with the Brothers of Liberty, a white supremacist organization. Allegedly, their goal is to encircle the White House, with you inside."

"What about the police?" Rachel asked. "Why didn't they stop it?"

"We found out too late, Ma'am. Trucks, buses, and vans are coming from every direction to join the convoy. It's extremely well-organized."

"Are they succeeding in their objective?" Nicole inquired.

"We're not sure yet," the agent replied. "Apparently, a mob of Unite the Left demonstrators on the mall somehow found out about the convoy. We picked up on all of the sudden Unite the Left chatter and that's how we found out about the convoy ourselves. At this moment, they're heading towards the White House and it looks like the two sides are going to collide at some point. D.C. police are just ramping up an emergency response."

"Oh, my God!" Rachel blurted. "So this could potentially turn into another January sixth riot, maybe even worse if both sides are involved—or, Heaven forbid, if there's guns." She shook her head solemnly from side to side.

Only one month into the job, I'm having to face a credible threat to my life, AND the nation's democracy!

She turned to Nicole.

"As soon as we land and get settled, get me in contact with D.C. Police so we can keep abreast of what's happening on the ground."

"Yes, Ma'am," Nicole answered.

"Also, get me in touch with the D.C. National Guard. We don't want to make the same mistakes they made on January sixth—I want them placed on immediate standby. I intend to be a President who's part of the solution this time—not the source of the problem."

"Should I plan a press release or a press conference?" Nicole asked.

"Not yet. I'll let you know after I've been in touch with DCMP and the National Guard."

Before she knew it, Rachel felt Marine One bank right and start its descent into Camp David. She felt her heart pumping and felt the tension in the muscles in her head, neck, and especially in her shoulders. Her adrenaline was flowing and she realized that she was about to face her first big test as President of the United States.

Five Days Earlier

AN AGING black service van, its windows heavily tinted and patches of rust around its doors and lower frame, pulled into an empty parking spot on K Street, only a few short blocks from the White House. Inside the van, invisible to outsiders, the driver let out a long sigh of relief. The forty-hour drive from Couer D'Alene, Idaho, had been gruelling, stopping only to refuel, grab some fast food, and take a couple of short catnaps. With no shower or change of clothes for over three days, the van was beginning to take on the odour of an NFL locker room.

Forty-two-year-old Bryson MacDonald, aka Scorpion8188 when he's online, unbuckled his seat belt, and squeezed his sizeable frame, also belonging in an NFL locker room, awkwardly between the seats and into the rear of the vehicle. He surveyed an electronic control centre that lined one wall of the van's cargo area: two large computer screens, a keyboard, and a trackpad occupied most of the desk's working surface, while a shelf above his computer desk held a row of electronic instruments, including a pair of police scanners. He eased himself into a swivelling captain's chair, flipped his greasy hair out of his eyes, and began turning on switches and booting up the computer.

Almost immediately, two police scanners on the upper shelf began squawking and hissing. Bryson skillfully manned the controls, tuning into the frequencies used by D.C. Metropolitan Police and U.S. Capitol Police. He turned up the volume to listen to the USCP channel. It became clear after a few moments that the USCP was in the process of setting up additional barricades around the Capitol in anticipation of Saturday's giant left-wing rally. The process appeared to be going smoothly and the radio chatter was uneventful.

Bryson turned his attention to the computer. On one screen, he logged into a messaging platform featuring full end-to-end encryption. But his eyes focused on another screen showing a local network TV station's news broadcast. He listened while an African American woman reported on today's news from Capitol Hill.

"... this coming Saturday, July 2, left wing supporters plan to gather on Capitol Hill to protest the Republican House's plans to further limit abortion rights, and to tighten up election and immigration laws ..."

Bryson typed a cryptic message, not taking any chances, even though his message was allegedly encrypted and safe.

"If there's one thing we learned from January sixth," he muttered under his breath, "it's that Big Brother's always findin' new ways to spy on us. There's no tellin' when the bastards'll get warrants to take away more of our freedoms."

Scorpion8188: How are logistics coming? Are all loads for destination on schedule?

Piggyback06: All carriers loaded, on the road, and on time.

Bryson's fingers resumed typing almost immediately.

Scorpion8188: What about smokescreen?

Piggyback06: Volunteers making lots of noise and starting to trend on SM.

In the background, the Capitol Hill news report droned on.

"... this just in ... social media platforms have been buzzing over the past couple of days about a number of truck convoys possibly converging on a number of State Capitals. States that have been mentioned include Florida, California, Arizona, and Virginia ..."

Piggyback06: How are things on your end?

Scorpion8188: Good, no sign of cop worries, they're so focused on the woke socialist assholes.

"... the social media buzz indicates that convoy organizers may be demanding a Senate investigation into former President Spencer's death and President Williams' unexpected ascension to power, amid rumours that Spencer could have been poisoned by left-leaning sympathizers who support incoming President Williams ..."

Scorpion8188: Let's switch to a call we got lots to discuss.

Bryson toggled a switch on his computer screen and then donned a headset with a mic.

"You there, Piggy?"

"Yep, Scorps. What's up?"

"I'm just listenin' to the news from the hill," Bryson said. "That bitch President has to be our worst nightmare come true! Thinks she can grab power an' sneak 'er woke agenda by us before we notice. She won't know what hit 'er after we're finished. You got the maps I sent?"

"Yeah, I got 'em," Piggy replied. "Wouldn't surprise me at all if she poisoned our boy Spencer."

"Any questions 'bout the routes and their targets?" Bryson asked. "Make sure all the drivers know their exact time of arrival, an' which intersection each one'a them is sealin' off. We wanna make sure we completely control who gets in, an' who gets out."

"I've gone over 'n over it with 'em. Can't wait to see the look on 'er face when our boys arrive!" Piggy said with a snicker.

"Hey Piggy, remind everyone in operation smokescreen to ramp up the noise 'bout Sacramento, Tallahassee, Phoenix, an' Richmond. It's gotta be totally believable, but tell 'em to be careful an' not too cocky: we don' need anybody spillin' the beans."

"I will," Piggy answered. "I got all the buses 'ranged fer the marshallin' points: they're spread out aroun' the area so we don't raise any eyebrows. An' we should have a ton o' bodies arrivin' along with them eighteen wheelers."

"Good work, Piggy," Bryson said. "I'll be leakin' the real target info to the other six team leaders Friday so they kin get their people to the marshallin' points on time."

"Have ya' told 'em how big the convoy's gonna be?" Piggy asked.

"Nah," Bryson replied. "I just told 'em we wanna have some protesters on the hill on Saturday too, just so the 'woke sheep' don' get all the attention. They don' need to know 'bout how big this is gonna be till they get here."

"... and finally, all eyes will be watching President Williams as she welcomes Republican Senate Leader Sherman Crowley, and Representative Michael Chen, Democratic House Leader, tomorrow. When asked about his visit, this is what Representative Chen had to say."

"I'm excited to meet with President Williams, and I look forward to finding possible areas for bipartisan cooperation over the next couple of years."

Following Representative Chen's comment, the news report switched back to the network's reporter.

"When we caught up to Senator Crowley for comment, this was his response."

The picture switched again, this time to Senator Crowley, who appeared to be doing his best to dodge reporters.

"I have no comment until after I've met with the President myself, to see what path she intends to follow. All I can say at this point is that Republicans in Congress would take a very dim view of the President colluding with any Democratic attempts to water down any of our proposed Bills."

The TV screen reverted back to the news reporter.

"That's all from Capitol Hill this evening. Now back to the studio ..."

"That's all I got fer ya', Piggy," Bryson continued. "Lemme' know if there's any problems. If not, I'll check with ya' Friday to make sure everythin's on track."

"Roger that, Scorps," Piggy answered. "I'll tell everybody to be extra careful. Y'all be careful too. Talk later."

Bryson heard a click as his connection with Piggy went dead. He turned his attention back to the police scanners to ensure that it was business as normal for the Capitol and D.C. Police. He leaned back in his chair and stretched. All was quiet on the police front, and he allowed himself a rare smile. Saturday was going to be his greatest accomplishment as leader of the Brothers of Liberty. The eyes of the nation, probably the entire planet, were going to be on him by the end of the day.

Then I'll have their attention: everybody'll finally listen an' pay me the attention I deserve!

DUSK SETTLED slowly over The White House. As daylight waned, a number of windows in the building gradually illuminated, including those of the Oval Office, where the country's new Black President, Rachel Williams, continued to work into the evening, along with her chief of staff.

Nicole closed the office door as she ushered out President Williams' last visitor of the day, a prominent union leader. She heaved a large sigh of relief, and then looked over at the Resolute Desk, where the President leaned back in her chair, yawning and stretching her arms high in the air, before emitting a large sigh herself.

"Is that it?" Rachel asked.

"That's it." Nicole replied. "But I'm sorry to say that tomorrow's going to be just as bad."

"What a day." Rachel sighed. "And I thought I was busy when I was the Vice President! If I'd known that Ron Spencer would keel over from a brain aneurysm five months after taking office, and leave this job to me, I'm not sure I would have signed on as his running mate. This isn't the way I wanted to see our country get its first Black female President."

"Regardless," Nicole answered. "You're *it* now. President Spence's death was a huge shock to everybody. But the different factions within the party are already jockeying for power."

"You mean they're all lining up to find out whether or not I'm going to stick to Ron's agenda, especially regarding the pro-life and gun control issues."

Rachel took a moment to pause and reflect.

"Good God," she continued. "The poor man's barely been in the ground two weeks and the vultures are already circling above me. Can't they even give me some space while I figure out my own policies and priorities?"

Nicole paused and looked Rachel directly in the eyes.

"Do you want my honest opinion, Ma'am?" Nicole asked.

"Of course," Rachel replied. "You know I value your opinions."

Rachel silently appraised the young woman standing before her. She wasn't quite thirty years old, yet she had worked her way up the ranks of Capitol Hill staffers quickly, becoming a staffer in Ron Spencer's office while he was still in the Senate. The former President rewarded the young staffer's hard work and her allegiance by choosing her as his Press Secretary after winning the Presidential Election. After

Spencer's sudden death, Rachel looked to the young woman as a source of continuity when choosing her own Presidential staff. Rachel had no doubt that Nicole had political ambitions of her own, possibly as soon as the next midterm elections. But, for now, she was relying on the young woman's drive and energy as her Chief of Staff.

"The party, and our new Republican Congress," Nicole began, "were ecstatic that voters accepted President Spencer's shift to the right. We know that Republican voters are expecting to undo much of the Democrats' damage from the last four years. So, the longer you wait before coming out to endorse President Spencer's agenda, if that's what you choose to do, Ma'am, the more worried voters and the rest of the party will become. If there's one thing the far right hates more than a Democrat, it's a moderate Republican."

"But, everybody in the party, including Ron, already knew that I'm a moderate," Rachel said. "That's why he chose me to run on his ticket. I was his token woman, person of colour, and a moderate: everything he needed to win over voters in the battleground states. And it worked!"

"Don't sell yourself short, Ma'am," Nicole continued. "You could be seen by those voters as a kind of Kamala Harris."

"My situation is *nothing* like hers!" Rachel blurted. "In fact, in many ways, mine is almost an exact opposite! Where Kamala rode onto the scene as the potential saviour of the Democratic Party, much of my own party sees me as an Antichrist, especially on the far right. Kamala replaced an elderly Presidential candidate, whom much of the nation was praying would be replaced. And she never *became* President! But, in my case, I'm replacing a man the nation saw as their new saviour. Let's be honest, once I'd helped Spencer win the election, most of the party faithful were hoping I'd just fade into the background and be a good girl. Kamala was born to be a leader, but I'm the most unlikely first female President this country could ever have predicted!"

"So, if that's the case," Nicole replied. "Do you mind me asking why you agreed to be President Spencer's running mate?"

Rachel paused to take a breath and to gather her thoughts.

"I accepted because I'm sick and tired of all the bipartisan fighting in this country," she began. "When is it ever going to end? When is somebody going to start thinking outside the box, and start finding a way to get people working together? America is decaying. And the only way to save it—and the world we live in, I might add—is for people to start working together as a team."

Rachel stopped for a moment and sighed.

"I want to make a difference, to be a voice of reason and moderation when it comes to legislation, to find ways for Congress to be less partisan. Do you think that's totally naïve?"

This time it was Nicole's turn to pause, taking time to choose her words carefully.

"That's not for me to judge, Ma'am." Nicole responded. "Like most people, I just assumed that you'd follow President Spencer's agenda for a while, if only to prevent a lot of uncertainty. The people, the markets, even the rest of the world, are looking for stability. I think you should start things off by throwing them a few small bones over the next few weeks, just to calm everybody's nerves."

Rachel let Nicole's words sink in, and she took a moment to process how to respond.

Not only is she smart, she's diplomatic as hell, too!

"Maybe you're right, Nicole. Rome wasn't built in a day. Let's start looking for areas where Ron and I were in agreement, and start with those issues. Hopefully, not everyone will be so restless, and it will buy me some time to look at my own agenda."

"Okay," Nicole answered. "So your first order of business is obviously that you've taken far too long to choose your cabinet."

"I agree," Rachel replied. "I think I needed to keep some of Ron's choices in the short term for continuity: the ones I thought I could work with. But I also need to make some of my own choices. I need to show people that I'm more than just a clone of President Spencer. I need to put some of my own stamp on this Presidency."

Nicole paused and looked like she had more to say, but after thinking it over for a few seconds, she appeared to think better of saying anything more. Instead, she swiped through the calendar on her phone, taking a close look at President Williams' agenda.

"Tomorrow's Tuesday," she began. "You'll be meeting with Senator Crowley and then with Congressman Chen from the Democrats. They're the two most influential voices on the Hill. After that, you should have more open time this week to work on some cabinet changes. Can I tell the press that you'll be able to announce those early next week?"

"Sure, that sounds manageable," Rachel agreed.

"Good. Is there anything else I can do for you tonight, Ma'am?"

"I don't think so, Nicole. Thanks for all your help. I don't think I could have made it through the day without you."

"You're welcome, Ma'am. I'll just sort this pile of mail and paperwork for you before I leave."

Rachel removed her glasses and rubbed her tired eyes while Nicole moved stacks of paperwork off the President's desk, exposing a paperback book in the pile. She held it up for Rachel to see.

"Where did this come from?" Nicole pointed to the book, titled *The Night Class*, with an artist's rendition of a translucent, illuminated teepee at night on the cover.

"I'm not sure," Rachel replied. "It was sent anonymously. I think there's a note with it—what does it say?"

Nicole removed the note from the book.

"It says: 'I admire you for speaking out in support of Indigenous people at the 2021 Minnesota Pipeline Protest, despite taking heat from within your party. I hope this short book will help you to follow your spirit and find your own voice (as did the author, Samantha Bower), as you embark on your renewed life journey as our new President.' "

"That sounds intriguing," Rachel answered. "I'll take a look at it tonight. I was looking for something light to read, to help me clear my mind and fall asleep. Hopefully I'll sleep better tonight than I have for the past few nights."

"I hope so too, Ma'am," Nicole added.

Rachel extended her hand and Nicole handed the book over to her.

"That will be all, Nicole. I'll see you in the morning."

"Bright and early," Nicole replied. "Good night, Ma'am."

Nicole walked briskly to the door and exited the Oval Office. As the door closed, Rachel sank into her chair at the Resolute Desk, and allowed her eyes to take in the room's history and grandeur. The room was totally still, and she felt herself cherishing the silence that suddenly descended upon it. At that moment, the reality of her new role finally became clear. She turned her gaze to the cover of the book she was holding. The mood in the room at that moment seemed to mimic the pensive mood conveyed by the artwork on the book's cover. Rachel closed her eyes and took a few deep, relaxing breaths, immersing herself in her silent, peaceful surroundings. Then, after a few moments, she opened her eyes and opened the front cover of *The Night Class*.

CHAPTER 2—FREEDOM OF SPEECH

LATE SATURDAY morning, Jordan Marsh parked her vintage cobalt-blue Honda Shadow motorcycle on Constitution Avenue, near Fourteenth Street, then hurriedly removed her helmet and stowed it securely. She removed the rubber band from her ponytail, then shook out her shoulder-length brown hair. She stole a quick glance at herself in one of the bike's mirrors. Even in direct sunlight, her long hair and strategically applied makeup transformed her biological male face into that of a woman. Pleased with her look, she grabbed a small backpack from one of the bike's saddlebags, locked the bike, then took off towards the National Mall, half jogging and half walking. As she reached the mall, in front of the National Museum of American History, she glanced at her watch, noting that it was already 12:10 p.m..

Jordan gazed out over the gathering crowd at the west end of the mall. The peaceful march to East Seton Park was due to begin at 1 p.m.. The weather was perfect—sunny, but not too hot—for spending the afternoon covering the Unite the Left rally. Jordan looked eastward at the U.S. Capitol Building, which stood like a postcard image of the nation's democracy and freedom, shining a brilliant white in the midday sunshine, set against a cloudless azure sky.

It was a busy day on the mall, given that the Fourth of July created a rare long weekend by falling on a Monday. Scores of tourists: couples, families, and guided tours, had been filling the museums, lining up for the Washington monument, and snapping group photos or selfies since early that morning.

Jordan noticed that the crowd of demonstrators was growing quickly, a good sign for the organizers that the rally would likely be a smashing success. She estimated that there must already be a few thousand people lingering in the rally's marshalling area. Many of them carried banners and placards to advertise their favourite causes: Black Lives Matter, abortion rights, voter rights, climate action, and LGBTQ2+ rights were the most visible. As a transgender woman, Jordan identified closely with the movement for LGBTQ2+ rights, and she wished she was participating in the march.

But Jordan wasn't here to demonstrate today. She was here for work. From her vantage point, her eyes roamed slowly over the crowd, looking for organizers to interview for her article about today's events. While scanning, she was also vigilant for any signs of the rumoured right wing counter-protesters, who had vowed to show up and disrupt their political arch enemies' activities.

"No skinheads or angry-looking rednecks so far," she said to herself.

Her eyes scanned the crowd again, until they landed on a slim, medium height young woman with olive-brown skin and black hair. The two womens' eyes locked for a split second, the contact breaking when the other woman abruptly turned and wandered in the opposite direction.

That was odd. It's like she didn't want me to see her.

Shaking the encounter out of her mind, Jordan continued her scan of the crowd until she spotted a tall, confident African-American woman talking with a group of demonstrators. She immediately recognized the woman as Cecilia Robinson, the prominent progressive activist and organizer, and spokesperson for Black Lives Matter and the NAACP. She was also the leading spokesperson for this afternoon's demonstration. Jordan caught the woman's eye, waved to her, and then approached the group, hoping for an interview. Cecilia stepped away from the group of demonstrators and turned to greet Jordan.

"Looks like you're going to have a big crowd, Cecilia. Do you have a few minutes?"

"Well, if it isn't Jordan Marsh, one of my favourite freelancers. Sure, I've got some time. I'm encouraged by how many people are coming out to spend this beautiful afternoon with us."

Jordan used her pointer finger to turn on the recording app on her phone, then she held the device in front of Cecilia.

"Are you worried at all about the rumours that some of the Brothers of Liberty are supposedly coming here to counter-protest?"

"Those fascists?" Cecilia scoffed. "Not at all. Our people and our guest speakers are here to demonstrate peacefully. I'll be reminding everybody in the crowd not to let themselves be provoked if the Brothers do try to disrupt things."

"As you can see," she continued. "There's a visible police presence around the entire mall."

"I noticed that," Jordan answered. "Hopefully, that's a good sign. So, tell me, who are your co-organizers, and what do you all hope to accomplish here this afternoon?"

"Well, we're here to bring together any group that promotes progressive social policies: people who want to see an end to racism against people of colour, people who don't want to lose the voter rights or abortion rights we gained during the last Democratic administration. People who want to see more commitment to fighting climate change, and people who continue to advocate for the rights of refugees and the LGBTQ2+ community."

Cecilia stopped for a moment and looked around her.

"There's Colorado state Senator Sandra Delgado," she said, pointing to a middle-aged Hispanic woman nearby. She continued to scan the crowd

"And there's Dudley Morris, the Aussie scientist and climate change expert over there. He's also spearheading efforts to limit the spread of misinformation over social media."

As Cecilia pointed towards Dudley, Jordan noticed another familiar face, but she couldn't put a name to it.

"Do you know who that young Asian woman is, behind Dudley?" Jordan asked.

Jordan caught Cecilia rolling her eyes.

"That's Danielle Chen, the actress," Cecilia replied. "She's so flighty, and she's constantly on the prowl for any opportunities for more social media coverage. She'll support any cause that will get her more attention."

"Isn't she Michael Chen's daughter?" Jordan asked.

"One and the same," Cecilia said. "Most people think she was pretty much born with a silver spoon, and that she never would have made it in Hollywood without riding on daddy's coat tails."

Jordan was startled by the sudden ringing of her phone. She tried to ignore it, but it continued persistently, until it finally went to voicemail.

"Sorry about that," Jordan said. "Where were we? ... Oh, right, Danielle Chen."

Interrupted by her phone again, Jordan took a quick look at her call display.

"I'm so sorry, Cecilia. Do you mind if I take this? It might be a source with information on counter-protesters."

"Not at all, my dear," Cecilia replied. She pointed to a nearby group of people. "I'll just be talking to that group over there."

"Thanks," Jordan said, while she pressed the phone's answer button. She turned away and answered the call.

"Hi Jess, what's up?"

"Holy shit, Jordan, you're not going to believe this!"

It was one of Jordan's sources, Jessica Murray, an Indigenous activist from Minnesota. However, Jessica wasn't just a source: she was also Jordan's girlfriend. Her voice was excited, but hushed.

"Don't you dare tell anybody you got this from me, but that fascist weasel, Bryson MacDonald, has been lying to everybody."

"What do you mean, lying?" Jordan inquired.

"You know all the rumours about truck convoys going to some of the State Capitals, and the Brothers possibly showing up to hassle you guys on the mall today?"

"Yeah, ..." Jordan answered, her face puzzled.

"Well, it's all lies! We showed up here today, expecting a few small bunches of people from various right wing groups. But when we got here, there were hundreds of people gathering!" Jessica replied.

"The organizers here aren't too worried," Jordan said. "There's a sizeable D.C. police presence at the mall."

"That's just it, Jordan," Jessica blurted. "Threatening to disrupt the left wing demonstration is just a diversion: their real target is the White House. They're planning to block off Pennsylvania Avenue, Fifteenth and Seventeenth streets, and Constitution Avenue with dozens of semi-trailer trucks. They're going to surround the White House and the President while the left is demonstrating peacefully at the mall! You gotta do something!"

"What the ... what do you expect me to do?" Jordan answered, her mind going totally blank.

"Get to the organizers! Tell them they have to change their plans! They gotta turn around and march—no, run—towards the White House, and try to clog up the streets with people before the trucks get there! You gotta hurry, Jordan! They plan to be there shortly after 1 p.m.! And Jordan, I think I saw guns go into some of those trucks!"

Jordan looked around frantically to see where Cecilia had gone. She finally found her about fifty feet away.

"Okay, Jess. Thanks for the tip, I'll do what I can. Wish me luck. Gotta run!"

Jordan rushed over to where Cecilia was talking to Senator Delgado and Dudley Morris. Breathing heavily, she burst into Cecilia's conversation.

"Cecilia! You've got a major problem! I just got a very hot, very reliable tip that the Brothers of Liberty aren't targeting your demonstration today. They're targeting the White House, while all of the D.C. police are watching over you guys this afternoon!"

Looks of alarm flashed on the faces of all three organizers.

"What do you expect us to do about it?" Sandra Delgado asked.

"You've gotta talk to this crowd and tell them what's going on!" Jordan answered. "Then you've gotta march them up to the White

House and clog the surrounding streets so that far right truck convoy can't take over the White House!"

Jordan looked anxiously at her watch, and then back at Cecilia and her two colleagues.

"There's no time to waste!" Jordan shouted. "My source says they're gonna be there in about forty-five minutes!"

Dudley Morris, the aging science guru, turned to Cecilia and Sandra.

"She's right! There isn't a moment to lose. We could be looking at another January sixth fiasco. Should I grab the bullhorn right now?" he asked.

Cecilia and Sandra looked at each other anxiously, each waiting for the other to come up with an answer.

"There's no time to talk with the rest of the committee," Cecilia blurted, at last. "Let's do it! Now!"

The three organizers pushed through the crowd towards a flatbed truck that was serving as a stage for rallying the demonstrators. Sandra Delgado reached the truck first. She climbed a ladder onto the flat bed and then reached out to help Cecilia and Dudley up onto the stage. Dudley grabbed a bullhorn that was lying on the wooden floor, and quickly switched it on. A squeal of acoustic feedback alerted the crowd that Dudley was about to address them. He moved the bullhorn away from his face.

"Can you hear me?" he shouted, looking down at the crowd.

When he saw people nodding affirmatively, he wasted no time.

"Your attention, please!" he continued. "We have an urgent security situation that demands everybody's immediate attention. To tell you what we know, here's our lead organizer, Cecilia Robinson."

Dudley nodded to Cecilia and promptly handed the bullhorn to her. The crowd, sensing that something ominous was brewing, waited in silence.

"We've received a credible tip that members of the Brothers of Liberty have secretly organized a massive truck convoy and protest, with plans to encircle the White House and the President. Our informant tells us that the convoy is coming together at this very moment, and will start blocking off streets surrounding the White House in just over thirty minutes!

A loud murmur washed over the crowd.

"We fear that this far right convoy could pose a security threat to the nation, equal to or greater than that of the January sixth protests. Are you going to let that happen?" Cecilia shouted.

"No!" the crowd shouted in return.

"Are we going to try to stop them?" she shouted again.

"Yes!" the crowd roared.

"Then here's what we're going to do!" Cecilia bellowed. "We need everybody to start marching with us, as fast as we possibly can, up Fourteenth Street to Constitution Avenue. Dudley and I will lead you. When we reach Fifteenth Street, we'll split in two. Half of you will follow Dudley up Fifteenth Street towards Pennsylvania Avenue. The rest of us will continue to Seventeenth Street, where we'll take over that street and try to reach Pennsylvania Avenue before the trucks arrive.

Cecilia paused for a moment to look over the crowd.

"Are you with us?" she yelled.

The massive crowd answered with a unanimous roar.

"One more thing! While we march, we need each and every one of you to message everybody you know to spread the word about what's happening! Beg them to join us as soon as they possibly can! We can't let the fascists succeed!

The crowd roared its approval.

"Then let's go!" Cecilia continued. "Unite the Left! Unite the Left! ..."

The mass of humanity below picked up on the chant immediately. Cecilia, Dudley, and Sandra clambered down the ladder from the flatbed and started marching west towards Fourteenth Street. As the organizers passed members of the crowd, demonstrators handed them placards saying *Unite the Left*, *No More Fascism*, and *No More Racism*, then they fell in behind their leaders. What began as a chant quickly became a roar as the mass of humanity poured out of the mall and onto the streets of Washington D.C.

"Unite the Left! Unite the Left! Unite the Left! ..."

Jordan Marsh, her phone held high in the air to record the spectacle, slipped into the flood of protesters, just behind the three organizers. She felt the adrenaline pumping through her bloodstream, suddenly realizing that she was in at ground zero of what might be the biggest scoop she had ever uncovered as a journalist.

BRYSON MACDONALD continued to glance in his sideview mirrors. He grinned as he saw semi-trailer trucks, buses, and vans packed with people continue to merge into his Liberty Convoy, seemingly coming out of nowhere. Bryson was behind the wheel of his van, which would serve as the convoy's control centre, following two lead semi-trailer trucks. They were all heading eastbound on Pennsylvania Avenue now, nearing their destination.

Bryson's face beamed with pride as they approached the intersection of Seventeenth Street and Pennsylvania Avenue, and he chuckled as he saw the White House ahead on his right. But his joy was short lived, and his face fell as he saw Marine One rising into the air behind the Presidential residence. At the same instant, his eyes locked onto a mass of people converging onto Pennsylvania Avenue at Fifteenth Street. He grabbed for the radio microphone on his dashboard.

"Liberty One, come in!"

"Liberty One, here. What's with all them people? They ain't s'posed to be there!"

"Fucked if I know!" Bryson shouted. "Get to that intersection an' block it off so they can't go no further! Now!"

The convoy's lead truck picked up speed and raced down Pennsylvania Avenue towards Fifteenth street and the demonstrators, blowing its air horn and startling protesters. Bryson clicked on the radio's mic again, this time calling the truck directly in front of him as they were making a right turn onto Seventeenth Street.

"Liberty Two, continue to our target, and step on it!"

As Liberty Two and Bryson's van raced down the street towards Constitution Avenue, anger and determination were etched on Bryson's face. But, the closer they got, the more obvious it became that their plan had sprung a leak. His eyes grew wider and his suspicions were confirmed when he saw another mob of demonstrators coming towards them on Constitution Avenue.

"What the ...? How the fuck did they know? ... We gotta rat somewhere!" Bryson muttered.

He clicked on the mic button once again.

"Where the fuck are y'all, Piggy?" he shouted. "You were s'posed to be here by now!"

"Sorry, Scorps," Piggy replied. "Got held up by an accident. Couldn't help it, just a block away now. Holy shit! Where did all them people come from?"

"Just shut up an' get there!" Bryson screamed. "Help Liberty One seal off the intersection, then start securin' every side street off Pennsylvania!"

"Roger, got it!" Piggy answered.

Bryson clicked the mic again, this time calling the truck in front of him.

"Liberty Two, beat them fuckers to the intersection and turn onto Constitution, jus' like we planned! Give 'em a few blasts on yer air horn to scare 'em outta the way, then seal off Constitution with yer rig. All other trucks behind me, help Piggy secure all them side streets off Pennsylvania and Seventeenth as planned!"

Bryson watched as Liberty Two slowed and then started turning left onto Constitution Avenue. Suddenly, the truck's brake lights blazed red and the trailer jerked to a sudden stop. Bryson heard the rig's air horn giving blast after blast.

"Liberty Two, clear that fuckin' street!" Bryson commanded.

"Sorry, Scorpion," the driver replied. "They're all lyin' down on the street in front'a me, and they're not movin'!"

Bryson's face turned crimson while his mind scrambled for options. He pressed the mic button.

"This is Scorpion to all units. Help the trucks seal off the side streets, then everybody outta yer vehicles an' show them woke bastards who's boss! Pick 'em up an' carry 'em away if ya have to!"

As more convoy trucks, along with buses and van loads of people arrived, Bryson's far right Liberty Convoy protesters, many of them clad in camouflage gear, poured out of their vehicles and onto the streets, where they attempted to start forcibly removing the Unite the Left demonstrators who were lying on the street.

Cecilia Robinson saw Bryson's army coming towards them. She felt her heart pounding and her body tense as she filled with rage.

She turned on her bullhorn and pivoted around to address the mob behind her.

"Save your comrades!" she shouted. "Fight for your freedom! Are you gonna let these Nazi assholes take over? Show them they're not gonna get away with this!"

The Unite the Left mob bellowed their support and surged forward past Cecilia. Clashes broke out as they ran to defend their prostrate comrades on the pavement, using their protest signs to ward off their opponents. Other far right supporters surged into the fray, some of them wielding batons. Blood splattered onto the pavement.

Bryson sat in shock in the driver's seat of his van, trying to decide whether or not he was safe, as he watched the Unite the Left mob push forward. At that moment, he saw a surge of his own supporters coming up from behind his van, and then dividing into two waves on either side of the vehicle. They waded into the melee, keeping the progressive demonstrators from making any further progress.

Jordan Marsh clambered up onto a street light control box at the corner of the intersection to escape the danger. She stood atop the metal box and watched in horror at the violence transpiring below her. Nobody was closer to the unfolding story, or had a better view than herself. Her eyes swept over the mass of humanity, instinctively looking for the best story angle. At that moment, her eyes landed unexpectedly on a young olive-skinned woman standing on the fringe of the crowd. A shiver shot down Jordan's spine.

It's her, and she's looking at me again. What's up with her?

Jordan blinked and the woman was gone, disappearing into the sea of human chaos. The roar of the crowd jerked Jordan back into reality. She held up her phone and began live-streaming the hideous scene for the entire world to see.

"This is Jordan Marsh, reporting to you live from Constitution Avenue in Washington, D.C."

BLOCKS AWAY, at the intersection of Pennsylvania and Fifteenth Street, a similar scene was unfolding. Dudley Morris' eyes went wide with terror as he turned the corner and saw a semi-trailer truck bearing down on them, its air horn blaring a gruesome warning. There was no time to think. He threw himself prostrate on the ground, then closed his eyes and waited, wondering if he would feel any pain when the truck thundered over him.

Other Unite the Left demonstrators beside him wasted no time. They threw their bodies to the pavement beside him. Dudley heard the truck's engine howl and its tires squeal on asphalt. He opened his eyes and saw the truck's trailer starting to jack-knife. He saw the terror in the driver's eyes as he struggled to maintain control of his rig. Dudley's world slowed, dragging out a moment that he wished would end, regardless of the outcome. All around him, fellow protesters froze with fear. Finally, the screeching of tires and the growling of the trucks engine stopped, mere feet away from Dudley and his sprawled comrades. The air reeked of burning rubber and the truck's trailer now blocked Pennsylvania Avenue completely.

Everything went still and silent for a few seconds. Dudley turned his head and he was barely able to see the driver's eyes over the hood of the truck, as the driver spoke into a microphone. Within seconds, other vehicles—buses and vans full of far right protesters—roared up behind the jack-knifed trailer and began to spew its occupants onto the street.

Dudley's eyes opened wide as the newcomers surged towards him and his fellow demonstrators. A bearded, middle-aged man dressed in camouflage and wearing a bandana on his head, grabbed Dudley's torso, while another protester grabbed his ankles. His arms flailed and he attempted to kick his legs free, but this didn't stop his body from being lifted off the ground. After only a moment in the air, Dudley's torso fell to the pavement as fellow Unite the Left demonstrators came to his defence. He kept kicking and finally his legs came free as well, allowing him to haul himself to his feet. Dudley's entire body trembled from terror and shock, while his mind went into survival mode. Mind over matter, his wobbly sixty-five-year-old legs managed to carry him to safety on the White House side of the street. He leaned against the fence and watched the horror that was unfolding in front of him.

Without warning, Dudley felt a hand on his shoulder, causing his startled body to jump. He wheeled around and saw Senator Sandra Delgado beside him, with a cut over her left eye oozing blood. Despite her shocking appearance, Dudley relaxed at the sight of his colleague.

"Dudley," she shouted. "We're too old for this shit! Are you hurt badly? Can you walk or run?"

Dudley lifted his shirt, his hand shaking almost uncontrollably, revealing a number of sizeable scrapes and angry red contusions on his rib cage. He tried to take a deep breath and winced.

"My ribs hurt, especially when I breathe," he responded. "But more than anything, I just want the trembling to stop!"

"I'll help," Sandra called out over the crowd noise. "Come on, let's get out of here!"

She lifted his arm over her shoulder and began leading him back, away from the front lines of the fighting. The pair worked their way upstream, struggling against the current of Unite the Left demonstrators that continued to surge into the intersection.

Finally, Sandra and Dudley reached a spot around the corner where the crowd had thinned. Sitting on the curb to catch their breath, Sandra turned to the badly shaken Aussie scientist and shook her head from side to side sadly.

"Can this really be happening, Dudley? Is this what America has become?"

CHAPTER 3—CAMP DAVID

D.C. METROPOLITAN Police Captain Dewayne Robby felt the adrenaline coursing through his bloodstream as he listened intently to the reports from his front line officers on Pennsylvania and Constitution Avenues. A fifty-three-year-old Black police officer, Robby had worked hard to rise to his current position, in charge of the DCMP Special Operations branch for Homeland Security. He and his three subordinates huddled around a table at the rear of the DCMP Mobile Control Center, studying a large map of the area surrounding the White House.

"They've managed to completely seal off an entire block on every side street off of Pennsylvania Avenue and Seventeenth Street," Robby said, pointing to the map. "And they're already unloading their trucks: it looks like they're planning on settling in for an extended stay."

"That's not good," muttered one of the subordinates.

"No, it's not," Robby commented. "On a more positive note, it's good to hear that Alpha unit now has some separation between the two mobs at Constitution and Seventeenth. We need to bring in some fencing to separate the two groups and maintain some distance between them."

"I'll get on that right away," said another of the subordinates.

"Bravo unit, come in?" Robby said into his headset.

"Bravo unit here," said a voice over the radio.

"What's the situation like over there?"

"We've finally got some distance between the mobs over here. We managed to make room for the ambulances to come in, so they're finally able to tend to the injured. So far, no life-threatening injuries reported. Any plan for keeping these two groups apart, sir?"

"We're working on it, Sergeant," Robby answered. "Good work, Bravo."

Robby heard a commotion coming from the front of the bus. He turned around in time to see a familiar Caucasian man in his fifties flash his badge and then walk towards the rear of the control center.

Oh, shit. Just what I need right now!

"Well, if it ain't Agent Matt Butler. As you can see, I'm pretty busy right now. So, what brings the FBI to our neighbourhood?"

"I'm here to relieve you, Captain," Butler said, curtly. "This incident was quite clearly an attempt to take over the White House, so it's federal jurisdiction. It's time to call in the National Guard to clear this mess up."

"Like Hell it is!" Robby bellowed. "You know that the White House and the President's security is Secret Service jurisdiction, not federal. And now that the President's safe at Camp David, the threat towards her has ended. So, surely you're not going to try to pretend that skirmishes on our city streets aren't MDCP jurisdiction."

"Those are my orders, Captain," Butler replied. "You can take it up with my superior, if you don't like it."

Butler held out his cell phone to Captain Robby.

"You can call him yourself if you like."

"Listen, Butler," Robby shot back. "I don't have time for this bullshit! I don't care what your superior says. We worked all of this through after the January sixth riots. And we fine-tuned the process after we saw the massive failure of communications between police services in Ottawa in their 2022 convoy occupation—so we'd know exactly who's responsible for what, in case we ever have another similar situation. Capitol Police and MDCP will only get you Feds or the National Guard involved if it looks like our resources are being overwhelmed, or if federal crimes are being committed. And at this point, neither of those two things are happening. So, why don't you just go and fuck yourself!"

Butler shook his head from side to side.

"My bosses are not going to like your attitude, Captain."

"Well, tell them to bring my attitude up with the Mayor and Police Commissioner," Robby responded. "Right now, if you don't mind, we have a job to do here."

Robby turned to his colleagues and ignored Butler. Realizing that he wasn't about to get his way, Butler huffed and then made his way out of the bus. He walked away until he was out of earshot, then stopped and dialed a number on his cell phone.

"Butler here, sir ... Robby won't budge ... no sir, I didn't ... I tried, sir ... I ... I ... he told me to go through the Police Commissioner and Mayor ... you must have some connections with them ... no, sir, I'm not questioning your competence at all ... yes, sir ... I'll keep working on it ... I'll try to find a way ... yes, I'll keep you updated ... good night, sir."

Back in the van, Robby continued to huddle with his team.

"Okay," he said. "Let's get more bodies in between those two groups at both intersections, and make sure we can get more ambulances in there. We need to create a no man's land at those two key intersections."

"We're on it," answered the third subordinate, a Lieutenant.

Robby took another look at the TV screen showing live-streaming drone footage over the two camps of protesters. He was amazed at how quickly the far right protesters were unloading their trucks and building their encampment. A large tent, a decent sized stage, eating areas, portable toilets, and even a hot tub were already in place.

But even more amazing to Robby was how quickly the Unite the Left protesters were responding. Hordes of people were flooding into the side streets behind the Unite the Left camp, bringing small tents, sleeping bags, barbecues, food, and water. He expected as much from the far right, seeing as it appeared to be a well-organized and well-funded occupation. But Robby was shocked at the power of social media and how fast it was allowing the left wing protesters to pivot and reorganize.

Robby paused to think for a moment, considering his next step. He shouted to an officer at the Comms desk near the middle of the bus.

"Sergeant," he shouted. "Have we established communications with that guy in the van? What's his name again?"

"No contact yet, sir," the Sergeant replied. "His name is MacDonald—Bryson MacDonald. He calls himself Scorpion8188 on the radio, and he's the founder of that far right group, The Brothers of Liberty. He's from Idaho."

"Just wonderful," Robby muttered. "Right wing extremists."

"Seems that way, sir. I've found their frequency and I'm monitoring them now."

"Good work, Sergeant," Robby called. "What's up?"

"He sounds real pissed, sir. Apparently, he thinks they have a mole who leaked details of the convoy to the Unite the Left group, and ruined their plan to encircle the White House."

"Is that so," Robby mulled. "I think it's time I had a little chat with Mr. MacDonald: maybe ask him what he plans to do, now that his surprise party's been crashed."

Robby made his way to the Comms desk.

"Patch me in, Sergeant," he ordered.

The Comms officer hit a few keys on his keyboard.

"You're good to go, sir," he answered.

"Scorpion8188, this is MDCP Captain Robby speaking, come in?"

Robby listened to the background noise as he awaited a reply. Finally, the background hissing stopped and a voice came through.

"This is Scorpion. Good to hear from you Captain. What kin I do fer ya?" Bryson said.

Robby paused for a moment, choosing his words carefully before answering.

"I think the better question is what can I do for *you*?" Robby responded. "I don't think you came all the way from Idaho just for a camping trip, am I right? So why don't you tell me why you really came here, and what I can do to help?"

The airwaves went silent again, except for the background hissing. Finally, Bryson's voice came through again.

"Nobody don't ever take people like us seriously," Bryson began, "'cept fer President Spencer. He unnerstood us, an' he was goin' to make this country great again. Now the progs have poisoned 'im, an' that new, moderate, bitch of a President is goin' to take us backwards again. So, we came to talk some sense to her: it's time she listened an' heard what the people in this country really want!"

"I hear you, Scorpion," Robby said. "But I'm afraid I can't speak for the President."

"Of course you can't," Bryson replied. "So, let me know when our new President's ready to listen to us. We're here to exercise our democratic rights under the Constitution: to gather peacefully an' speak freely. So we're content to stay as long as it takes fer her to listen to our grievances, an' we ain't goin' nowhere till then. It's goin' to be a gorgeous summer evenin'. Think we're gonna fire up the grills, have some brews, an' sit aroun' the campfire tonight. Lemme know if y'all hear from Madam President, Captain. Cuz we ain't goin' nowhere! Over an' out."

Bryson's voice went dead, and the gentle hissing of the empty airwaves resumed.

"Scorpion8188, this is Captain Robby."

The airwaves remained silent, except for the uninterrupted background hissing. Robby turned to the Comms Sergeant.

"Better patch me through to the Mayor," he said. "Looks like we've got us a situation that isn't going away unless he takes this right to the top."

THE FAINT fragrance of wood emitted by the room's wood panelling and finishings gave the Aspen Lodge a completely different vibe from the opulent, officious decor of the Oval Office. Outside, the sun was setting over the forested Maryland countryside, but inside the cabin, the room felt cozy and welcoming. Although Rachel had only been here a few hours, she was already more relaxed than she was in the White House, where she still felt like an imposter who didn't belong.

Rachel and Nicole sat in lime-green plush velvet chairs, across a coffee table from Senator Crowley, who occupied a matching love seat. Near the informal seating area, a large flat screen TV flashed video clips of the afternoon's skirmishes between the two opposing protest groups on the streets outside the White House. The sound on the TV was muted while the room's three occupants conducted their business.

"Given that I didn't have two months to select a cabinet, like President Spencer did after the election, and given today's serious events and our ongoing issues with China, I've decided to ask Ron's entire cabinet to continue on for at least the next few months," Rachel announced.

"I'm glad to hear that," Senator Crowley replied. "I think you would have been making a grave mistake if you'd tried to start from scratch."

"I agree with the Senator, Ma'am," Nicole said, while nodding her agreement. "I think you've got more than enough on your plate right now, without putting extra pressure on yourself."

Nicole noticed a video reporter on the TV. She was interviewing Captain Robby outside his mobile control center about the clashes on Washington's streets, and about the two camps that were quickly becoming entrenched on them.

"Excuse me, Ma'am," she said. "I think we should watch this. It's Captain Robby."

Nicole reached for the remote and unmuted the TV.

"We've managed to separate the parties at the two major intersections," Robby was saying. "We've created a couple of so-called no man's land areas between the camps, and the situation is now stabilizing."

Robby pointed into an unseen crowd of reporters for his next question, and a woman's voice could be heard over the crowd.

"Will there be any charges laid against the instigators of this riot?"

"We haven't yet determined exactly what, or who, instigated the two riots. At this point, we don't have enough evidence to start prosecuting individuals. I should note, however, that we're reviewing all available CCTV and social media footage. If we see evidence of individuals committing crimes, we will identify them and consider pressing appropriate charges. Next question."

Robby pointed to another reporter, this time a man.

"Is there any plan yet for ending the occupation of the streets surrounding the White House?" the reporter continued. "Any timeline for when it's safe for the President to return?"

"In answer to your first question, that call will come from the Mayor's office. As for your second question, I believe it's the President's security team who will advise the President as to when she might be able to return."

"There are rumours that some of the protesters have demands for the President. Can you comment?" the reporter continued.

"I can confirm that," Robby said. "Both camps are saying they won't leave until somebody listens seriously to their demands, and until those demands are met."

Nicole held up the remote and muted the sound again, before turning to the President.

"What do you think, Ma'am? Do you think you should intervene?"

"I think it's premature for me to make any kind of decision like that. We haven't even heard what demands they have, if any. I'd like to withhold comment until we have more information."

"Madam President, you don't want to appear weak," Senator Crowley responded. "This is an opportunity to show the American public what you're made of. Take back the streets from those hoodlums!"

Rachel paused for a moment to ponder the situation.

"I think we need to tread very lightly here," she answered. "We don't want to appear like we're denying these people—on both sides of those barricades—their freedom to congregate and their freedom to speak freely."

"But this has turned into much more than peaceful protests!" Crowley insisted. "It's erupted into violence. And who knows what would have happened if you weren't evacuated!"

"I agree, Ma'am," Nicole chimed. "I think that the longer this standoff goes on, the worse you're going to look."

Rachel paused for another moment to reflect. Finally she looked up at Nicole and Crowley with determination.

"I'm sick and tired of all the division in this country," she announced. "And I don't want to be the one who is seen as making it worse. Just look at what happened with the standoff in Ottawa in 2022: bringing in police and clearing the protesters, without at least listening to their grievances. It only deepened divisions across Canada. So, can we afford more demonstrations that close major border crossings across *our* country, like they did at the Ambassador Bridge in Detroit in 2022?"

Rachel paused and reached for a glass of water, then took a sip while she considered the situation.

"The American people, on both sides of the political spectrum, are becoming increasingly dissatisfied and restless," Rachel continued. "We know that they're becoming more cynical of us, their politicians, and with our bureaucrats. Just look at how many people across the country—and around the world, for that matter—refused to accept public health guidelines, and the science behind it, during the pandemic!"

Rachel's eyes narrowed, and she glared at Crowley.

"What if we actually take some time to listen to both sides?" she continued. "What if we see this as an opportunity to learn, instead of seeing it as a crisis that we need to squash? What if I were to recommend bringing in an objective, non-partisan team to hear the grievances from both sides?"

Senator Crowley huffed and shook his head from side to side.

"And just where do you think you'd find such a thing in this country? It doesn't exist. It's a pipe dream, Madam President!"

Rachel paused one more time.

"Then maybe I'll just have to reach outside the country to find that kind of objectivity."

Rachel's words hung in the air, leaving both Nicole and the Senator with puzzled looks on their faces. Finally, Senator Crowley rose to his feet and gave his President a stern look.

"Just don't wait until it's too late," Madam President. "The entire nation is watching: not just the people, but the House and the Senate too. They're all waiting for you to screw up so they can move in for a kill, and I hope that doesn't happen."

Crowley looked at Nicole, who took the Senator's cue and rose to her feet.

"Thank you for coming, Senator," she said. "I'm sure we'll be in touch soon, especially as more information becomes available. Let me show you out."

Senator Crowley nodded to Rachel, then he turned and followed Nicole to the cabin's front door, and then outside onto a pathway. Once outside, he turned to Nicole.

"I hope you can talk some sense into her, young lady. Her talk about bringing in somebody from outside the country: what an absurd idea!"

"I'm glad you agree," Nicole replied. "Between the two of us, and our mutual connections, I'm sure we can find ways to put some pressure on her, and to help her change her mind."

She gave the Senator a knowing glance. He smiled at Nicole and then chuckled.

"You're an ambitious one, young lady. And smart, too! I admire that. You play your cards right, and maybe it will be *you* sitting in that cabin someday."

With a nod of his head, the Senator ambled down the pathway towards the parking lot and his waiting ride. Nicole watched for a moment, allowing herself to let Crowley's words sink in. She smiled while she allowed her mind to wander, secretly envisioning his prediction coming true.

CHAPTER 4—AND I'M TAYLOR SWIFT

A WARM, dry breeze blew through Samantha Bower's hair as she cycled along College Avenue, past the entrance gates to the University of Saskatchewan and then past the Royal University Hospital. She was on her way downtown to celebrate with some fellow grad students, but as she reached the University Bridge, she paused to enjoy the view across the South Saskatchewan River to Downtown Saskatoon.

Sam had to admit that she'd come to prefer the dry prairie heat to the frequently oppressive humidity of Ontario summers. This pleasantly warm prairie evening was a far cry from the many treks Sam had made on foot across the same bridge over the past two winters. Sam shuddered as she recalled bone-chilling -40°C wind chills, driven by the bitter north winds that funnelled down the river valley during those frigid winter days, when the sun set so early in the afternoon.

Now, although it was past nine o'clock in the evening, the summer sun still cast its golden rays over the city, thanks to Saskatchewan's northerly latitude. To the west, Sam saw the distinctive black girders of the old railway bridge and the green riverbank and pathways along the opposite bank of the river. To the south, the venerable old Bessborough Hotel and the Broadway Bridge took on the golden hue of the sun's fading rays. Sam's supervisor, Dr. McCulloch, a long-term resident of the city and a self-confessed "old hippie," had shown Sam an old Joni Mitchell LP, containing the singer's own painting of the city landscape at this same time of the evening. Looking down over the city, Sam now appreciated why the artist was inspired to capture that famous landscape and to use it on her album cover.

Sam's earbuds signalled an incoming call. Glancing down at the screen strapped to her arm, she smiled and picked up.

"Hi, Sam here," she said cheerfully.

"Samantha, dear. It's your aunt Rose. How did your defence go today?"

"I passed!" Sam squealed excitedly. "It was unanimous from both Departments, Psychology and Indigenous Studies, and I only have a couple of minor revisions to do!"

"Congratulations! I knew you would do well. Wasn't it a bit strange for them to be holding your defence on a Saturday?"

"Yeah, it was a bit weird," Sam answered. "But Dr. McCulloch leaves on Monday to spend the summer at her cottage up north. And my external Indigenous examiner had to squeeze it into her itinerary before flying back to Vancouver tomorrow morning."

"And what did they have to say about your research?" Rose asked.

"They praised my sensitivity towards the residential school survivors that I interviewed, and they agreed that my qualitative approach to gathering their stories was ideally suited to working with that particular Indigenous population," Sam said.

"Well, I'm so happy for you," Rose said. "You deserve their praise. How are you doing otherwise?"

A significant pause followed as Sam pondered the question.

"Okay, I guess," she answered, finally. "I didn't realize how much I miss seeing Hunter, Arjun, and Terri, after seeing them and getting their input on *The Night Class* manuscript last summer. And I really miss you and the Healing Lodge!"

"I miss seeing you too," Rose replied.

Sam felt her eyes starting to water, and she was sure she detected a sniffle or two coming from Rose.

"How *is* Hunter?" Rose asked. "Do you talk to him often?"

Sam smiled at Rose's question. She knew Rose had been trying to play matchmaker with her and Hunter, ever since Rose met him at Charlie's funeral.

"Not too often," Sam admitted. "It's hard to have any kind of a relationship when he's in Ontario and I'm in Saskatchewan. I don't know if there's anything there, or not."

Feeling like the conversation was growing awkward, Sam quickly changed the subject.

"I was thinking of going back home for a couple of weeks to visit Uncle Bob and Aunt Melanie," Sam said. "Things are going to be slow at school during the summer, with Dr. McCulloch being away. I can't do much more until she finishes reading the draft proposal for my doctorate."

Sam paused to take a quick drink of water from a bottle mounted on her bike.

"And I'd love to come and visit you, that is, if you're going to be around," she continued.

"You just tell me when you're coming, and I'll be sure to make time for my favourite niece," Rose answered.

As Sam opened her mouth to reply, her earbuds chimed for another incoming call. Her aunt's voice faded into the background, and her mind momentarily checked out of the conversation with Rose as she read the caller ID.

Unknown Caller

Maryland, USA

"Are you there, Sam?" Rose asked. "Is everything alright?"

Sam let the unexpected call go to voicemail and brought her mind back into the present.

"Uh, yeah ... I'm okay," she said. "I just had another call come in on my phone. It was weird—said it came from Maryland. Probably just another scam. That's all I seem to get on my phone lately."

"I know," Rose said. "It happens to me all the time too. But, about your visit, just give me a call and let me know when you're coming."

"Okay, I'll do that ..."

Sam's earbuds started chiming once more. She glanced at her phone and realized the call was from Maryland again.

"My phone's ringing again, Rose. I'll look into booking a flight and I'll phone you back in a day or two, okay?"

"Of course, dear. Talk to you soon. Love you!"

By the time Rose's call disconnected, Sam's phone stopped ringing. She removed the phone from her armband and dialed to check her voicemail. There was one unheard message.

Hello. My name is Nicole Davies, and I'm the Chief of Staff for Rachel Williams, President of the United States. Please call this number back when you hear this message.

Sam huffed as the message ended.

"Right, and I'm Taylor Swift," she scoffed. "Do they think I was born yesterday."

Once again, Sam's earbuds started their relentless chiming. This time, she tapped an earbud to take the call, and waited to hear who was on the other end.

"Hello? Is this Samantha Bower?" the voice asked.

After a short pause, Sam decided to reply.

"Yes," she said, tentatively. "This is Sam."

"My name is Nicole Davies. Did you get my voicemail message? I'm calling for Rachel Williams, President of the United States."

Sam's patience was running short and she started laughing.

"Right," she said indignantly. "Who is this ... really? What do you want from me? I'm just a poor university student, so why don't you go and try to scam somebody who's actually got some money to steal!"

There was a pause on the other end, while the voice spoke to somebody in the background.

"I'm going to hang up now," the voice said. "But, after I hang up, we'll be calling you on FaceTime. This call is for real, so please answer when we call."

Sam's phone went dead. She was tempted to fasten it back on her arm, and to continue riding downhill across the bridge. But, true to the mysterious Nicole Davies' word, the screen on Sam's phone lit up again, advertising that a video call was indeed coming from Maryland. And this time, she saw the caller's name:

Rachel Williams, POTUS

"Hello?" Sam said, tentatively.

A woman's face appeared on the screen and Sam found herself holding her breath, unable to find any words.

"Samantha, I'm Rachel Williams," the woman said. "I understand that this call must come as a huge surprise, but I have something I'd like to discuss with you."

Sam swallowed hard, unsure what to say.

"Okay, but why in the world would you want to talk to me? And you can call me Sam."

"Sam it is. Have you been watching the news on TV?" Rachel asked.

"Uh, no. I've been busy all day. Why?" Sam answered.

"I'm sure you're aware of the convoy that occupied Ottawa in 2022. Well, we've just had the same thing happen today in Washington, D.C. Only this time, the far right protesters in the convoy clashed on the streets with demonstrators from a Unite the Left protest. Right now, both sides have become entrenched in a standoff on the streets surrounding the White House."

Sam began to feel the urgency in the President's voice. But the call from Rachel Williams still left her confused.

"I've read your memoir, *The Night Class*," President Williams continued. "I was extremely impressed by your objectivity and your ability to bring that very diverse group of people together, especially at that difficult time in your life."

"Thank you," Sam replied. "But it was the team who finally got their act together and did the work."

Sam saw President Williams smile warmly.

"You're too modest," the President said. "You appear to have that rare ability to bring out the best in people, and to put their talents to their best use. So, I have a proposal for you."

"For me?" Sam asked.

"Yes, for you," the President replied. "Like the protesters in Ottawa, both encampments in Washington are demanding that I listen to their ultimatums before they will even consider leaving the streets. As you know, that didn't happen in Ottawa, and it likely prolonged the occupation in that city. Are you following?"

"Sort of," Sam said. "But what does that have to do with me?"

"Good question," the President responded. "While both sides want me to listen to their demands, neither side really trusts me: the Unite the Left because I'm a Republican, and the far right because they think I'm too moderate and I won't take them seriously. That's where you come in. I'd like you to consider bringing your team from *The Night Class* to Washington. I'd like you to objectively listen to the protesters' demands and convey those demands to me, along with your recommendations for how to address them."

The reality of the FaceTime call was beginning to hit Sam, along with a familiar feeling from her past: that feeling that she was an imposter.

"I see your dilemma," Sam said, hesitantly. "But why me? I don't know anything about your country's politics. I don't belong in your world."

"I think I understand how you feel," President Williams replied with a chuckle. "How do you think I felt after I suddenly, and totally unexpectedly, became President of the United States? Do you think I feel like I belong here?"

Sam paused for a moment, thinking about the other woman's situation.

"I suppose not, Madam President," Sam answered. "But that still doesn't answer my question. If *you* don't feel like you're qualified to negotiate with the protesters, then why *me*?"

"Don't sell yourself short," President Williams replied. "And please, skip the formalities. You can call me Ma'am, or even better, Rachel. Like I said before, I need somebody who is objective, and I doubt that I'm ever going to find anybody like that here in my own country. I need somebody from the outside: normal, everyday people who can relate to the normal, everyday people in those camps.

"So, why you?" she continued. "I love how you described yourself in *The Night* Class: how you learned to see things through two sets of eyes after learning of your Indigenous roots. I'm hoping you can help both of these camps to see things through two sets of eyes as well."

Sam watched as President Williams reached off camera for a water bottle, took a sip, and then replaced the bottle.

"Sam," the President continued. "I need a team who can listen to people whose opinions are extremely far apart, and still be able to help them find common ground, even through times of adversity. You and your team check all of these boxes. So, what do you say? Will you think about my offer?"

Sam, still in a state of semi-shock, swallowed hard and took a moment to think.

"Even if I were to say yes, Ma'am," Sam said, "I can't speak for the other members of the team."

"I understand," the President answered. "You need time to think about it, and to talk to the team. But I hope you realize that time is critical for me. I need to make a decision within the next day or two, at the very latest. So, can you at least take the night to think over my offer, and also to give your team some time to do the same?"

Sam went silent again, her mind still reeling after the President's offer came completely out of the blue. Finally she managed to gather her thoughts and find some words to reply.

"Okay," Sam said. "But I'm not going to promise anything. And if my team doesn't want to do it, then I'm out too."

"That's all I ask," President Williams said. She flashed a warm, reassuring smile that felt genuine to Sam.

"And one more thing," the President added. "I'm sure I don't need to remind you to keep this between you and your team. I'll call you tomorrow night, about the same time, for your answer. I look forward to your reply, and I hope that we'll be working together soon. Good night, Sam."

"Good night, Ma'am," Sam replied.

Sam's phone beeped twice as the video call ended.

She gazed out over the South Saskatchewan River at Downtown Saskatoon, which was now glowing deep gold as the sun edged its way slowly towards the horizon. Lights were beginning to turn on in buildings. Finally, Sam took a deep breath, letting the reality and the great significance of the last fifteen minutes sink in. As she switched on her bike's flashing LED lights for the ride downtown to the bar, she resigned herself to having an abbreviated thesis celebration. Even worse, she resigned herself to a sleepless night, at least until she resolved the many conflicting thoughts that were swirling around in her mind.

SOON AFTER Rachel Williams decided to address the nation, the serenity of her rustic Camp David office in the Aspen Lodge was replaced by the hustle and bustle of a TV news production team. Rachel chuckled to herself as she watched the proceedings, likening the scene to ants who had just discovered and invaded a nearby picnic. The space was now full of TV cameras, teleprompters, lights, reflectors, and a myriad of cables.

Rachel sat at her desk, reviewing a paper copy of her speech and the last-minute changes she had made to her address. The crew's makeup artist applied finishing touches to a couple of areas on Rachel's face where it was reflecting too much light from her dark skin. The team's director hovered nearby and glanced nervously at her watch, as she listened in her earpiece to instructions from the network's New York production team. Finally, she looked up at Rachel and the makeup artist.

"One minute! Everybody ready?" she said.

The director looked around the room at every team member, each of whom flashed her a quick thumbs up. The makeup artist hurriedly picked up the tools of her trade and scurried out of the room.

Rachel placed her speech on the desk in front of her and reached for one last sip of water. She felt her heart rate increase slightly. No matter how many times she faced the cameras, the nervous anticipation never failed to show up. But Rachel always took it as a good sign: that she was pumped and ready to go.

The director held up both hands, displaying all ten fingers.

"Ready, Madam President?"

Rachel nodded as the director's fingers counted down the seconds.

"In five, four, three ... " she continued. As she finished counting down the final three seconds silently with her fingers, she pointed to Rachel, who saw a red light illuminate on the TV camera directly in front of her.

"Good evening, my fellow Americans," she began, looking directly into the camera. "I come to you in your homes again tonight, only weeks after becoming your President, and two days before our nation's birthday, to discuss this afternoon's events on the streets of our nation's capital, which I'm sure you've all had a chance to see by now. On one hand, we saw a large crowd of peaceful demonstrators preparing to exercise their Constitutional rights to congregate freely, and to speak freely. On the other, we saw a highly secretive plan unfold, which would have seen a convoy of trucks, buses, and vans lay siege to my Presidential residence and office, had the plan not been foiled by the first group of protesters. In the end, street fighting broke out between the two groups. If not for the rapid and professional response of the Metropolitan D.C. Police, the protests and the fighting may have led to more serious injuries, or even deaths.

Rachel paused to let her words sink in with her audience.

"Thankfully, most of those who were injured in today's rioting were not seriously hurt, and there were no deaths."

Rachel reached for her glass of water and took a sip while she watched the next segment of her speech appear on a teleprompter, which was mounted on the TV camera. The director nodded her approval to the President.

"Now that both of these large groups of protesters have shown their intent to occupy the streets, and now that we have a standoff between the two political factions, you are all likely asking yourself: What's next? What is my President going to do?"

Rachel paused again for effect before continuing.

"There are those around me who favour calling in the National Guard to clear our streets, very much like how the police in Ottawa, Canada ended the occupation of that city's streets in 2022. But that decision led to a great deal of dissension across that country. One of the lessons we learned from studying the Ottawa police intervention, was that nobody in a position of power cared to sit down and listen to the protesters—to ask them why they were so disenchanted—before forcibly removing them from the streets. 'Nobody would listen,' they cried! And that failure to listen only caused more disenchantment and division within that country in the aftermath of their convoy protest!"

"I CAN'T believe this!" Cecilia Robinson shouted, as she and the Unite the Left organizers all watched the Presidential address. "Is she trying to say that we're just as responsible as the fascists for what happened today?"

"Shhhh!" Senator Delgado hissed. "Let's listen to what she's saying!"

Cecilia, Delgado, and Dudley Morris sat in front of Cecilia's laptop computer, which she had set up on a small table in a modest twelve foot by twenty foot tent that had been donated to their movement, and had only been erected about an hour before the President was to go on the air. Another five organizers, representing a variety of progressive groups and issues, were gathered behind the threesome to watch the address as well.

Thirty-three-year-old Nasir Hazrat, an Afghan refugee who aided U.S. Forces while they were occupying his country, was now living in Newark, New Jersey. Like Cecilia, he was an avid supporter of progressive, social democracy. It was his dedication to pursuing immigration reform and laws against hate crimes, especially Islamophobia, that prompted him to volunteer to help Cecilia organize the weekend's Unite the Left festivities.

Kymberly Babineau, a twenty-one-year-old university student from Florida, was a college shooting survivor who had also lost an older sister in a mass high school shooting. Predictably, she was an advocate for the reform of gun laws. However, she was also a realist, who understood that her fellow Americans were never going to give up their guns without a fight. She came to Washington to push for a "third way" which finds common ground and agreement in regulating guns. She was also a supporter of social media controls for any speech or activities that endorse hatred.

Stephen Danilenko, a fifty-five-year-old lawyer from New York City, was a son of Jewish immigrants from the Ukraine. A devout advocate for laws against hate crimes, he was also an avid supporter of ANTIFA. Like Kymberly, he supported limits on social media freedom that would ban online posts containing hate speech, or any kind of hate crimes.

Idris Mohammed was a gay Islamic man in his mid-twenties who had fled Africa, fearing for his life in the face of laws against homosexuality. He came to America to seek asylum and safety, and was living in Miami when he survived a mass shooting in a gay night club. In addition to being active in the LGBTQ2+ and African communities, he was also an advocate for bans on guns and hate crimes.

The last of the Unite the Left organizers in the tent was Danielle Chen, the Asian-American actress and daughter of Democratic Representative Michael Chen. Much to her father's chagrin, she took great pleasure in proclaiming her bisexuality and her support for the LGBTQ2+ community. She also advocated for sweeping bans on virtually all guns. Finally, she was a loud and proud pro-choice advocate, as well as being a supporter for a living wage, something that her father vehemently detested. "After all," her father had argued repeatedly, "If I can claw my way to the top from being a poor immigrant, anybody can do it if they work hard enough."

A hush fell over the organizing group as Rachel continued her address.

"First of all," she continued firmly, "Let me assure you that I do not condone what happened on our streets today. The planned siege of the White House was quite simply an attack on democracy, and particularly on the President's role in that sacred process. However, it is not the siege itself that disturbs me so deeply."

She stopped purposely again for effect, and stared directly into the camera.

"What disturbs me the most is the fact that so many people, on both sides of the political spectrum, are so dissatisfied with our democracy that they feel justified in going to such lengths to disrespect it, and possibly destroy it!"

She paused again, reaching for another sip of water to pace herself.

"The widespread dissatisfaction and partisan protests we witnessed today are not new. If we study our history, we see that those deep divisions go back almost two-hundred-fifty years, to the time when the Fathers of our nation were crafting our Constitution. And those partisan divisions have persisted ever since that time. The Constitution, to which both sides cling, is no longer working for either side. Thus, it is no longer working for our country. Our drastically different partisan interpretations of the Constitution are tearing us apart."

Rachel paused again and took a deep breath. The red light on the camera in front of her went dark, and the light on a second camera, to her left, turned on. She turned towards the second camera.

"Too frequently, I have heard people around the world say that the term 'United States of America' is a joke. Instead, those people often refer to us as the 'Divided States,'" Rachel said solemnly. "I don't know about you, but I'm sick to death of this divisiveness and the image we are portraying to the rest of the world. As a nation, we must find a way to overcome our differences. And we must do it soon, before our nation tears itself apart!"

"Why isn't she pointing the finger squarely at Bryson MacDonald?" Dudley shouted. "He's the one who planned the siege. He's the one who should be arrested for sedition. We were just gathering to protest peacefully. I don't get it!"

"I disagree," a strong voice said from behind the organizers, where Jordan Marsh had been watching the broadcast from just inside the tent's entrance.

All heads turned to see who had disagreed with Dudley so boldly.

"It seems to me that she's being careful *not* to pick sides," Jordan continued. "She's calling on both parties to find ways to work together."

"Shhhh, she's still talking!" Senator Delgado shouted.

The organizers' voices became more muted as the President's words continued to come from the laptop.

"So, I'm not going to be a President who makes the same mistake that they made in Ottawa. I intend to be a President who listens to what the people want: *all* of the people! After all, we in government are here to represent and to work for each and every one of you, to make your lives better."

IN STARK contrast to the hastily assembled and modest headquarters of the Unite the Left encampment, an eight-by-ten foot projection screen occupied only a small portion of one side of a huge mess tent and entertainment venue in the Liberty Convoy encampment. Bryson MacDonald, owner of a gun shop in Idaho, and far right podcaster Anna Dahl shook their heads in dismay as they watched President Williams' address, along with six other convoy organizers.

Thirty-two-year-old Jessica Murray was a well known Indigenous activist who accepted Bryson's invitation to join his Liberty Convoy as a way of getting the new President to listen to Indigenous land claims across America. She was a prominent member of the White Earth Nation in Minnesota, which successfully protested against a pipeline crossing of the Mississippi River in her state. Her convictions in that protest landed her in jail. She hoped to use the Liberty Convoy as a platform to lobby for informed consent from Indigenous people for any developments on their lands.

Sean Pritchard was a fourth generation rancher from Oregon who was having a progressively harder time making a living, now that the Upper Klamath Lake was drying up and water was becoming increasingly scarce. He was one of the ranchers who had set up a camp outside the Klamath Dam, eventually attempting to open the dam's flood gates, because they felt that Washington hadn't lived up to its promise of "guaranteed" rights to water along the Klamath watershed, a claim that conflicted with the nearby Indian reservation's claim of having rights over their resources.

John Gregg was the owner of a family-run grocery store that had been in Jasper, Texas for three generations. However, in recent years, he had been finding it increasingly difficult to compete against the local big box store. His family had been Republicans for as long as anybody could remember, and John blamed the Democrats for everything that was wrong in America today. He came to Washington to lobby on behalf of rural Americans, who were finding it increasingly difficult to make a good living in their communities, and who were feeling increasingly marginalized. John was a dedicated pro-life and Second Amendment advocate, who also supported legislation to limit immigration and to regulate voting access.

Pastor Luke Kessler was an extreme Evangelistic Pastor who adhered strictly to the Bible for the guidance of members of his cult-like flock. He eschewed anything that had to do with any form of government. He was young, and his enigmatic personality attracted members who shared his ultra-conservative views on abortion, public health mandates, traditional medicine, public education, and the traditional media. In the past, his members had been investigated by the local Child Welfare agency for possible abuse and neglect of children, as well as elder abuse from denying members access to essential medical treatment. Unlike other protesters who felt increasingly ignored or marginalized in society, Pastor Luke preferred to claim that his congregation was continually being persecuted by government agencies.

Norm Barfield, also known as piggyback06, was a fifty-eight-year-old long-haul trucker from Bryson MacDonald's home town of Couer D'Alene, Idaho. He was Bryson's right hand man in the Brothers of Liberty. Norm had little formal education due to severe dyslexia, and he had known no other jobs besides long-haul trucking since he was old enough to drive the big rigs. He was a clear case of a marginalized American white male, who had become increasingly bitter over the marginalization caused by his poor education and limited employment possibilities. He shared Bryson's view that the label "Redneck," as applied to marginalized white Americans, was the most racist term in America today. Like Bryson, he was in the convoy to fight for his Constitutional rights and freedoms, and to make America great again.

Sitting apart from the remaining organizers, and paying little attention to Rachel Williams' address, was twenty-two-year-old gamer, Ming "Martin" Lee. His family immigrated to the States from Hong Kong when he was a child. Unlike everybody else in the tent, Martin held very few strong political views, apart from a strong dislike of the establishment. Consequently, he simply enjoyed using his gaming and hacking skills to fight the establishment, a modern day version of sticking it to the man. His purpose for being in the convoy was to be Bryson's tech advisor and general "shit disturber."

"Whatta load'a horse shit!" Bryson cursed. "The people already spoke. They voted in November, an' they voted fer President Spencer's brand'a change! This bitch was just his runnin' mate—it's her job to carry out his policies an' his plan fer the country. If she was doin' 'er job properly, we wouldn'a had to come here to talk some sense back into her."

The rest of the committee, along with a tent full of convoy supporters, shouted their collective support for Bryson, along with jeers for the President.

Oblivious to the far right camp's distain for tonight's address, Rachel Williams' words continued to travel over the airwaves and the internet.

"So, I plan to listen to those of you who came to Washington to protest: *all* of you, whether you support the left or the right." Rachel continued.

The red light on the second camera turned off, while the main camera, directly in front of Rachel, now had its light turn red. She turned her head towards the camera, her face now wearing a softer, more sincere look.

"I realize that very few of you trust me, because you haven't had a chance to really get to know me," she said. "As a result, I plan to bring in some non-partisan experts to help negotiate, and to help defuse the standoff on our streets. As of this moment, I have not selected such negotiators."

Rachel reached for her glass to take a sip of water. She looked back into the camera, wearing a look of genuine sincerity.

"So, I call on both sides of this standoff to be patient," Rachel continued, "while I work on a plan to bring in people whom you can truly trust to listen to your concerns, and to convey those concerns to me."

Jeers and heckles filled the convoy's tent.

"Oh, sure," Anna Dahl shouted. "More of the same old bull shit! She'll bring in some old, retired hacks from the 'objective' press, or some so-called experts from the universities. Same old Cathedral crap!"

A renewed roar of jeers for the President, along with cheers for Anna, arose in response to the podcaster's accusation, drowning out Rachel Williams, whose words were now falling on deaf ears in the Liberty Convoy tent.

NICOLE DAVIES stood just outside the Presidential Office as Rachel continued her address to the nation. She spoke into her cell phone in a hushed voice as she retreated further away from the national broadcast.

"I said I'm sorry," Nicole whispered loudly. "Both Crowley and I did our best to steer her away from this stupid plan. We both urged her to call in the National Guard ... I understand ... look, I don't see you doing anything to solve the problem! ... just tell him we're still working on her. And you've gotta stop calling me here, somebody's going to notice! I gotta go."

Nicole ended the call and slipped back into the rear of the Presidential Office to hear the end of the speech.

"Finally, I know this last announcement will come as a great disappointment to everybody who came to Washington to celebrate the Fourth of July," she said, her facial expression changing from one of sincerity to one of disappointment. "However, the Mayor and I have agreed that, out of an abundance of caution, this year's Fourth of July celebrations in Washington on Monday, including the fireworks, are cancelled. In addition, all major tourist attractions will be closed during the holiday."

One last time, Rachel paused for effect, and then she changed her expression back to one of friendly sincerity.

"Thus, we are asking all tourists for their cooperation, and we are asking them to leave the Capitol area as soon as possible, so that we can dedicate our security personnel to the occupation and standoff on our streets. God bless America. Good night to you all."

The broadcast's director nodded at Rachel as the TV camera's red light extinguished. After only a second of complete silence, the room erupted again into the same frenzy as before the show, as all of the worker ants went to work disconnecting cables and disassembling equipment. Rachel rose from her desk, walked around it, and shook hands with the director. She saw Nicole approaching her from the rear of the room.

"Thank you," Rachel said to the director. "How did I do?"

"Just fine, Madam President," she answered. "If you had some jitters, it certainly didn't show."

Rachel turned to Nicole.

"What did you think?"

The pregnant silence that followed told Rachel all she needed to know.

"We'll see," Nicole answered, her voice devoid of emotion. "It shouldn't be long before the reviews start coming in."

CHAPTER 5—CRANBERRY FLATS

A WARM, southeasterly wind blew through Sam's hair, giving her a much needed sense of freedom and escape from reality, as she pedalled up the road towards the conservation area's entrance. On her back, she carried a backpack with a small beach towel, sunblock, and her cell phone. Sunglasses shielded her eyes from the summer sun, which had initially peeked over the horizon three hours earlier and was now rapidly warming the Sunday morning air. She felt herself starting to sweat as she slowed her bike and the cooling breeze gradually disappeared.

She arrived at the park entrance just as a young female conservation officer unlocked a road barrier and swung it aside for the park's 8 a.m. opening. Sam pulled up to a bicycle rack inside the park's entrance, locked up her bike, and then set off on a footpath that wound its way down the steep, sandy riverbank to the South Saskatchewan River valley below. The river had gradually eroded the riverbank over millennia, creating a sandy flood plain alongside the river that was dotted with small pools that remained whenever water levels rose and then receded. Sam found one of those pools close to the riverbank. She removed the pack from her back, pulled out her towel, and spread it on the sand. Then she took off her shoes and let the warm sand flow between her toes and around her feet. Finally, she unbuttoned her blouse and wriggled out of her shorts until only a simple, orange bikini remained.

Sam sat down on her towel, took a deep breath, and allowed the serenity and the natural beauty of the conservation area to steep into her pores and calm her body. She allowed her mind to roam freely, letting go of the racing thoughts that had preoccupied it since the previous night. She watched as water fowl flew over the river or floated on the surface, listening to their calls and the soft, soothing gurgle of the fast-flowing river, only a few feet away. She watched as a young couple paddled a canoe across the river to an uninhabited island, access to which was forbidden to park users. She heard their giggles floating over the water, and she watched as they reached the island, pulled their canoe out of the water and hid it in the bush. She chuckled as the young couple threw caution to the wind and stripped off their clothing, before jumping into the chilly, fast-moving water. Their uninhibited and carefree laughter felt like medicine for Sam's conflicted soul.

Finally, the young couple climbed out of the river and giggled as they spread towels behind bushes on the island to avoid prying eyes. For a moment, Sam felt a faint trace of envy for the young couples' ability to be so free. Then she laid down on her back, took another long protracted breath, and exhaled slowly. As she repeated the cycle over and over, she closed her eyes and allowed the sounds of her natural surroundings to envelope her. She heard the caw-cawing of a nearby crow over the soft, gurgling and swishing sounds of the river.

As her breathing continued to slow, Sam felt the soothing warmth of the sun on her body, as if it was caressing, holding, and supporting her. She drifted in and out of the no man's land between consciousness and sleep. As she did so, the sounds surrounding her underwent a surreal transformation: the sounds of the river were voices whispering to her, spirits of the people who once inhabited the valley over thousands of years, their voices calling to her to return to the land and their ancient ways.

The caw-cawing of the crow now sounded increasingly human and more insistent. At the same time, a lone cloud moved in front of the sun and Sam felt a sudden chill that caused her entire body to shiver. She opened her eyes and looked up at the cloud. As the morning breeze blew in the sky above, the airborne droplets transformed into a prominent nose, chin, and then the profile of a human head.

"Charlie?" she said. "Is that you?"

The crow cawed again, followed by a flapping sound that gradually grew louder and closer, until the large black bird landed in the sand, just beyond Sam's reach.

"Are you trying to talk to me?" she asked.

Once again, the crow cawed. The whispering voices from the river seemed to rise and fall, as if the water was also trying to converse with the young woman lying on the river bank. Sam drifted back into a semi-conscious trance, envisioning her ancestors living in a simple, peaceful community beside the river: children playing, men returning from a hunt carrying the carcass of a deer, and women tending fires and preparing food. The images permeated through her body, until Sam felt them viscerally: messages from beyond the grave from her departed father, Charlie, and the rest of her ancestors.

I hear you ... I hear your message ... you want me to use my two sets of eyes ... you want me to help integrate your ways of seeing into the colonial ways of seeing the world ...

The sun's warmth started to creep gradually upward from her feet until her body once again felt as though she was being held and supported. Sam's eyes flickered open and she gazed up at clear blue sky. Her father's misty profile had morphed again and completely dissipated.

The sound of more giggling from the young lovers echoed across the water. Sam smiled, then reached into her backpack, removed her cell phone and earbuds, dialled a number, and waited while she listened to the phone ringing in her ears. Finally, she heard her aunt Rose's voice.

"Hello, Rose?" Sam said.

"Sam? This is a surprise," Rose answered. "It must still be early out west. Is everything alright?"

"Yes, I mean, sort of. I'm down by the river. I needed Mother Nature's peace and quiet so I could think. I really need your advice about something that's come up—something big."

"What is it, dear?" Rose asked. "Are you in any trouble?"

"No, nothing like that. Remember last night, when I had to answer another call?" Sam said.

"Is that what this is about?"

"Yeah. You're never going to believe who it was that called me."

Sam paused, feeling a bit foolish and a bit afraid that Rose wouldn't believe her. She hesitated for a moment before continuing.

"You know the demonstrations and the street fighting in Washington, D.C. yesterday?"

"Yes," Rose replied. "What about them?"

"Well, it was Rachel Williams who called—the President. She said she's read *The Night Class* and my story made a big impression on her. She actually asked if I'd bring the team to Washington to help negotiate with the two camps to try and end the occupations. Why would she think I, or we, could possibly help?" Sam asked.

A brief silence followed while Rose allowed the unexpected information to sink in.

"That certainly *is* a surprise! Maybe she identifies with you in some way," Rose answered.

"Me?" Sam asked. "Why would she identify with me? Half the time, I still feel like an imposter in grad school, like I don't ever really belong there."

"But you do," Rose replied. "Look at all the praise you received from your examiners the other day. They believe in your knowledge and skills. And obviously, the President must feel that she needs those skills right now."

"I just remembered something she said to me," Sam said. "She said something about her feeling like an imposter as the President. Do you really think she doubts herself like I do? She's the most powerful woman in the world right now. How can that be?"

"Why not?" Rose said. "She's human, just like the rest of us. What else did she say?"

Sam paused for a moment to think back to her conversation with the President.

"She said that she liked what I said about having two sets of eyes for seeing the world."

"Ah, she values the wisdom you've learned from our Indigenous culture and how you used that with the team in *The Night Class*," Rose answered. "What do you think you can bring to negotiations that non-Indigenous negotiators wouldn't bring?"

Sam paused to think again, noticing that the young couple on the island had returned to the river, shouting and laughing, seemingly without a care in the world.

"Well, there's the Healing Circle," Sam responded. "It was important for everybody on the team to feel like equals around the table. And Hunter taught me to think differently about time and its circular nature."

"Anything else, dear?" Rose asked. "Don't forget about our holistic perspective on life. How *all* lives are sacred, and that humans aren't above or below any other creatures, or other people. That our individual wellbeing depends completely on the wellbeing of everything around us in nature. If you can remember those basic, sacred teachings, you can navigate the waters that frighten you."

Sam gazed across the water to the young couple, who were climbing out of the river again. Their laughter floated across the water and Sam found herself smiling and talking to herself.

They've stripped themselves down to their natural selves, much like my ancestors. They've shed their fears and trusted themselves in the water. They don't seem to have a care in the world.

"So, you think I should do it?" Sam said, finally. "But I won't do it if the rest of the team isn't up for it."

"Then call them," Rose said. "Seek their thoughts and their wisdom. Then you will be able to follow your heart. You will know what to do. When does the President want an answer?"

"By tonight. I don't have much time."

"Well then, I think you'd better get busy, and I hope that you reach your team members. I should let you go. You have work to do. Good luck, Sam. I believe in you!"

Sam wiped away a single tear that escaped from one eye.

"Thanks, Rose. I miss you. Love you, I'll call you later."

Sam ended the call, then took a long, deep breath and allowed her surroundings to permeate her one last time. Then she made a decision.

Following the young couple's lead, she slipped out of her bikini. She glanced at the pool of standing water beside her, tempted to wade in and soak in its relatively warm, safe water. But instead, she wheeled around and made her way to the river, wading into the chilly waters until she was waist deep. She took a deep breath and submerged herself in a slower moving eddy near the shore, allowing herself to feel the cool, refreshing water flow over every inch of her bare skin as she held her breath and felt her body come alive. When she could no longer hold her breath, she surfaced and felt fresh air surge into her lungs.

She turned and waded back out of the water. As she did, she felt the wind flowing over her skin, simultaneously chilling and invigorating it. She slowed her breathing and felt the small, fine hairs on her arms and legs standing up and tingling as she made her way back. Finally, she laid down on her towel and closed her eyes, paying attention to every sensation in her skin. Her breathing slowed even more. While parts of her still felt cool and tingly, she sensed other parts being warmed by the sun. And as the feeling of warmth spread slowly across her body, she felt a sense of freedom and calm—of being unburdened—of feeling connected again to her ancestors and the message they had sent to her earlier.

She took one last slow, calming breath, then reached for her phone. She opened her contact list, selected a contact, and then waited for the call to connect.

ONLY HOURS after Rachel Williams' broadcast to the nation, Camp David's Laurel Lodge was a beehive of activity. Between the two TV cameras, the production crew, their cables, Secret Service agents, and a hand-picked audience of journalists, there was little room to move, except at the very back and along two narrow aisles on both sides of the room. Jordan Marsh counted herself lucky to be amongst the couple of dozen journalists the President had invited to be in attendance. The crowd was buzzing with conversation when Nicole Davies strode in and stood behind a podium. The Presidential Flag and the Stars and Stripes stood to the left and right, respectively, of the President's Chief of Staff.

"Good morning, everybody!" Nicole began. "Can I have your attention, please!"

Nicole stood patiently until the buzz in the room gradually gave way to a few hushed whispers.

"Thanks, folks," Nicole resumed. "The White House understands that the events of the past twenty-four hours in Washington have been unprecedented, and have progressed quickly. We've called this press conference to answer any questions you might have about the occupations on our streets, and about the President's address last night. So, let's begin ... you, sir?"

Nicole pointed to a middle-aged, balding man in the front row.

"For the Washington Post—I have a question about the so-called *Liberty Convoy* and their plot to surround the White House. Was the President's life really in any danger, and if so, who made the call to evacuate the White House?"

"Thank you," Nicole replied. "The White House only became aware of the convoy's existence about forty-five minutes before the first trucks were expected to arrive. We had no more information than that. It was extremely well-planned and was executed in secret, so we had no prior intel about its existence. The Secret Service, which is responsible for the President's security, made the determination that she should be evacuated from the White House out of an abundance of caution, given the unknown nature of the threat."

"I have a follow-up question," the reporter said. "Given what happened on January sixth in 2021, was there any consideration given to calling in the D.C. National Guard right away?"

"No, there was no such consideration," Nicole said. "One of the things that we learned from the January sixth riots was to have a protocol in place for responding to similar events. That protocol has laid out the areas of jurisdictions of the Capitol Police, MDCP, the D.C. National Guard, and federal agencies such as Homeland Security and the FBI. In this case, where the actions took place away from the Capitol buildings, on the streets of the city, the jurisdiction for responding to the alleged siege clearly belonged to MDCP. The Mayor and MDCP were in constant contact with the National Guard, but they felt they had the situation under control, and did not require any external resources to back them up. Next question?"

Nicole pointed to a short Asian woman in the second row, who was dressed in a cream-coloured suit. The reporter rose to her feet.

"I'm with CNN. There are rumours swirling around that the Brothers of Liberty have an arsenal of firearms hidden in their trailers. Is there any evidence that the White House is aware of, that this rumour might be true?"

"No," Nicole answered. "At least not that we are aware of. However, nobody really knows for sure what's in all of those trailers. All we've seen so far are their tents and sleeping bags, grills and mess tents, portable toilets, and so on. So, at this point, MDCP is assuming that there *might* be firearms, and they are preparing for any possible eventualities. Next?"

"I also have a follow-up," the woman said, as she waved her hand to keep Nicole's attention.

"If MDCP determines there are weapons, will the White House be calling on the FBI to investigate?"

Nicole smiled at the CNN reporter.

"I'm glad you asked that question," she responded. "I believe the FBI would have to be involved if they felt there was credible evidence of any federal laws being broken, including the presence of illegal firearms, or any evidence of a conspiracy against the President."

Nicole's eyes wandered over the invited reporters to the back of the room, where they met those of FBI Agent Matt Butler. In a very subtle gesture, he nodded his approval to Nicole. Her eyes resumed scanning the invited journalists and stopped when they reached a young woman wearing a bright multicoloured hijab. Nicole pointed to the woman.

"I believe you're next," she said.

"I'm from Al Jazeera," the woman announced. "Has the President received any demands yet from either side in this standoff?"

"No, she has not received any demands. To date, the White House has not had any communication with anybody on either side of this standoff."

The young woman raised her hand again.

"Are there any plans yet for establishing communications with both camps of protesters?"

"Not at this time," Nicole said. "We believe that emotions are still running high in both camps right now, and the President wants to allow some time for those emotions to cool, especially with tomorrow being the Fourth of July … I believe the New York Times is next."

A tall, redheaded Caucasian woman rose to her feet and made eye contact with Nicole.

"Thanks. Can you explain the President's reasoning for wanting to bring in outside, independent negotiators, instead of meeting personally with the demonstrators, given her expressed desire to take both sides seriously in this standoff?"

"Absolutely. Given the little information we have about the agendas of both groups of protesters, both Homeland Security and the Secret Service will not allow the President to put herself in any situation where her safety might be compromised, even if that were something she might contemplate. It's just a non-starter. Does that answer your question?"

"Not really," the reporter continued. "I get the security concerns. But why outsiders? Surely there's an abundance of experts here in Washington who are more than qualified to negotiate on the President's behalf."

Nicole flashed a friendly smile at the redhead.

"I'm afraid I can't speak for the President and her thought processes on that subject," Nicole answered.

A murmur arose within the cramped confines of the room. The reporters now had what they wanted: a sign of discontent within the White House.

"She must have her reasons for wanting to take that approach," Nicole added.

A slightly smug smile spread across Nicole's face as her eyes once again searched the attending journalists. Her eyes stopped when they reached Jordan Marsh, standing at the back of the room. Nicole's smile vanished and her eyes narrowed as the two women's eyes met.

"Ms. Marsh," Nicole said, trying not to let her displeasure show. She had done her best to dissuade the President from inviting the outspoken freelance reporter, but she was unable to sway her boss.

"Always a pleasure to have you in attendance," Nicole continued. "Your question?"

"I'd like to revisit the previous question about possible arms in the Liberty Convoy trailers. Does the White House have any theories about who's behind those rumours?"

Nicole's eyes narrowed and she glared suspiciously at Jordan. The woman was a relentless pain in the ass, who was like a bloodhound when it came to trying to disprove false news.

Jordan responded to Nicole's stony stare with a smug smile.

"No," Nicole said curtly. "We have no idea where those rumours are coming from. Perhaps you should ask your CNN colleague where she's getting her information."

Nicole looked up at Matt Butler, still standing against the back wall. She was pleased to see the concern on his face, and that he was equally displeased with Jordan's presence, knowing that the reporter could be an ongoing thorn in their sides. Suddenly, Butler glanced down at his phone, then he rushed from the room and out into an adjacent hallway. Nicole turned her attention back to the press conference.

"Next question ..."

"WHAT DO you want, Crowley!" Butler hissed into his phone, not hiding his anger. "You shouldn't be calling me, especially here!"

Senator Crowley ignored the FBI agent's admonishment.

"Our mutual friend wants to know why the President hasn't changed her mind yet about bringing in outsiders. What have you and Davies been doing? Besides fucking each other, I mean."

Matt's face went red. As a veteran field agent, he wasn't used to having people show such little regard towards him.

"Haven't you been watching the press conference?" Matt hissed. "We've called in some favours from the press and planted some rumours. We're trying to stir up the pot to justify getting the agency involved. And for your information, it looks like that seed is starting to take hold!"

"So what about getting the National Guard involved, ASAP? What have you been doing about that?" Crowley pressed.

"We're doing the best we can, sir. That Captain fucking Robby isn't about to let anybody else onto his turf. I'm working on a plan, but it will take some time."

"Well, work faster!" Crowley growled. "Our friend says to do whatever it takes to derail any of that bitch's plans for negotiating with those protesters!"

"Anything?" Matt asked bluntly.

"Anything!" Crowley replied. "Just don't get caught, is that clear?"

"Understood," Matt confirmed.

The call ended. Matt slid his phone back into his suit pocket, but he was no longer interested in returning to the press conference. His mind was more preoccupied with satisfying his and Crowley's mysterious and powerful mutual overlord. As he exited the Laurel Lodge and walked quickly to his car, he revisited the plan that had been germinating over the past twenty-four hours. Now that he had a green light from above, it was time to put that plan into action.

CHAPTER 6—REUNION

DRESSED IN his new tennis whites, the young South Asian man in his early twenties searched feverishly through his living room, but his tennis racket was nowhere in sight. He didn't want to blow it with Maryam by being late for their first date. He glanced anxiously at his watch, knowing that he was already running late, and he wasn't going to miraculously find an extra ten minutes of time. He hurried back into his bedroom and his eyes did another systematic scan around the room. Finally, he caught a glance of the missing racket's grip, sticking out from under one of the many piles of dirty clothes on the floor. He made a mental note that it was definitely time for a laundry day. He grabbed the racket and ran to the entrance of his apartment, where he stuffed it hurriedly into his backpack.

Before Arjun Patel's hand reached the doorknob to leave, he felt his cell phone buzzing in his pocket.

"Damn," he cursed. "Of course, when I'm already late!"

Tempted to let the call go to voicemail, he quickly scrapped the idea in case it was Maryam who was calling. He glanced at the phone, and his face lit up in surprise. He swiped to answer the call.

"Sam, is that really you? How are you?"

"Yes, it's really me," Sam said. "I'm fine. How are you, and how's Harvard treating you?"

"I'm good," Arjun answered. "I really like it here, and the people are great."

"So, any regrets about switching from medicine to political science?"

"You mean apart from my mother still complaining about it?"

Both Arjun and Sam chuckled, knowing that his mom had always had her heart set on her son becoming a doctor.

"But seriously," Arjun continued. "This is the direction I want to go. I think this is where I belong. So, what's new with you?"

Sam paused for a moment, searching for the right words.

"Have you been watching the news from Washington?" she said, finally.

"Are you kidding," Arjun replied. "I can't avoid it. That's all we see on the news down here. Why do you ask?"

Sam went silent again for a moment, before she finally responded.

"You're never going to believe me, but hear me out. I got a call last night from the President."

"Which President?" Arjun asked. "Of your university?"

"No. *THE* President—of the United States!" Sam blurted. "Apparently, she read *The Night Class* and she loved what the team managed to accomplish on the Reconciliation project. So, she wants us to go to Washington to help negotiate with the protesters in both camps."

Arjun was momentarily lost for words.

"You're joking, right?" he asked, finally.

"I'm afraid not," Sam said. "She's given me until tonight to contact the team and to let her know if we're willing to do it. I told her I wouldn't consider it unless you, Hunter, and Terri are all willing to join me. You're the political brains of the group: we're nothing without you. So, if you say no, I won't even bother phoning the others."

"You know this is right in my wheelhouse. My thesis topic's about why people are losing faith in democracy. But, the President? The standoff in Washington? I don't know. Why us?"

Sam chuckled at Arjun's response.

"That's exactly what I said when she asked," she replied. "But she said that she wants somebody from outside Washington: outside the U.S., in fact. I guess she thinks we'll be more objective, given how the country is so polarized. And she really liked the Indigenous approaches that Hunter and I brought to the Reconciliation team."

Sam paused to give Arjun time to digest her information.

"So, what do you say?" she asked. "I won't be offended if you say no."

The line went silent as Arjun mulled things over. Finally, he made up his mind.

"The way I see it," he said. "this is either the biggest break I'll ever get in my new career, or it will be the end of my credibility, but what the hell, why not?"

"You're in?" Sam said incredulously. She hadn't believed that he would actually take the President's offer seriously.

"You actually want to do it?" she repeated.

"Sure," Arjun answered. "It's the chance of a lifetime. I'd be crazy to pass this up. And it would be great to be working together again. So again, why not!"

Because she hadn't actually expected Arjun to be on board, Sam was momentarily speechless. She realized she hadn't thought any further ahead about the implications of getting involved in the Washington occupation, and reality was setting in quickly.

"Alright, then," she said, finally. "If you're in, I guess I'm in too! You and Hunter both have your shared interest in constitutions. Can I get you to call him and see if he's on board? I'll try to track down Terri before tonight."

"You're sure you don't want to call Hunter yourself?" Arjun asked. "I thought you two were close."

Sam paused again. Arjun had touched a nerve.

"It's complicated," Sam answered. "You know, long distances and everything."

"I see," Arjun said. "Okay, I'll phone him. I just have to find a tactful way to postpone a tennis date first."

"Sorry about that, but thanks," Sam said. "Call me as soon as you've talked with him. I'll phone you once I've talked with Terri. It was great talking with you again."

"You too, Sam. Talk to you later."

HUNTER MACMILLAN glanced at the weather app on his phone, and then looked towards the west. The wind was already picking up and the angry grey clouds in the distance told him the app's severe weather warning was one to be taken seriously. It was another hot, hazy, and humid summer day in Southwestern Ontario, but it looked like an incoming cold front was going to put an end to the heatwave.

He picked up his pace, hurrying the last four blocks towards *Spirits of the Seven Generations* and shelter from the incoming summer storm. He enjoyed volunteering at the Indigenous support centre every weekend, and he was looking forward to a traditional drumming session on this hot, sticky afternoon.

Ironically, and without warning, the sound of traditional drumming and chanting blared from his pocket, signalling an incoming call. He came to a stop while he fished his phone from his pocket. When he saw Arjun's name on the screen, he quickly swiped to answer the call, and then continued to rush towards his destination.

"Arjun," he bellowed. "How the heck are you?"

"I'm great," Arjun replied. "And you? How's law school? Just one more year before you graduate, right?"

"Yup. I've been packing four years of classes into three, so the time's been flying by," Hunter answered. "What's up with you these days?"

"I just had a call from Sam, in Saskatchewan," Arjun said. "She's got a proposal for getting the team back together: something really big. She wanted me to call you, to find out if you're interested."

Hunter went silent as soon as he heard Sam's name.

"Any reason why she didn't call me herself?" he asked.

"A couple of reasons," Arjun said. "The biggest reason is that there's some urgency to her proposal, and she needs to reach Terri as soon as possible. She needs to hear from all of us by tonight."

"And the second reason?" Hunter asked.

"I sensed some awkwardness about phoning you," Arjun said. "I didn't push her."

"Okay," Hunter huffed. He was starting to breathe heavily as he rushed the last block towards his destination. "So, what's this project that's so important."

"You're not going to believe this; I didn't at first," Arjun began. "She got a call from President Rachel Williams, asking if our team would consider coming to Washington to negotiate with both sides in the current street occupation."

"What?" Hunter bellowed. He skipped up four steps to a front porch at *Spirits of the Seven Generations*, grateful to have some shelter from the wind and the inevitable heavy rain coming his way.

"She's not just pulling your leg?" Hunter continued. "Why us?"

Arjun laughed out loud.

"That's exactly what I said! Apparently, the President doesn't think she can find anybody in the U.S. who is unbiased enough for the job. Sam sounded reluctant at first, but I think she'll do it if the rest of us are onboard."

"So, I take it you said yes?" Hunter asked.

"Yup. And that's why Sam has to reach Terri this afternoon," Arjun added. "I'm pumped for a chance to get the team back together. What do you think? Are you even available?"

Arjun waited patiently while his friend and former colleague pondered the situation.

"I've got a month off before we're back to classes for the fall," Hunter said. "And it would be great to see all three of you again. So, I guess I'm in if everybody else says yes."

All of a sudden, huge drops of rain started to splatter on the sidewalk below, and a giant gust of wind hit the side of Hunter's face. He saw flashes of lightning in the angry grey clouds, and the sound of thunder rumbled ever closer.

"That's great!" Arjun answered. "I'll let Sam know. She'll be calling each of us this afternoon to let us know if this is a go or not."

The huge droplets of rain transformed into a torrent within seconds, with the storm's preceding wind shear driving the rain sideways. Giant maple trees in the old neighbourhood were whipped back and forth like rag dolls, shedding leaves and small branches. A fat, wet maple leaf smacked Hunter in the side of the face. Seconds later, a brilliant flash of lightning lit up the sky and a crash of thunder followed almost immediately, as he peeled the soggy leaf from his face.

"I'd better go inside," Hunter shouted. "Don't want to get struck by lightning! Talk to you soon!"

"THAT'S IT for this week," Terri Fortin shouted. "Good work, ladies. And you too Jason!"

She wiped the sweat from her forehead with a towel, as the students in her Introduction to Pole Dancing class gulped water and wiped sweat from their beet-red faces.

"That's our last class of the season, but I hope to see you all back again in the fall for Level Two."

She reached for her water bottle and took a lengthy guzzle, then she started gathering her belongings. After two years of attending university in Ontario while her husband got his certification in Oral Surgery, being back in her Edmonton pole-dancing studio this past year was a breath of fresh air. It wasn't like she disliked being a university student, it just felt great to be back home and doing the things she loved best, while university took a backseat in the evenings.

A sudden blare of dance music erupted from Terri's phone, the ring-tone startling her out of her brief reverie. When she saw the caller's name, she broke into a wide grin.

"Sam! How the hell are you? It's been a while!"

"I'm good," Sam replied. "How about you? How's the dancing school going?"

"Busy as ever," Terri said. "But things will be slower over the summer. It'll be a nice change."

There were a few seconds of dead air before Sam responded.

"So, how would you like to get away for a little while?"

Terri roared with laughter.

"You inviting me on a girls' trip?"

They both had a good laugh before Sam's laughter trailed off.

"I have a potential gig for the team," Sam said, her voice suddenly becoming more serious. "If you're up to it, that is."

"You're serious, aren't you," Terri answered. "Well, don't keep me in suspense, girl, what's up?"

Sam brought Terri up to speed on President Williams' offer and her call to Arjun. Terri's mouth dropped open as she listened, and the typically bombastic woman went uncharacteristically silent. Finally, Sam finished her story.

"So, what do you think?" Sam asked.

"You're shitting me, right?" Terri replied. "You had me goin' there for a minute!"

Sam remained silent.

"Wait. You're not shitting me, are you?" Terri continued. "You're serious! What did Arjun and Hunter say?"

"Arjun said he's in, as long as you and Hunter are in," Sam answered. "And I'm in, if all three of you say yes."

"Why us?" Terri asked.

"I've been thinking about that all day," Sam said. "I think it comes down to our diversity. Arjun's our political brain, Hunter's politically aware and progressive, I've become good at seeing both sides of things. And I think we need you to play good cop with the *Brothers of Liberty*!"

The two women burst out laughing.

"So, you wanna know if I'm up for the challenge, eh?" Terri said, still chuckling.

"And are you?" Sam answered.

Terri went quiet for a moment while she turned over the pros and cons in her brain.

"I'll have to run this by the hubby," she said, finally. "But I don't think he'll mind having me out of his hair for a while."

"So you're in if he doesn't object?" Sam asked.

"Hell yah, sister!" Terri proclaimed. "When do we have to leave?"

THE PRESIDENT stole another quick look at her watch. It was past 5 p.m., Eastern Time, but two hours earlier on the prairies where Sam lived. Rachel sighed. It was beginning to look like she was going to have to come up with a Plan B to deal with the occupation, and she dreaded the politics that would come along with that process.

She rose from her desk, yawned, and strolled out into the cottage's living room, where Nicole had slipped off her shoes and was napping on the couch. With the entire city in a state of crisis since the protesters hit the streets, neither Rachel nor Nicole slept much last night. They managed to keep working into the early morning only with the aid of a steady stream of coffee. Rachel continued walking to the front door and stepped outside for some fresh air, hoping it might help to keep her awake. A Marine, posted on guard duty outside the cottage, snapped to attention and saluted Rachel. She still hadn't got used to that.

"At ease, soldier," she said. "A hot one today, isn't it?"

"Yes, Madam President," the soldier replied.

"I just want to go for a short walk. Is that allowed?" Rachel asked.

"Yes, Ma'am," he answered. "I just have to keep an eye on you."

Rachel was about to answer the Marine when the cell phone in her hand started vibrating. She raised the phone and saw Sam Bower's name on the display.

"Please, let her say yes," Rachel muttered to herself.

She tapped the phone to answer the call.

"Hello, Sam," Rachel said. "I trust you've had a chance to talk with your team?"

"Yes, Ma'am," Sam replied.

"And?" Rachel inquired.

"Looks like we're all in," Sam replied. "As long as I still agree after hearing more details. And they all asked for a day to tie up loose ends. Are you okay with that?"

"Absolutely," Rachel answered. She glanced at her watch and paused a moment while she worked out the details in her mind. "The Secret Service can have a private jet on the ground to pick you up at eleven o'clock. That's at the Saskatoon Airport, right?"

"Yes Ma'am," Sam answered. "Is that 11 p.m., tonight?"

"Yes, that's right. I'm afraid it will be a red-eye flight so I can get you here as soon as possible, and bring you up to speed before your team arrives. I'll arrange to have the rest of the team on a plane first thing tomorrow morning, so they can get here by tomorrow afternoon."

Sam peeked at her watch and realized she only had a few short hours to eat, pack her suitcase, and get to the airport. She took a slow, deep breath to calm herself, before the reality of the moment could overwhelm her.

"I think I can make that work. I'll be ready," Sam replied. "Will there be anything else?"

"No. Thank you Sam, I look forward to meeting you tomorrow morning."

SAM GAZED out through the helicopter's window at the wooded Maryland landscape below, as the U.S. Navy aircraft carried her closer to her final destination. Golden rays from the newly risen sun contrasted with dark early morning shadows, and a small lake below sparkled as the chopper passed over it. The last day and a half seemed like a blur to Sam, and it still seemed surreal that she was only minutes away from landing at Camp David, and meeting President Rachel Williams, possibly the most powerful woman in the world at that moment.

Sam had never felt more like an imposter than when she boarded the U.S. Government private jet in Saskatoon late last night. The crew's lone flight attendant was totally focused on ensuring Sam's comfort on the long transcontinental flight. Looking around at the plane's opulent leather seats, wood accents, casual seating, and entertainment amenities, Sam felt internally conflicted. She had grown much closer to Mother Earth over the past couple of years, since she met Aunt Rose and embarked on the journey of discovering her Indigenous roots. At the same time, her changing moral compass had turned her into an ardent environmentalist. So, accepting this solo flight on a private jet did not sit well with her conscience.

During the flight, Sam alternated between studying the documents that President Williams had provided for her, and nodding off to compensate for her many sleepless hours over the past two nights. The documents contained a security brief, with information about all of the people who were believed to be organizers of the Unite the Left protest and The Liberty Convoy. If Sam thought that working with the eight members of Team Reconciliation in Dr. Sanderson's team building class had been a challenge, the wide range of personalities present on both sides of the Washington occupation likely quadrupled the complexity of the task that lay ahead for Sam and her team.

In the Unite the Left camp, the team faced a dedicated Black Lives Matter and ANTIFA organizer, an Islamic Afghan refugee, a college shooting survivor and advocate of tightening gun legislation, a Jewish lawyer and supporter of bans on anti-semitism and hate crimes, a gay Islamic man and avid LGBTQ2+ crusader, a State Senator and pro-immigration campaigner, a world famous environmentalist, and a young Asian American Hollywood actress.

In contrast, she faced a whole different kettle of fish with the far right Camp. Bryson MacDonald, the apparent lead organizer of The Liberty Convoy, was the proprietor of a gun shop in Idaho and a card carrying NRA member. His organizing committee contained a well-known far right podcast host, an Oregon rancher with a history of demonstrating against local governments, a struggling midwest business owner, an outspoken Evangelist and pro-life advocate, a long haul trucker who was Bryson's best friend, and a young tech whiz who apparently enjoyed throwing a wrench into anything that smelled of the establishment.

Reading the security brief had only increased Sam's sense of being an imposter.

What in the world am I getting myself and the team into?

She felt the helicopter lean slightly to the right, and it began to circle an area in the woods where a number of small buildings were situated. The area was surrounded by tall wire fencing, and she saw a helipad near the area's perimeter.

This must be it ... Camp David!

Sam felt as though she must be in a movie. She took out her phone and flipped the camera to make sure she was presentable. She was thankful that her hair was no longer dyed purple, but her nose piercing and the new tattoos on her arm only increased her sense of being a stranger in a strange land. Fortunately, her dark brown hair was short and didn't look any worse for wear after the long flight. She realized that she'd completely forgotten to put on any makeup that morning when her plane landed at Joint Base Andrews.

Good thing my face is tanned. At least I don't look like a ghost.
Oh, well, I guess this is what the President gets when I have to take a red-eye flight.

The aircraft's internal vibrations increased as the chopper gradually stopped moving forward and began dropping slowly towards the landing pad. Finally, she felt a thump and the aircraft shifted slightly from side to side as it settled. The co-pilot left his seat and motioned for Sam to approach him. He opened the aircraft's side door, which turned into a short staircase as it dropped from the side of the chopper. Through the open door, Sam saw a tall Caucasian woman with short dark hair and wearing an expensive blue suit, ducking down and approaching the aircraft.

"Off you go!" the co-pilot shouted. "Keep your head down"

"Thank you!" Sam shouted in return.

The co-pilot took her arm and helped her down the stairs. The woman in the suit stepped forward and extended her hand to greet Sam. With her other hand, she passed Sam a security badge to wear around her neck.

"I'm Nicole Davies, the President's Chief of Staff," she shouted. "Glad to meet you, Samantha. Here's your security clearance. Keep your head low and follow me. President Williams is waiting."

The two women took a pathway that led from the helipad towards the President's cottage.

"Did you have a good flight? And did you have a chance to review the information we gave you?" Nicole asked.

Nicole's question was curt, and not exactly welcoming in tone. Sam felt her own guards start to come up, and she found herself wondering if she'd made a mistake coming here.

"It was great, and the food was delicious. Thank you. And yes, I did read over the documents."

"If you have any questions, President Williams will be glad to answer them, I'm sure," Nicole answered.

They walked briskly and silently along the path for a few moments, until a cottage appeared on their right. Two U.S. Marines stood guard in front of the door.

"This is the Aspen Lodge, the President's cottage," Nicole said, as they approached the guards. Nicole flashed her security badge at one of the guards.

"She's expecting us," Nicole said to the guard.

"Yes, ma'am," the guard said. "Go ahead."

Sam flashed her new security badge at the guard and followed Nicole through the Aspen Lodge's front door and into a living room. As they entered the room, President Rachel Williams rose from a couch and walked over to greet Sam.

"Ms. Bower!" the President said, as she shook Sam's hand and placed her other hand warmly on the younger woman's shoulder. "So nice to finally meet you. Please come in and have a seat. Can I offer you something to drink?"

A young Black man, a member of the White House kitchen staff, appeared out of nowhere.

"Do you have some coffee?" Sam asked, tentatively.

She was instantly in awe of the President. The woman seemed much taller than she appeared on TV, and Sam noted that she held her head high. Her warm smile and confident nature had an immediate calming effect on Sam's anxious nerves.

"Two coffees, please," the President said to the young man.

"Yes, Madam," he replied, before he wheeled around and disappeared into the rear of the lodge.

President Williams turned her attention to Nicole.

"Thank you, Nicole," she said. "I think that will be all for now. I'll call if I need you."

Sam couldn't help noticing a faint note of resentment in the Chief of Staff's eyes as the President spoke.

"Yes, Ma'am," Nicole answered. "I'll be in my office if you need me."

With that, Nicole turned and left the lodge through the front door. President Williams turned back to Sam and smiled.

"Don't mind Nicole," the President said. "Some of the people around me, including Nicole, don't approve of my plan to listen to the protesters, or to bring in your team to negotiate with them. It's hard to get people to try something different these days. She'll come around."

The young kitchen staffer returned and poured coffee into two elegant china coffee cups, before pivoting smoothly and retreating from the room.

"You must be hungry by now, and we'll be having breakfast soon," President Williams continued. "Until then, let's chat and get to know each other. I'm sure you're feeling a bit overwhelmed, and you must have a thousand questions for me."

"I do ... I mean, *we* do," Sam replied. "How do you think America is going to react when they find out you've brought in a bunch of university students: and Canadians at that?"

Sam held up the brown envelope with the documents provided to her by the President.

"And, do you think we can really get these two diverse groups of organizers to respect us, and to trust that we're working for *them*, as much as for you?"

The smile faded slightly on Rachel Williams' face. She nodded her understanding of Sam's questions.

"Were you able to listen to my address to the nation?" she inquired.

Sam shook her head from side to side.

"I only caught highlights on social media," she said.

"Then I'll give you a quick recap," the President said. "This country is more deeply divided than ever before, and I believe it's tearing us apart and threatening our very democracy. The two sides in this standoff represent two sets of ideals that are miles apart. And *neither* side trusts me."

Rachel paused and shook her head from side to side. Sam read sadness in the other woman's eyes.

"The left believes that I'm going to repeal everything that the Democrats did over the past eight years," she continued. "And the right thinks I'm going to betray the ideals and policies of my predecessor, President Spencer. I can't think of anybody within this country that both sides in this standoff would respect!"

"So, why us?" Sam asked. "Why do you think we're the answer?"

"Why you?" Rachel repeated. "Because, during these deeply divisive times, this country needs somebody like you and your team: with your unique political insights, your respect for diverse views, and your deep commitment to the causes of democracy and justice for all. Everybody in this country should be honoured to have you!"

Sam felt herself blush. She wasn't used to receiving praise, especially from somebody important like the President.

"If you've read *The Night Class*, you'll know that I'm far from perfect. I made a lot of mistakes while I was mentoring those students."

"But you learned so much from those mistakes, Sam!" Rachel insisted. "Like I said before, I admire what you accomplished in your team's Reconciliation Project. Whether you believe it or not, I think you've got an innate talent for bringing people together. And most importantly, none of you are politicians. You're common, everyday people, just like the organizers that are listed in those documents I gave you."

Rachel paused for a moment, then she looked directly into Sam's eyes.

"Have you ever heard of a man named Thomas Paine?" she asked.

Sam's forehead took on wrinkles of concentration as she searched her memory for the name.

"I don't think so. Why?" Sam asked.

"His name is often overlooked in history books," Rachel replied. "He was an Englishman who worked as an excise tax collector, and who decided to lobby King George III and the British Parliament for higher wages for those in his profession. But, instead, he lost his job and was living off the charity of friends in London, when he had a chance meeting with Ben Franklin, who was in England lobbying the King and Parliament to repeal a number of harsh laws in the American colonies following the Boston Tea Party. To make a long story short, Franklin admired Paine's skills for organization, his persuasive writing style, and his dedication to causes of injustice. So he invited Paine to join the staff of his Philadelphia newspaper. Paine's subsequent pamphlets were instrumental in spreading word through the colonies of the need to rebel against the English, and he was also instrumental in drafting the Declaration of Independence. And even though he wasn't involved in actually creating the Constitution, many of his ideas were eventually incorporated in the first ten amendments, the Bill of Rights portion of the Constitution."

"So, what does that have to do with me?" Sam asked.

"Don't you see? You're my Thomas Paine!" Rachel replied. "Like him, you seem to have similar organizational and communication skills, and you're dedicated to the causes that you're involved in. But most importantly, you're a foreigner, just as Paine was. And like him, you don't have the pre-existing biases that most Americans have. You and your team could conceivably have the same kind of impact today, that Thomas Paine had on America back in his day."

Still reluctant to receive such high comparisons and compliments from the President, Sam shrugged her shoulders.

"You know that what I did in *The Night Class* with Team Reconciliation was pretty much a fluke ... bringing the team members together, I mean. I can't see us inviting the Unite the Left and the Liberty Convoy organizers to a potluck dinner to resolve their differences."

The smile returned to Rachel's face, and she nodded her agreement.

"Perhaps, but the important thing is that you learned a lot along the way. You learned to rely on each other's strengths, and to become something much greater than the sum of your individual attributes. You trust each other. That's why I think your team can do it, if *anybody* can."

The kitchen staff member slipped into the room and nodded to the President. She gave him a quick nod, and then turned back to Sam.

"Come, they're serving breakfast on the patio," Rachel said. "I'm sure we have a lot more to discuss while we're eating, and until your team arrives late this afternoon."

SAM COULDN'T believe that it was already Monday, the Fourth of July. And while the rest of the United States was celebrating the holiday, a palpable tension still hovered ominously over Washington D.C., especially over the two camps of political adversaries now living on that city's streets. It was hard for Sam to believe that not even two full days had passed since she received her shocking phone call from President Rachel Williams. Yet, here she stood beside the helipad at Camp David, eager to reunite with her friends and colleagues from *The Night Class*, and anxious about the task that lay ahead of them.

Behind Sam, in a nearby parking lot, a black Harley rumbled slowly into the lot and came to a stop. The lone rider, dressed in black leathers, dismounted and took a moment to stretch. Hunter MacMillan removed his helmet. He watched as a helicopter gradually slowed, reduced altitude, rotated ninety degrees in the air, and then descended slowly until it came to rest on the helipad. He recognized Sam, standing by the edge of the pad, waiting for the aircraft's occupants to disembark, and a sly smile spread across his face.

A moment later, the aircraft's door opened. For the second time that day, Nicole Davies ducked and scurried to meet the incoming Presidential guests. Arjun was the first to poke his head out of the door and descend the stairs, with Terri following close behind. The gusts from the helicopter's propellers blew Terri's long blonde hair in every direction. She reached into her purse, withdrew an elastic, and hurriedly tied her hair back into a ponytail.

As Nicole greeted the two travellers, Sam felt a flutter of anxiety and she caught herself holding her breath.

Where's Hunter? Is he a no-show?

Nicole motioned for Arjun and Terri to follow her, after which they ducked and hurried away from the helipad to where Sam stood. Both Terri and Arjun noticed right away that Hunter was standing behind Sam, but he held his finger over his lips as a signal for them not to say anything.

Terri was the first to reach Sam. The two women embraced as the roar of the helicopter's turbines escalated. Finally, the chopper lifted off the ground, swung around and headed back towards its base at Joint Force Andrews. As it flew away, the team could finally talk to each other at normal volume.

"You're here!" Sam squealed to Terri, her voice rising an octave in pitch. "It's soooo good to see you!"

"And you, too!" Terri answered. "It's been way too long!"

Before Sam could greet Arjun, she unexpectedly felt three heavy taps on her right shoulder.

"Looking for somebody?" Hunter asked, at the same time as he tapped Sam's shoulder.

Instinct took over. Sam jumped and screamed, then wheeled around, only to see Hunter and Arjun doubled over with laughter. Nicole Davies seemed less than amused.

"You're an ass!" Sam shouted at Hunter, trying not to laugh. "You scared the shit out of me! You were supposed to be on that helicopter!"

"I didn't see the point of sending a private jet, when it's only an eight-hour ride down here from Ontario and there's no traffic at night," he answered. "The President seemed okay with that. And I have to admit that it was pretty sweet going through U.S. Customs when the President's left word to let me through without question!"

Terri looked around in awe at the military encampment surrounding them.

"I just can't believe we're really here," she remarked. "Is this a dream?"

"I don't think I'll really believe it till I see the President for real," Arjun said."

He and Sam laughed and then gave each other a friendly hug.

"I hope I didn't screw up your tennis date the other day!" Sam said.

"It's all good," Arjun replied. "She understood about the team reuniting, but it was hard not to tell her where I was going, or why."

"She'll probably figure it out real soon when she sees your face all over the news."

Sam's eyes met Hunter's again. Finally, she stepped towards him awkwardly for a friendly hug. She felt his arms tighten around her waist and felt her heart flutter briefly, before the rest of her body stiffened. Her mind scrambled to find the right words, but it was Hunter who broke the awkward silence.

"Good to see you, stranger," he said.

"You too," Sam answered meekly. "I'm glad you could come."

"Okay, everybody," Nicole called out. "Let's not keep the President waiting. Here's your security badges: you're to wear them at all times while you're in the camp. Follow me."

The three new team members hung their badges around their necks. Then Sam and the team fell in line behind Nicole as she strode along the path to the Aspen Lodge. The newcomers showed their badges to the Marines outside the lodge, followed Nicole and Sam into the building, and entered the living room, where President Rachel Williams stood to greet them. She smiled warmly as Arjun, Terri, and Hunter filed into the room.

"Welcome to Camp David," she said. "I'm President Williams. But, since we're going to be working closely, please feel free to call me Rachel. I'm sure you must be tired after your flights, and after your ride, Hunter."

The President turned to Terri and took her by the hand.

"Especially you, Terri, coming all the way from Alberta."

"No problem," Terri answered. "It wasn't like I was crammed into an economy seat all day. I'm pretty sure I could get used to flying in a private jet!"

They all laughed, the tension within the group easing gradually as they felt Rachel Williams' easy-going interaction style and kindness.

"Nicole will show you to your quarters in the Birch and Dogwood cabins, so you can freshen up," Williams said. "Shall we meet on the back patio in thirty minutes for dinner?"

Sam and her team members all nodded in agreement.

"And after dinner," she added, "Sam and I would like to bring everybody up to date, so we can start discussing strategy and get right to work tomorrow morning."

The President nodded to Nicole, who led Sam and her team out of the living room and then out of the Aspen Lodge.

Rachel watched as they filed out of the lodge. She knew her decision was going to be unpopular, but deep down, she knew that this unprecedented crisis needed somebody who was willing to risk thinking and doing things outside the box. Whether her strategy would work or not, only time would tell.

LATER THAT evening, Sam, Terri, Hunter, and Arjun sat around a circular table, along with Rachel Williams and Nicole Davies, in the Aspen Lodge's cozy Presidential Office.

"I think my teammates will agree that I was extremely naïve when I took on the job of mentoring Team Reconciliation in their school project," Sam said to Rachel. "I had no idea there was such a diversity of views within the team. I think that diversity is what kept the group from jelling for so long."

"I'd say that was an understatement," Hunter said, and then he flashed her a mischievous smile.

"About what? My naïvety or the diversity?" Sam answered. She winked back at Hunter.

"Very funny," Arjun said, "but I think Sam made a great point about the diversity. It took a long time to find some common ground within that group of eight students. But this time, the two sides in this standoff are already separated into two distinct camps that are more homogenous. So, theoretically at least, it should be much easier to find some initial common ground within those groups. That should help us to build some trust within each group."

"True," Hunter added. "But that's also our biggest obstacle: how are we going to find a way to have those two homogenous, but very different sides, learn to trust and listen to *each other*?"

"We need to organize," Terri said, "to take advantage of each other's strengths for working with these two camps, but also to minimize any individual weaknesses we might have. I think we can all admit that we each have our own strengths, as well as our own emotional triggers."

"I was thinking the same thing," Sam added. "I think we should split into two teams. Arjun's always calm and cool, and he's our political brain."

Sam turned her attention to Terri.

"You're friendly and have a big heart. And you tend to lean to the right, politically."

She then turned her attention to Hunter, still feeling somewhat awkward in his presence.

"Hunter, you like to be a bit of a rebel: you don't accept the status quo and you love to push for change. Am I right?"

Hunter shrugged his shoulders and nodded with Sam's assessment.

"And Sam," Terri interjected. "You're our best listener. But we know that you're still uncomfortable with conflict, right?"

Sam nodded reluctantly, knowing that Terri had an excellent read on her.

"Based on those strengths and weaknesses, I'd like to propose a plan," the President observed. "I think that within each sub-team, you're going to find that you'll sometimes need to play the 'good cop, bad cop' routine. Can I suggest having Hunter and Terri work with the Liberty Convoy camp, while Sam and Arjun work with the Unite the Left camp?"

The four friends looked at each other, and then they all nodded their agreement.

Nicole, who had been silently observing the team, continued her silence. However, her posture grew increasingly closed off and her face showed no emotion.

Hunter cleared his throat and he looked in Rachel's direction.

"I'd like to suggest one more thing, if I may," he said. "I notice that you and our team are all sitting in a circle right now, which is a sacred thing in our Indigenous culture. It shows that each one of us around this circle is an equal, regardless of our title or position. And, like we're doing now, I hope we can incorporate more of our culture and traditional learning into how we interact with the people in each of our camps."

He turned his gaze towards Sam.

"Do you agree?"

"Absolutely," Sam said. "I learned a lot from the small bits of Indigenous culture that I learned from Hunter and my Aunt Rose. It helped my confidence to grow as the Reconciliation project went on."

Rachel looked at Hunter, and then at Sam, with a look of genuine sincerity in her eyes.

"I wouldn't have it any other way," she said firmly. "It's one of the things that attracted me to your team in the first place. I'm open to your suggestions."

"As we move forward," Hunter said, "I hope we can bring an awareness within both camps that each one of our individual decisions affects all other people and life forms in the circle of life around us. That all forms of life are sacred and interconnected. That the wellbeing of Mother Earth is essential to our survival. And, that no human is above or below others in the eyes of The Creator."

"I've also learned a lot about time from Hunter," Sam said. She looked at Hunter and saw him smile. "We have to remember not to rush our negotiations. It will take listening, empathy, and time to earn the protesters' trust, like plants that take a whole season to grow. We have to think of our suggestions as seeds that we sow carefully: seeds that need to be tended, and take time to mature and harvest."

Hunter chuckled as he remembered their repeated arguments about the concept of time during *The Night Class*. Everybody else around the table smiled and nodded their agreement with Sam.

"If we can all keep those things in mind as we move forward, I'm sure it will have a positive effect on your negotiations," Rachel said. "However, your concept of time is going to be a hard sell to the American people, to the press, and especially to Congress. I just want to warn you that you'll be under immense pressure to produce results, and produce them fast. So, before we go ahead with this, are you all sure you can deal with that?"

Sam went around the table, taking time to look into each team member's eyes, and eventually receiving a positive nod from each. Finally she turned towards Rachel.

"Looks like we're all on the same page, Ma'am!"

A broad smile spread across Rachel's face.

"Thank you," she said. "I think we've made an excellent start this evening, and I'm sure you're all very tired. I'll see you all here tomorrow morning at 8 am."

As the team rose and filed from the room, Sam couldn't help but glance in Nicole's direction, making brief eye contact. And in that short moment, Sam caught a flash of anger that caused an ominous shudder to shoot through her entire body.

AS THE clock crept closer to midnight, Rachel did her best to stifle a yawn. She had always tried her best to get a good night's sleep. However, since being thrust unexpectedly into office after former President Spencer's untimely death, the never-ending tide of Presidential business had a way of keeping her up until midnight much of the time. And the unforeseen clash between the two groups of political protesters, plus the resulting standoff and occupation of the Capitol's streets, was only making things worse.

Captain Robby had just completed his nightly update report to Rachel, but Agent Matt Butler, as well as Nicole, refused to accept Robby's assessment. They continued their attack over how Rachel and Robby were handling the crisis.

"I simply can't agree with this ridiculous plan to negotiate with a bunch of thugs!" Butler insisted. "They tried to lay siege to you and the White House—in the name of so-called peaceful protest, for God's sake! Your plan just legitimizes them and encourages them to keep up their occupation! At some point in this country, and I'm not sure when it happened, so-called 'peaceful protests' crossed the line into passive resistance. And believe me, passive resistance is nothing more than a disingenuous, dishonest form of aggression!"

"How so?" Rachel asked.

"Just look at what happened in 2022 in Canada: in Downtown Ottawa, on the Peace Bridge to Detroit, and at the Coutts border crossing between Montana and Alberta. Not to mention the student standoffs in support of Palestinians in 2024. In each of those cases, the passive resistance created situations where the governments, or other institutions like universities, had no choice but to eventually react with some form of force. And as soon as they did that, they were instantly seen as the evil aggressors. It creates a no-win situation that ultimately invites force, and it's about time somebody did something to call a spade a spade, and stop calling it 'peaceful protest.' It's effin' bullshit, if you'll pardon the expression!"

"I agree with Agent Butler, Ma'am," Nicole echoed. "I think that by allowing these two so-called peaceful protests around the White House to continue, it sends a dangerous message to every fringe group in America that has a beef with the President. And even if negotiations were the way for you to go, choosing that bunch of unknowns from Canada to negotiate on your behalf makes no sense at all: an insecure psychology student and her ragtag group of friends? You'll be the laughing stock of the country—maybe even the world. It's political suicide!"

Robby shook his head slowly from side to side, frustrated with the continued opposition from his FBI colleague and the Presidential aide.

"Look, Butler," he answered. "We're sitting on a powder keg out there right now. We've got one group of very frustrated convoy protesters, who are dying to vent their anger somewhere after their grand scheme was derailed. And then we have the Unite the Left group who wants us to round up the so-called fascists on the other side of the fences. If we make one bad move, the whole thing could erupt into full-scale violence! As far as I'm concerned, negotiations are the only way to move forward."

Rachel paused to consider all of the arguments. Finally, she turned to Butler.

"Captain Robby's right," she said confidently. "I hear your arguments, Nicole and Agent Butler. But, I'm just not willing to take on the responsibility for what might erupt if we activate the National Guard and march them into that convoy camp. If nothing else, I want to be known as a President who listens to my people!"

She turned her attention back to Nicole.

"And, as for my decision to recruit Ms. Bower and her colleagues, it may appear to outsiders that she and her team are completely out of their league," the President observed. "But I believe they've proven that they know how to listen, that they know how to work together, and that they know how to get the job done under pressure. So, I'm willing to go to bat for them and give them a chance, and I'll take the heat if it doesn't work out."

As the President finished speaking, Robby turned to face Butler.

"And as for you and your jurisdiction, just because you managed to find a judge who agreed that your alleged intelligence showed the possibility of arms caches in the convoy trucks, and she justified your involvement in this operation on the pretense of significant Homeland Security risks, I'm still running this show! So, until the Mayor or President Williams say otherwise, you report to me—got it?"

"Well, if that's the case," Nicole blurted indignantly, "then what exactly *is* Agent Butler's job?"

Robby turned and looked to the President for the final word on the subject. She paused for a long moment to ponder the issue.

"It's not just the current standoff that I'm worried about," Rachel replied. "I'm looking at the longer term implications of how we act now. If I don't sit down and listen to these peoples' concerns, and especially if I send in the troops to break up what they believe is a peaceful protest, I think there's a genuine risk of similar protests breaking out all over the country. If you remember, the government's refusal to meet with the so-called Freedom Convoy in Ottawa, was the main reason that led to those major protests and their economic consequences in Canada. And the fallout from that debacle continued to haunt the Trudeau government. I don't want to risk having that happen in our country."

She looked Butler squarely in the eyes.

"So, for now Agent Butler, your job will be limited to using your intelligence resources to rule out or confirm the presence of guns or seditious activity in the convoy trailers. Under no circumstances will I allow you to deploy your tactical team, or to make a public plea for calling in the National Guard, unless you receive the order directly from me! Do I make myself clear?"

Matt Butler's flushed red face couldn't hide his anger. On the other hand, Nicole donned a stoic, emotionless expression to hide her deep disagreement and anger towards her boss.

Rachel turned back to Robby.

"Captain, I expect you to allow Agent Butler to carry out the job I've given him, and to keep him informed of any issues that fall within his jurisdiction. Does that work for you?"

"Yes, Madam President," he answered.

"Good," Rachel continued. "It's been a long day. Unless something unforeseen happens during the night, let's touch base again tomorrow morning. And, let's make it virtual, I don't think there's any need to meet in person. Let's say 11 am."

Rachel rose to her feet, signalling that it was time for everybody to leave. As Nicole left the room and closed the door behind her, Rachel exhaled a long breath and allowed herself to relax just a little. Yet, at the same time, something inside told her that she should keep an eye on her ambitious assistant. She knew she couldn't afford to make the mistake of underestimating anybody within her inner circle, especially so early in her unpopular Presidency.

CHAPTER 7—ULTIMATUM

THE FOURTH of July had been hot and muggy, and the evening showed no signs of any significant relief overnight. Intermittent bursts of fireworks lit up the sky above the Liberty Convoy encampment, as the organizers drank beer and alternated between slamming the new President, mocking their woke" opponents on the left, laughing at crude jokes, and celebrating the nation's birthday around a fire pit.

"Enuffa this sittin' round on our asses," Norm Barfield, shouted. "I'm tired o'waitin' fer that bitch to do somethin'. When are we gonna do what we came here to do?"

"Yeah, my patience is wearin' real thin," Sean Pritchard moaned. "I didn't drive all this way to sit aroun' roastin' weenies. The only thing those assholes in govermint understand is guns an' action. Ya shoulda seen how fast the govermint got off their asses when we started openin' the floodgates on that dam back home in Oregon!"

"I hear y'all," Bryson MacDonald answered. "Y'all are heroes for comin' out here an' standin' up fer freedom, far as I'm concerned. Jus' like them patriots up in Canada an' their Freedom Convoy: they totally sacrificed theirselves fer freedom, an' look how they got treated an' disrespected. Ain't nobody took time to listen to them!"

Bryson tipped back his can of beer and drained half of it.

"Ah," he sighed. "I've pretty much had ma fill'a that cunt's 'let's be patient' song'n dance BS. We're fed up an' we ain't gonna take it anymore!"

The other organizers raised their beer cans into the air, randomly shouting slogans like 'Hell yah!'or 'fuck patience', but they were definitely not in unison.

Anna Dahl, organizer and far right podcaster, picked up on Bryson's momentum.

"I think it's about time to send the Commander-in-Chief a manifesto: a list of our demands. Are y'all with me?"

Another motley mixture of cheers arose from around the fire pit. Anna took out a note pad and started taking notes.

"Okay, Bryson," she said. "What's our first demand?"

"None'a this negotiatin' team BS. We wanna meet face't face with the President," he shouted. "An' no fuckin' with our Second 'mendment rights!"

"You tell'er, brother!" Norm shouted.

"We ain't gonna stand fer nobody takin' way our right to defend ourselves," Bryson added. "B'sides, it ain't guns that kills all them kids in schools, it's them weirdos with mental problems. If they din't have guns, they wouda used a car, a bomb, or a machete anyway!"

"Alright," Anna called out. "That's a great start. How 'bout each one'a y'all givin' me the biggest thing *you* wanna tell 'er. Jessica?"

"I wanna know if she's gonna act on the U.N. Declaration, and do something about giving us back our land, our resources, and our culture."

"Beg yer pardon," Sean blurted. "When the govermint built them dams, over a hunnert years ago, we was promised we'd 'ave that water fer our crops'n livestock. Now they's goin' back on them promises, jus' t'save some so-called sacred fish."

"Well, that water flows through our ancestral lands," Jessica retorted. "They shouldn't have made promises about land that wasn't rightfully theirs in the first place. *We* should be the ones to manage that watershed, and the U.N. Declaration says so!"

Bryson glared at Jessica.

"We all didn't come here to Washington to right the wrongs o'the past" he retorted. We don' need you to be stirrin' up new problems, missy! We jus' wanna put things back the way they were when this here country was great, before them progs started ruinin' everythin' an' takin' our freedoms away."

"And that's all my people want," Jessica shot back. "We want our freedom just like you. Our freedom to engage in our culture and to live on our ancestral lands. We want the government to put things back the way they were before you settlers arrived!"

"So, why're you here with this convoy, sweetie pie?" Bryson shouted. "Sounds kinda like y'all should be on the other side o' the fence, sittin' round singin' Kumbaya with them progs."

"I'd like to remind you that I'm here in Washington because I was lied to, you asshole!" Jessica blurted. "I was told that I was coming to Virginia to join a convoy that was gonna drive through Richmond to the State Capitol in the name of freedom. And then, at the last minute, I'm suddenly told the plan has changed—to come to this location in Washington, with no mention of surrounding the White House! And you have the nerve to ask why I'm here?"

Jessica's face was red, on its way towards purple, with rage.

"I thought the purpose of this convoy was to preserve liberty and freedom," Jess continued. "I was coming to Richmond to lobby for liberty and freedom for my people, just like the rest of you!"

"Well, you're here now," Bryson said, smugly. "If ya don' wanna be here, ain't nobody stoppin' ya from leavin'. Fer all I know, maybe y'all are the rat who tipped off the progs an' caused this standoff!"

Jessica continued to glare at Bryson. If he wanted her to look guilty, he had not succeeded.

"What if it was me? Or Anna, or any one of the people in this room?" Jessica shouted. "Was there ever a requirement that each and every one of us has to agree with everything the great Bryson MacDonald says?"

Like the rest of the group, Anna looked increasingly uncomfortable with the mounting animosity between Bryson and Jessica. She hastily scribbled her thoughts in her notepad.

John Gregg, the grocery store owner, raised his hand and Anna pounced on the opportunity to end the standoff between Jessica and Bryson.

"John," she interjected. "What message do y'all wanna send to the President?"

"What's she gonna do 'bout savin' farmers an' small town America, so farm families an' businesses like my grocery store kin survive? When's somebody gonna protect us from them big corporate farms, from big box stores, an' from greedy businesses that outsource everythin' to India an' China?"

"Excellent question," Anna answered.

A pause ensued while she scribbled John's comments in her notepad. Finally, she looked up at Pastor Luke Kessler.

"Pastor, what about y'all? What do y'all wanna tell the President?"

"I came to deliver God's message to the President," he said. "To tell her to end the murderin' an' ban *all* abortions. I came to demand that she respect our Constitutional right to freedom of religion: to keep government outta our congregation's affairs, and to let God guide us and tell us how to live our lives!"

"Do you have any examples of how you feel the government has interfered with your affairs?" Anna asked.

"Absolutely," the Pastor replied. "The Bible tells us that we have the right to educate an' discipline our children so's they respect the absolute authority of God, his representatives on earth, and their fathers. We don' need no Child Protection Services tellin' us how to parent, how to educate 'em, or to force us to take our children to *their* doctors. We leave discipline an' healin' up to the Will of Almighty God.

Anna continued to scribble notes as the Pastor rambled on.

"And that means protectin' us from Public Health declarations," the Pastor added. "It's God's will that we should congregate in His House to worship. It's up to our Lord whether or not we're afflicted by disease, or whether He will cure us. But, to deny us our right to gather to worship, just because of a pandemic, is unconstitutional!"

"Thank you, Pastor," Anna said. "Anybody else have anything to add? ... Norm? Martin?"

Martin Lee looked up from his cell phone, in which he had been engrossed while the rest of the group aired their grievances.

"Huh?" he grunted.

"What message did you want to give the President when you came to D.C." Anna asked.

"Oh," Martin said. "Just get government outta stuff that's none of its business. Give us back our freedom. No more 'hate crime' laws or policing the internet. Give us *real* freedom of speech!"

"Thanks, Martin. I'd like to add one more message for Williams that y'all haven't mentioned yet. What about the flood of illegal immigrants coming over our borders? What's she gonna do to stop that?"

The group came alive at Anna's message for the President, with a chorus of unanimous support.

"Yeah, when are they ever gonna finish that wall?" Sean shouted.

"An' whatever happened with deportin' all them illegals, anyway?" Norm chimed. "That's somethin' Spencer done promised us. Williams fuckin' well better keep that promise!"

"I've added that to our list, an' we'll see what she has to say," Anna replied. She looked around the campfire circle at the other seven organizers.

"Is that it? Anybody else have anythin' to add?"

Her question met with a silent chorus of shaking their heads from side to side.

"Okay then," she said, finally. "If y'all are in agreement, I'll bring Bryson onto a special live-streamed edition of my podcast tomorrow at 11 a.m. And I'll let him issue the ultimatum to the President, live for the entire nation to hear!"

ON THE other side of no man's land, at the intersection of Constitution Avenue and Seventeenth Street, the Unite the Left organizers gathered around two picnic tables that they'd pushed together, end-to-end, in their mess tent. Jordan Marsh sat at the far end of one table, taking notes. She mopped the sweat from her brow yet again.

"Damn this humidity," she muttered. "I don't know how much of this I can stand!"

"Quit your bitching!" Stephen Danilenko shouted. "You're not camping on the street like we are. You get to go home to your cozy bed and your AC every night."

Without thinking, he too wiped his forehead, then turned his attention back to the other organizers.

"So, now that we've managed to disrupt MacDonald's big plot," he continued, "what do we do now? We never planned for anything like this." His question was met initially with silence. Finally, a voice broke through the stillness.

"I think that our first priority is to get Bryson and his friends off the streets," Kymberly Babineau said. "But, at the same time, we have to be careful not to make this all about them. We have to remember why we came to Washington in the first place: for a peaceful rally, and to continue the fight for freedom and equality, for every single person in this country!"

"Kym's right," Cecilia Robinson added. "We all came to D.C. to protest and stand up for all the social progress we made over the past eight years. And now, thanks to Bryson, his band of fascists and white supremacists, and their failed plot, we now have a spotlight on us as well. This is an opportunity to keep deliverin' the same kinda messages, as long as we have that spotlight on us."

"I agree," Senator Delgado said. "We're all here to support a lot of different progressive causes: universal health care, Black Lives Matter, voter rights, immigration reform, LGBTQ2+ rights, gun control, and environmental protection. Why don't we release a series of press releases that will basically tell *all* Americans what we were going to say at Saturday's rally on the mall?"

"Excellent suggestion," Dudley Morris added. He looked toward the far end of the picnic tables, where Jordan was seated.

"How would you like to do a series of interviews with each of us about those issues?"

"Absolutely," Jordan remarked. "That's why I came to D.C. in the first place. The news outlets are clamouring for news from inside the two camps. Right now, all they're getting is whatever they pick up from social media, mostly what they pick up from Anna Dahl and Bryson on the other side."

Jordan turned her head to her right and gave Danielle Chen an icy stare.

"And mostly from Danielle on our side."

"What's *your* problem?" Danielle said, sneering. "Are we going to put a muzzle on everyone in this camp, except for you?"

"Absolutely not, Danielle," Stephen replied. "You know I stand for freedom of speech, and I'm sure all of us do. But, I think it's also important for this group to be consistent in our messaging. If one of us goes rogue, Bryson will jump all over it and find a way to divide us."

Idris Mohammed, who had been watching the proceedings in silence alongside Nasir Hazrat, raised his hand to speak.

"I would like to suggest that we appoint Stephen to be our media coordinator," Idris said. "I am not suggesting that he censor our posts. But, with his legal and media experience, perhaps we can ask that everybody at this table gets his opinion before posting, only so we can be consistent. It is always good to have a second pair of eyes look at anything we write."

"I agree with that," Nasir added, as he looked across the table at Danielle. "Would that be acceptable?"

Danielle screwed up her face, obviously not happy with anybody possibly limiting her social media presence. Finally, she exhaled a final huff of defiance.

"Oh, alright," she said. "I'll try to cut back on my posts, and I'll run things by Stephen first."

"I'll do the same with my reports," Jordan said. "But I hope you all realize that the interviews with me are all mine. As a journalist, it's my job to report and comment on the news. Is everybody okay with that?"

She looked around the table, registering nods of agreement from everybody in the group, even Danielle. Jordan turned her attention back towards Dudley and Cecilia at the other end of the table.

"Do you think this group can give me one solid interview each day for at least the next eight days, if this standoff lasts that long?"

The group of eight spent a moment looking around the table at each other once again. Gradually, they all nodded their agreement.

Cecilia Robinson rose to her feet and smiled at Jordan, and then at the rest of the group.

"Ladies and gentlemen, it looks like we have a plan. I'll go first, as long as nobody objects. And we might as well do this in the same order that we'd planned for Saturday's speeches."

"Perfect!" Jordan declared, returning Cecilia's wide grin. "Can you have something for me by noon tomorrow?"

"No problem at all," Cecilia answered. "I'll look for you tomorrow morning. It's time to let our new President hear what we all came to Washington to say. And the first thing on our agenda is to tell her that we're not leavin' here till Bryson and his fascist buddies pack up an' go home!"

TUESDAY MORNING in Washington dawned cloudy, but the previous day's sticky, clinging heat and humidity lingered. Anna Dahl checked the weather for the rest of the day and shook her head.

"Shit," she muttered. "Severe thunderstorm warning for this afternoon. Ain't that just perfect!"

She did the best she could with her hair and makeup before crawling out of her tiny tent. She held her phone up and used it as a mirror, attempting to wipe out the most noticeable wrinkles from her clothing with her free hand. She shrugged, realizing she wasn't going to do any better. She glanced at the time on her phone and then dropped it into her purse.

Anna hurried to the mess tent and found that her production assistant was almost finished setting up her small, mobile studio on the mess tent's modest performance stage. Satisfied that preparations were well on the way, she headed towards the lineup for the convoy's morning breakfast buffet, where Jessica Murray had just arrived at the end of the line. Anna slid into position behind her while Jessica was preoccupied with her phone.

"Good mornin'," Anna chirped.

Jessica jumped, startled by Anna's presence, and her face flushed. She stuffed her phone into a rear pocket in her blue jeans.

"I'm sorry," Anna continued. "Didn't mean to scare y'all."

"No problem," Jessica replied. "That was rude of me not to notice you."

She caught a glimpse of Anna's producer up on the stage, testing the lighting and microphones, as he neared completion of setting up Anna's mobile studio.

"Almost ready for the podcast?" Jessica asked.

"Yes, ma'am," Anna answered. "Things are gonna get interestin' after Bryson makes his ultimatum."

Anna paused for a moment, appearing as though she was deciding whether to say something, or not. Finally, she found her nerve and spoke up.

"Y'all was pretty tough on Bryson last night," she said. "What's with that?"

Jessica pursed her lips and the muscles in her jaw tightened.

"I don't like being lied to," Jessica answered. "In my culture, a person's word is sacred."

"It's still a Liberty Convoy," Anna said. "He had to keep the plans secret, or the FBI wouda been all over it. You know that. But the message is still the same: we just wanna make sure the President preserves all our rights and freedoms."

"You know I'm always up for a good, old-fashioned passive protest, if the time, place, and issue are right," Jessica answered. "But, I feel used this time. I feel like Bryson just wanted to use my reputation to add to the group's credibility. This isn't what I signed up for."

"But, y'all are gonna stick around to see what happens, ain'tcha," Anna said, smirking.

"Might as well, I guess," Jessica replied, guardedly. "Nothin' else better to do right now."

They reached the front of the line and Jessica filled her plate with hearty helpings of bacon, eggs, and French toast. Anna grabbed a bagel, and they both filled large paper cups with coffee from a row of carafes. Anna spied Bryson arriving at her podcast set, and she waved to him. With coffee and bagel in hand, she turned to Jessica.

"Gotta run! Wish us luck!"

She scurried off to meet Bryson. Jessica shrugged, then picked up her coffee and her breakfast plate.

"Might as well get a front row seat," she said under her breath.

"Mornin', Bryson! Y'all ready to do this?" Anna shouted. Her cheerful voice exuded excitement and anticipation. A story this big was going to boost her podcast audience to stratospheric heights, along with her advertising revenue.

"Ready when you are," Bryson answered. "Just tell me where you want me."

"We're justa 'bout ready, Anna," said her production assistant. "One minute to go, so y'all can take your seats."

Anna motioned for Bryson to sit to her left. She noticed his leg vibrating up and down anxiously as they waited.

"Nothin' to be nervous about," Anna said. "Just be yourself an' this'll be great."

She placed her warm hand on his arm in an attempt to calm him. The assistant began counting down from ten using his fingers. When he'd counted down to one, he pointed to Anna to indicate they were now live and streaming.

"Good mornin', my fellow Americans!" she began, cheerily. "Thanks to y'all for joinin' me on a special edition of the Anna Dahl podcast. I know y'all have been holdin' yer breath since I posted 'bout this last night. Today, I'm streamin' live from the Liberty Convoy camp, just steps away from Constitution Avenue in Washington, D.C. And, for my special guest this mornin', I have the man who masterminded this historic convoy and encampment: the one and only Bryson MacDonald of the Brothers of Liberty. Welcome, Bryson."

"Thanks fer havin' me, Anna," he answered. "It's a pleasure to be on yer show."

Bryson's leg still vibrated up and down. Anna smiled warmly at him and went to work. She had a knack for being able to charm and relax her guests, if that was the effect she wanted.

"So, tell me, Bryson," she asked. "What prompted you to come up with the idea for the Liberty Convoy?"

"Well, the last eight years under the Dems an' their woke agenda has been rough on our basic rights an' freedoms," Bryson began. "President Spencer heard our concerns. An' when the people voted 'im in last November, he promised us that he was gonna make things right again. But now, we got ourselves a wolf in sheep's clothing in the White House, an' it ain't right!"

"By a 'wolf in sheep's clothing' I assume you're referring to President Williams?" Anna asked.

"Damn right, I am," Bryson added. "She claims to be Republican, but we all know she's nothin' but a moderate: a Dem when push comes to shove."

Anna smiled inwardly. She had Bryson in his zone now, and he was starting to loosen up.

"But there are people out there—people behind a fence only a hundred yards or so from here—who would say that the swearing in of President Williams is a sign of our democracy in action. What would you say to them?"

"We didn't vote fer her!" Bryson blurted. "We voted fer him! We know he picked her as his runnin' mate, just to win over prog voters:

but he never meant fer her to become President. We voted fer the Spencer agenda, an' we demand that the new President abide by that agenda!"

"On another issue," Anna continued, "what do you think about the comments from DCMP Captain Robby 'bout the possibility of layin' charges against protesters?"

"That's gonna be our first demand," Bryson snapped. "They wanna lay any charges 'gainst anybody in our Liberty Convoy, an' take away their Constitutional rights an' freedoms? Then I guarantee we ain't movin' from this spot till every damn one of them charges are dropped!"

"I hear y'all," Anna answered. "An' I also hear that y'all and yer organizin' committee have put the rest of your demands in writin'. Would you care to share any of those demands with my audience?"

"Damn right, I would," Bryson bellowed. "First, we wanna make it clear we're here peacefully. We have no intentions of harmin' the President. We jus' demand a face-ta-face meetin' with her, an' we wanna hear her agenda comin' from 'er own mouth! No secrets, no lies. Jus' the straight-up truth. An' no bullshit negotiatin' team either—we ain't gonna negotiate with nobody but the President herself!"

"That's a pretty strong statement, Bryson," Anna replied. "Is there anything else y'all wanna say to the President right now?"

Anna's video operator zoomed in on Bryson's face as he turned to stare at the camera.

"Ya, I got somethin' else to say," he said firmly. "This here convoy's got support all 'cross the country. We got people with deep pockets supportin' us. So we're here fer the long haul—we ain't got no place else to go. We're gonna kick back'n relax, an' enjoy the summer. We aint' goin' nowhere till you sit down with us, an' listen to the rest of our demands."

The camera operator zoomed out and panned back onto Anna, who looked straight into the camera.

"Well, there it is folks," she said emphatically. "Bryson MacDonald of the Brothers of Liberty. It looks like the Liberty

Convoy has drawn a line in the sand here on Constitution Avenue. So, it seems the ball's now in y'alls court, Madam President. The big question is: What are y'all gonna do with it?"

Still sitting in her front row seat, Jessica Murray's thumbs hurriedly tapped out a secret text message. She hit send and the message hurtled into cyberspace.

U watching this J ???? Shit's gonna get real now!

CHAPTER 8—VODKA SHOTS

SAM, HUNTER, Arjun, and Terri sat around the large round table in the Aspen Lodge's Presidential Office, along with Rachel, Nicole, Captain Robby, and FBI agent Butler. Nicole hit the pause button to stop the replay of Bryson MacDonald's interview on Anna's podcast. She sat down quietly while her boss digested what they had just witnessed. However, it was Robby who finally broke the silence.

"Well, looks like they've finally thrown down the gauntlet, Ma'am."

Rachel let out a sigh of frustration.

"Indeed it does," she answered. "But, now we know what they want, so we can start moving ahead with our strategy."

She looked directly at Robby, then at Butler and Nicole.

"Now that you've all had a chance to meet Sam and the rest of the team, and we've given you a rough outline of how they plan to proceed, are there any questions?"

"Sounds like a good beginning to me," Robby answered. He turned his attention from the President to Sam.

"But, I'm anxious to hear more details. I guess my biggest question at the moment is when do you plan to start?"

"As soon as possible, as far as we're concerned," Sam replied. "I've asked the President to have Nicole set up a press conference for tomorrow morning, where the President can personally introduce us to the nation."

Nicole pursed her lips and shook her head slowly from side to side.

"It's not much notice, but I suppose it's doable," Nicole replied. "They're forecasting a series of severe storms for the rest of today and tomorrow. Any chance we can put it off for another day?"

"Absolutely not," the President insisted. "We need to get the ball moving on addressing the standoff as soon as possible, or the country's going to think I'm waffling and weak!"

"But how are we going to deal with Bryson's refusal to deal with anybody else but you, Ma'am?"

"Enough with the 'buts', Nicole!" Rachel admonished, her tone expressing her clear frustration with Nicole's repeated hesitancy. "I don't think that either the short notice, or some thunder storms, are going to pose a problem."

Rachel frowned and her glaring eyes stared Nicole into submission.

"The entire nation, especially the press, has been holding its breath for three days," Rachel continued. "They're hungry for information right now, so we know they'll be fighting for a chance to attend the press conference. Schedule it for noon in the Laurel Lodge. I'm betting that your biggest problem will be deciding who gets credentials to attend."

Butler threw his hands in the air and shook his head angrily from side to side.

"That's absolutely crazy!" he shouted. "How do you expect to sell Bryson on accepting Sam's team, when he's made it clear that he won't talk with anybody but you?"

"Well, Agent Butler," Rachel replied. She shifted her body towards the FBI agent and her eyes narrowed. "That's where you come in. I'm counting on the FBI and the Secret Service to make it perfectly clear that it's an unacceptable security risk for me to meet face-to-face with protesters, who have already shown themselves to be violent."

"After that," Sam interjected, "the rest is up to us. What Bryson and his friends want most is for somebody to listen to them, so that's exactly what we're going to do."

"The critical part, to some extent," Arjun continued, "is knowing that our team needs to use a completely different set of listening skills for each side of this standoff. I'll need the rest of today to bring the team up to speed on the two different ideologies we'll be facing, and on the very different types of strategies that both sides tend to use habitually."

Hunter turned his attention to Nicole and Butler.

"That's why we're lucky to have Arjun on our side," he said. "The difference between those two different ideologies happens to be his area of research. He's already done a lot of the legwork for us while he was doing the background reading for his Master's proposal."

At that moment, ominous, distant rumbles of thunder penetrated the walls of the Aspen Lodge, signalling the approach of a storm towards Camp David.

Terri took advantage of the pause in the conversation to join in the effort to reassure Nicole and Butler.

"We're confident that we'll have a much better understanding of whom we're dealing with, have a more involved plan of action for how we're going to deal with each set of protesters, and have a plan for how we're going to approach tomorrow's press conference, by the end of today."

Sam noted Matt Butler's and Nicole's body language: crossed arms, pursed lips, and stern faces. She jumped back into the conversation to support her team members.

"It's all about listening to both teams," she said. "It's about getting to know them as people, and then trying to build trust with them. And that's going to take some time."

"Our biggest challenge," Arjun said, "is trying to find some common ground between the two groups. In reality, there are lots of things that most of those protesters agree on, although they don't realize it. Even most of the contentious issues have lots of shades of grey. But when emotions are running high, like they have been since Saturday, people only see things in black and white. They become blind to the things they have in common with the other side. The only way we're going to make any progress is to listen ... and to let both sides know that we *understand* their concerns and frustrations, and are willing to find ways to address them."

"That's crazy!" Butler shouted. "Time is something you might not have, especially if the Brothers of Liberty have the guns we think they have. All we need is to have one impatient, angry protester with an itchy trigger finger, and you can flush your listening skills down the shitter!"

Rachel had heard enough. She focused her eyes on Butler, as if they were lasers, and glared.

"Once again, Agent Butler," she answered sternly, "I believe I left that issue up to you. Just how *is* your intelligence gathering going in that regard? Do you have any confirmable evidence yet to corroborate those suspicions?"

Butler's face flushed and he swallowed hard.

"Uhh, not yet, Ma'am," he replied quietly.

"Why not?" Rachel pressed. "Are you telling me you aren't up to the job?"

Butler's face was now bright red and he was clearly flustered, trying his best to cover his growing anger.

"No, Ma'am. It just takes time to infiltrate groups like this, and for undercover operatives to earn their trust."

"Didn't you just tell me that time is of the essence when it comes to guns?" Rachel demanded.

"Yes, Ma'am," Butler mumbled.

"Then I suggest you get back to work and get those operatives of yours into action!"

Rachel Williams turned her attention back towards Nicole.

"I still have some things to discuss with Captain Robby and Sam's team. I'll let you go now, along with Agent Butler. I need you to get working on press releases for tomorrow's press conference."

"Yes, Ma'am," Nicole said, her voice devoid of any sign of emotion.

Nicole and Matt Butler rose from their chairs and exited the room together, closing the door behind them, and then proceeding down a hallway towards the lodge's exit. They stopped after they were a safe distance from the Aspen Lodge, just as another rumble of thunder rolled over Camp David.

"She just won't listen!" Nicole whispered.

"Don't worry," Matt answered. "I'll be working on something tomorrow while that press conference is going on."

"Is that something I should know about?"

Matt flashed Nicole a devious grin and shook his head slightly from side to side.

"Alright, then," Nicole answered. "Good luck with whatever that is. In any case, I'm betting that Sam's team can't handle the pressure tomorrow. I'll bet their inexperience causes *them* to self-destruct before they even get out of the starting gate. Then *we* won't have to do anything more to help things along."

BREATHING HEAVILY, Jordan wove her way as quickly as possible through the conglomeration of tents and shelters crammed into the Unite the Left's encampment. She stopped in front of a small blue tent and paused briefly to catch her breath. She slapped her hand against the tent's nylon fabric and waited briefly for sounds of life inside. After a few seconds of silence, she grabbed the tent's entrance zipper, and whizzed it up until there was an opening large enough to allow her to crawl into the tent.

Cecilia Robinson's body was curled up inside a sleeping bag, her chest rising and falling slowly as she slumbered soundly, blissfully unaware of the intruder in her tent. Jordan reached out and touched the older woman's shoulder lightly.

"Cecilia, it's me Jordan. Wake up!" she whispered loudly.

Cecilia stirred briefly, then settled back into sleep. Jordan grabbed her shoulder more forcefully and gave it a vigorous shake.

"Cecilia, it's an emergency. Wake up!"

This time, Cecilia's eyes flickered open, leaving her momentarily disoriented and gazing at Jordan. After a few seconds, she finally recognized the journalist and pulled herself up until she was resting on one arm.

"Jordan? What's going on?"

"It's MacDonald," Jordan answered. "He's finally broken his silence, and he's issued demands to the President."

Cecilia sat up fully and took a moment to process Jordan's message.

"What? When?"

"He beat us to the punch. He just finished a surprise, live-streamed guest appearance on Anna Dahl's right wing podcast!"

Jordan tapped a few times on her phone to bring up the link for the interview, then she handed the phone to Cecilia.

"Here, watch this," Jordan said.

The two women watched and listened intently as Bryson's voice filled the tent, airing his demands to the President.

"We ain't goin' nowhere till you sit down with us, an' listen to the rest of our demands!"

"Damn!" Cecilia muttered. "Now we have to play defence before we can start with our agenda and give the public *our* side of the story. Damn that Dahl woman. She surely knows how to keep us off balance."

Cecilia sighed, reached for her glasses and paused to think for a moment while she adjusted the frames on her face. Finally, she looked up at Jordan.

"We have to move up our press release, and we don't have much time," Jordan said.

"Okay. Can you give me fifteen minutes? I'll meet you in the mess tent so we can toss some ideas around."

"Sure, that works for me," Jordan replied. "See you then."

She backed out of Cecilia's tent, then quickly yanked down the zipper until the opening was closed. She stood and glanced anxiously at her watch, before she wheeled around and resumed her zigzag course through the mass of shelters on her way to the mess tent.

CECILIA RUSHED towards the Unite the Left mess tent, and her stomach rumbled as she inhaled the smell of fresh coffee and breakfast sizzling on the camp's grills. Fortunately, her closely-cropped curly black hair required little maintenance, so a quick makeup application helped her appear presentable enough to be seen on camera. As she came to the tent, she stopped and removed the sweater she'd pulled on as she rushed out of her tent.

"Damn, this weather's still hot an' sticky!" she muttered under her breath. "Ain't no way I need to be wearin' this. When is this friggin' heat dome gonna move on?"

She tied the sweater around her waist and continued into the mess tent. Most of the protesters in the encampment had little to get up for each morning, after staying up late, gathering around campfires, getting to know other protesters, laughing, drinking, chanting, and singing until the wee hours. Consequently, most of them were sleeping in late each morning as the standoff settled into a monotonous daily routine. Only a few early risers were present in the tent, so Cecilia had no problem spotting Jordan, who waved to her from a table at the far end of the tent, with two cups of coffee sitting in front of her. Jordan held out one of the cups for Cecilia as she reached the table.

"Coffee?"

"Absolutely," Cecilia replied. "Just what I needed."

She took the steaming cup of liquid from Jordan, sat down, and then reached for cream and sugar packages from a bowl to doctor her coffee.

"Sorry for waking you so early," Jordan said. "But the President's called a press conference for noon, and she'll have to at least acknowledge Bryson's demands at that time."

She glanced quickly at the time on her watch, then looked up abruptly as a distant rumble of thunder rolled slowly through the tent.

"It's eight now," Jordan said. "I need to upload a video by ten at the latest, so I have time to make it to Camp David for the press conference. And that thunder doesn't sound good. What do you think?"

"The thoughts have just been flyin' round in my head since you woke me up. But I think we still need to stick to the agenda the committee agreed upon last night, even if we need to play a little bit of defence first."

"So how do you want to start?" Jordan asked.

"I think I'd like to start by agreeing with Bryson's call for President Williams to clarify her agenda for her Presidency," Cecilia said. "Nobody will expect us to do that, so it might put them a little off balance."

Jordan nodded in agreement and started jotting down a quick note in her notepad.

"Smart. You don't want to come off as being too confrontational. And then?"

"Since Bryson's demanding that she meet personally with him and his sidekicks, we need to ask for equal time for our committee to air the issues and concerns we were going to raise at last Saturday's rally."

Jordan nodded again while she jotted down another note.

"That's only fair. She'll have to at least pretend to be bipartisan. Anything else?"

"Yup," Cecilia responded. "I need to make it clear that we're also continuing to raise funds from supporters across the country. We need to let her know that we're also prepared to stay as long as it takes. We aren't going anywhere until Bryson and his so-called Liberty Convoy pack up and leave D.C."

"What about President Williams' decision to use negotiators to represent her?" Jordan asked.

Cecilia shook her head slowly from side to side.

"I don't know what she's thinking," she said. "I think this is another thing we can agree on with Bryson. I want to appeal to the President to also meet personally with us. We need to reassure her that she's in absolutely no danger here in our camp. And besides, who are these negotiators she plans to use, anyway?"

"Don't know," Jordan answered. "Maybe she'll tell us more at the press conference."

Jordan glanced nervously at her watch again.

"Okay, I think I've got your main talking points. I'm already set up outside, with the Capitol building in the background. Are you ready to go on camera?"

Cecilia laughed heartily.

"No, I think I look like hell, like I've been camping out for three days. But, I guess I'm as ready as I'll ever be. I'm ready if you are."

Both Cecilia and Jordan gulped down the last of their coffee.

"After you," Cecilia said, as the two women rose from the table, exited the tent, and took up their positions against the classic background of the Capitol building's pristine white dome.

THE ROAR of Jordan's powerful Honda bike shattered the silence of the Maryland forest as she raced along straightaways and leaned hard into curves en route to Camp David. She sneaked occasional glances over her shoulder at the rapidly darkening sky behind her. Although she couldn't hear the rumbles of thunder in those clouds, she knew the storm was bearing down on her. Moments later, raindrops splattered on her helmet's visor.

"Oh shit," she murmured to herself. "Please hold off. Just ten more minutes, that's all I ask."

Her silent prayer fell on deaf ears. The rain picked up its intensity, turning into a downpour that rapidly transformed the asphalt into a slick, dangerous deathtrap. Jordan felt the bike's tires slip for a split second as she negotiated a turn, before the rubber managed to find some grip and she pulled the bike out of the turn.

"Fuck, that was too close!" she muttered. "Slow it down, girl."

The bike's engine howled as she geared down and reduced her speed.

Effin' hell ... Can't see an effin' thing ... How much further? ... It can't be that far!

Jordan felt her tires struggle to hold on through another couple of turns. She geared down and slowed again, but she was still pushing the envelope of safety as she pressed on through the deluge. Finally, as she pulled out of a particularly tight turn, a security hut and road barrier appeared out of nowhere in front of her. She geared down and braked quickly, barely managing to keep the bike under control on the slick surface. She came to a stop beside the security hut, and an armed Marine security guard wearing rain gear emerged to greet her.

"I.D. ma'am, and the purpose of your visit?" the Marine inquired sternly.

"I'm here for the President's press conference," Jordan answered.

She struggled to remove her gloves and open her rain gear to find her press credentials.

"They're in here somewhere," she mumbled, as she continued to fish for the credentials on the lanyard around her neck, beneath the rain gear. The rain was still coming down in torrents, making her clothing wet and sticky. Finally, she found the press badge and tugged on its lanyard to show it to the guard. He scrutinized the credentials thoroughly, then finally handed it back to Jordan.

"Nice bike, ma'am, but a pretty shitty day for a bike ride, if you don't mind me saying so," the Marine said, his face finally breaking into a wry smile. "You're lucky to be here in one piece."

"Thanks. Tell me about it," she answered.

The Marine walked around the vintage bike to get a better look at it, as the torrential rain continued its deluge. He stopped and knelt down when he got to the tail light, jiggling the light with his hand.

"You realize your tail light's flickering on and off, ma'am?"

"Really?" Jordan replied, genuinely surprised by the malfunction. "I had no idea. I'll look into it when I get back to the city. Hey, am I free to go? I can't miss this press conference."

"Oh, of course, ma'am. You're good to go," he said. "Parking lot's your first left. You can take a golf cart shuttle from there to the Laurel Lodge."

The soldier walked over to the barrier and raised it.

"Thanks," she said, then she tucked her ID badge back down inside her rain gear and flipped down her visor. She gave a quick wave to the Marine, then revved the bike gently and proceeded carefully to the parking lot, her tail light flickering in the rain. She parked the bike quickly, jumped off, and ran to a waiting golf cart.

THE GOLF cart slowed in front of the Laurel Lodge, but Jordan leapt from her seat before the cart even came to a full stop. Her boots squishing and oozing water, she rushed into the lodge and followed signs as she slogged down a hallway to the lodge's conference room. She managed to slide into the conference room just as the doors were beginning to close. The room was already packed with reporters and it was now standing room only. Dripping wet, she spotted an open space along the back wall. As she resumed walking, her soaked boots squished and sloshed with each step, causing all heads and eyes to turn in her direction.

Nicole had just taken her place at the Presidential podium when Jordan entered the room. She shot the reporter a quick evil eye for being such a distraction. Then she looked down at the front row of the crowd and spotted Anna Dahl, who had also been invited to attend the event, before she cleared her throat and addressed the gathered press corp.

"Good afternoon, everybody," she said. "Thank you all for coming on such short notice. Given last night's developments, the President wanted to update you in person on her plans for dealing with the ongoing standoff in Washington. So, without any further delay, I give you President Williams."

The audience rose to its feet to applaud politely as Rachel strode onto the stage and approached the podium. She acknowledged the crowd's applause, nodding her head in appreciation and then motioning for the attendees to take their seats, while she prepared to speak.

"Thank you everybody … thank you." she began. She paused briefly while the last of the crowd took their seats and an anticipatory hush fell over the room.

"I'd like to thank everybody in the nation, and especially everybody in this room, for your patience over the past few days, as we have tried to find solutions for the current standoff on the streets of Washington. In particular, I'd like to thank the Mayor's office and D.C. Metropolitan Police for their prompt response, and their professional handling of this incident. It's obvious that you all learned a lot from the aftermath of the January sixth riot, and you were able to apply those lessons to the current situation. For that, the nation owes you our deepest thanks.

Rachel paused again to look out over the room full of journalists, but a huge clap of thunder shattered the momentary calm. Waves of torrential rain could be heard pounding the lodge's roof as thunder continued to rumble in the background. Rachel raised her eyebrows and waited for the thunder to gradually subside.

"However," she continued, "we still have a standoff between two camps of people with very divergent ideologies, all of whom may be getting very wet as I speak."

The crowd responded with muted laughter, but Rachel's joke succeeded in brightening the mood in the room.

"Mr. MacDonald of the Liberty Convoy has made it clear in his recent demands, that he wishes to talk with me directly about his group's concerns. In my address to the nation a few days ago, I vowed to be a President who listens to the people.

Rachel's eyes focused in on the TV camera in front of her, and her face became more serious.

"So, while I would sincerely like to hear his concerns, as well as the concerns of the Unite the Left protesters, I must defer to the unanimous concerns of DCMP, the Secret Service, and the FBI for my security and safety. Thus, I am not able to meet with these groups personally, at least not at the present time."

A buzz of conversation drifted around the room. Rachel paused for a moment to let it settle down.

"But, in my previous address," she continued, "I also vowed to find a non-partisan party who could listen to the concerns of both camps in this standoff. Thus, I am here today to introduce that party to you."

Another wave of buzzing and anticipation washed over the room as journalists whispered to their neighbours and readied their phones, tablets, or notepads. Rachel paused until the buzz receded slightly, then she pressed on with her announcement.

"The team I have chosen is from Canada, our neighbour to the north, which as you know, has also had to deal with their own disruptive protests in recent years. The team is young, well-educated, and objective, since they have no connections with government, nor with any partisan political groups. They distinguished themselves by proposing a novel solution to the longstanding social and political issue of indigenous Reconciliation in Canada, and they published a memoir of their experience that I would recommend to everyone. So, without any further ado, I would like to welcome Ms. Samantha Bower, who will introduce herself and the rest of her team to you."

The background buzz changed into a low drone as Sam emerged from backstage and walked towards the podium. Rachel turned to her and welcomed her with a short embrace, before gesturing for her to take the podium. Rachel took up position a couple of steps behind Sam and to her left. The press crowd applauded politely, but unenthusiastically. Even after the applause subsided, a continuous buzz drifted around the room. Both Jordan Marsh and Anna Dahl wore expressions of surprise on their faces as Sam stepped tentatively up to the podium, cleared her throat, and looked into the lone TV camera for the first time.

"Good afternoon, everybody," Sam began. She swallowed nervously and felt sweat forming on her hands as she grasped the sides of the podium to ground herself.

"I know you're all probably wondering the same thing that I wondered, when I got a totally unexpected phone call from the President of the United States. 'Why me?' I thought. Why call upon a poor, part-Indigenous, Canadian grad student and her friends to negotiate on the President's behalf in the Washington standoff? I was just as skeptical as you are right now.

Sam turned and glanced briefly at President Williams, who smiled and nodded for her to continue. As she turned her gaze back towards the audience, another huge crash of thunder boomed over the constant sound of rain on the roof and filled the room.

"Hopefully, that's the storm before the calm in the Washington standoff," Sam said, smiling.

A few chuckles came from the audience, finally helping to quiet the background press corps' buzz and lighten the mood.

"But, all joking aside, President Williams said two things that eventually convinced me and my team to take on this task. First, we've proven ourselves to be good listeners, something that both the Liberty Convoy and Unite the Left protesters are asking of President Williams. And secondly, as non-Americans, we haven't been involved in the highly divisive and partisan political process in America, so we are highly committed to listening to both sides of the standoff as objectively as possible. Our goal is to listen, to bring the protesters' demands to the President, and to help negotiate a fair and peaceful end to the Washington standoff, with both sides satisfied that they've been heard.

Sam paused once again. Her hands were no longer perspiring and she felt her confidence growing.

"At this time, I'd like to take the opportunity to introduce you to the rest of my team."

She turned to her right and watched as Arjun, Hunter, and Terri took their places on the stage beside President Williams, and behind Sam and the podium.

"First, on your far left, Arjun Patel, our constitutional expert and all-around history geek," she said, smiling. "Next to him, Hunter MacMillan, our expert on constitutional law and Indigenous issues. And finally, Terri Fortin, our resident entrepreneur, who has the rare ability to keep us all grounded, focused, and real."

The audience applauded politely while Sam turned back to the TV camera.

"We'll be reaching out to both the Liberty Convoy and the Unite the Left organizers as early as this afternoon. We look forward to meeting with them, hearing and understanding their concerns, and getting down to work as soon as possible to find a way to end this standoff. Thank you, and now, back to you, Madam President."

Sam turned to her left and nodded to Rachel, who stepped back up to the podium. In the meantime, Sam stepped back beside Terri while some lingering audience applause subsided.

"Thank you to Sam and the rest of the team," Rachel resumed. "I want to assure all Americans, not just those involved with the Liberty Convoy and the Unite the Left protests, that we will be keeping America up to date on the progress of our negotiations."

The background buzz in the room was turning into a low roar as reporters conversed with their neighbours, texting their respective news desks, or some even rushing from the room to file their stories and to research information on Sam and her team members. Rachel looked out over the commotion and looked directly at Anna Dahl, and then at Jordan Marsh, before directing her next comments towards them.

"In fact, we'll be reaching out to some of you in the audience very soon to discuss press coverage of the coming negotiations."

Rachel paused one more time as she looked at her watch, and then over at Sam and the team. She gave an approving nod to Sam, who smiled and returned the acknowledgment.

"Alright," she said, almost shouting over the commotion, "that's all the information we've prepared for you at this time. But, I think the team and I have time to take a few quick questions before we get down to work."

Journalists' hands shot up into the air, vying for the President's attention. Rachel pointed to an Asian woman in the second row, who jumped up from her seat in excitement.

"Madam President, you said you want to keep Americans up to date on the negotiations. We know Americans are losing trust in where their news is coming from. The left doesn't trust Fox News and the right doesn't trust CNN or the other big networks. So, how are you going to ensure that Americans are going to hear the truth about the negotiations?"

"That's an excellent question," Rachel replied. "And I think I'm going to ask Ms. Bower to answer that one for me."

Rachel nodded to Sam, who stepped forward to the podium.

"Thanks Madam President, and thanks to the lady who asked the question," she said. "We haven't worked out the details yet, but my team would like to live stream the negotiations with both teams, if they are agreeable to that. We'd like to stream the raw, unedited proceedings over a video streaming channel, with no commentary whatsoever. That way, we think we can reduce the bias that inevitably gets attached to events by each different news outlet. We realize, of course, that every news outlet will put their own spin on what they see and hear, but my team won't have any control over that."

Pandemonium broke out in the audience, with every journalist jumping out of their chairs and waving their hands to be chosen next. Sam spotted Jordan Marsh at the back of the room, her arm also waving back and forth.

"Ms. Marsh, at the back," Sam said.

"I realize you haven't worked out the details yet," Jordan said, "but would it be fair to say that your team may be looking more towards independent journalists, rather than the usual network sources, to do this live streaming?"

The room buzzed with conversation while everybody awaited Sam's reply.

"I think that might be a fair assumption," Sam answered.

Once again, pandemonium erupted in the room. But Jordan Marsh quietly picked up her helmet and walked calmly out of the room, her mind silently putting two and two together while her soaked feet squished and sloshed along. It now made perfect sense as to why both Anna Dahl and herself had been invited to the press conference.

THE LIBERTY Convoy's mess tent vibrated and flapped wildly in the face of howling winds and driving rain, as the protest's organizers huddled around a table in the middle of the mess hall watching President Williams' press conference on TV. Anna Dahl, the only organizer not present in the tent, was still seated in the front row of the press corps attending the live event at Camp David.

Norm Barfield slammed his fist down on the table as he watched the President.

"Security concerns, my ass!" he bellowed in Bryson's direction. "That's just'a load'a chicken shit. She ain't got no intention o'listenin' to us. Whatcha gonna do to show 'er we mean business, chief?"

"Yeah, Bryson," Sean Pritchard shouted. "We need to do somethin' to show 'er we mean business."

"Ah'm all ears, guys," Bryson yelled. "Trouble is, we don' have as many options after those woke sons'a'bitches fucked up our plan. Anybody got any fresh ideas?"

"Why do we have to do anything?" Martin Lee asked. "Follow through on your threat. Just refuse to meet with them. Nothing pisses people off more than passive, peaceful protest."

"I'm not sure I agree," Jessica Murray answered. "You know I'm a big supporter of passive protests, like the one we pulled off at the Minnesota pipeline. But you know the left is going to agree to meet with those negotiators. And the rest of the country's watching us closely. As soon as we refuse to do the same, we'll be branded as the bad guys in this standoff, instead of being seen as peaceful and cooperative. I think we need to at least meet with Bower and her team."

"What?" Bryson bellowed, his face turning crimson. "We do that an' we lose face. We'll look like a bunch'a pussies!"

"Come on, Bryson," Jessica countered. "You're taking this too personal by making it about you saving face. You came here to make the President listen, but you'll never succeed if you sabotage yourself and this convoy by refusing to meet with her negotiating team. People on both sides are just going to see you as being inconsistent, at best."

"She's gotta good point," Pastor Kessler added. "What have we got to lose by meetin' with 'em? We don't want this to be a wasted opportunity to show the world that we're good, God fearin' Americans, who just wanna have our rights an' freedoms protected."

"Anybody else got something to say?" Jessica asked. "What about you, John?"

John Gregg looked around the table at the rest of the organizers, processing everybody's opinions, before he finally cleared his voice.

"I came here to tell the President what's happenin' to farmers an' small rural business owners 'cross this here country. It's gettin' harder every day to make a livin' an' feed our families, an' I ain't gonna leave here till I've managed to do that. So, I guess I'm with Jessica. I say we meet with the Bower woman an' her team."

Jessica turned to Bryson and the two organizers glared at each other. Finally, Jessica broke the stalemate.

"Looks like we have a difference of opinion, so let's do a show of hands. Who's in favour of hearing what the negotiators have to say, and telling them what we came here to tell the President?"

The seven organizers looked around the table at each other. Jessica raised her hand, followed by Pastor Kessler and John Gregg. Bryson, Norm Barfield, and Sean Pritchard sat with their arms crossed defiantly across their chests, refusing to raise their hands.

A huge clap of thunder followed immediately on the heels of a blinding flash of lightning, causing everybody around the table to jump.

As the thunder gradually rolled away into the distance and everybody managed to catch their breath and slow down their racing hearts, they all turned their attention to Martin Lee, who was once again engrossed with something on his phone.

"What about you, Martin?" Jessica inquired. "You still want to go the passive resistance route?"

"What? Oh, right," he answered. He took a moment to consider his options before finally making a decision.

"Okay, let's play their game for now," he replied. "Let's see if they're really willing to listen. We can always walk away if we don't like the way things are going."

With the vote clearly against him, Bryson locked eyes with Jessica and glared at her for daring to usurp his authority as the convoy's de facto leader.

"Then that's decided," she declared. "I'll be happy to speak on behalf of the group when they contact us."

She returned Bryson's icy stare with a sarcastic smile.

"That way, you won't have to worry about losing face."

ACROSS THE fences on Constitution Avenue, the Unite the Left encampment's mess tent wasn't standing up nearly as well to the storm as their Liberty Convoy counterpart. Volunteers worked feverishly to re-erect a couple of poles on the west side of the tent that had collapsed, while the unsupported tent fabric flapped violently in the wind. The group's organizing committee huddled around a computer screen at a table on the other side of the tent.

"What is that woman thinking?" Cecilia cried out. "Bringing in an inexperienced young team from Canada? I don't get it. Personally, this is one time I can agree with Bryson. I want to meet with the President in person too."

"I agree," Stephen Danilenko chimed. "She's up to something, and I don't know what. I just don't trust her. Surely, Washington is full of experienced negotiators from both sides of the floor. Why reach outside the country?"

"What?" Kymberly Babineau shouted. "You'd trust our politicians, on either side of the floor, to be objective? Wake up, Stephen. I, for one, think that Washington needs some newer, younger blood. I'm eager to meet this Bower woman and her team."

Nasir Hazrat, who had listened quietly to the others, cleared his voice and looked around the table at his peers.

"I am with Kymberly. I do not trust *any* politicians, especially after they abandoned us in Afghanistan!"

"Hey, everybody," Sandra Delgado answered. "Not all of us politicians are completely partisan or untrustworthy. But, I do agree with Kym that bringing in some new blood could be a good idea. What about you, Dudley?"

The veteran scientist paused, rubbed his chin, and took a moment to ponder the arguments on the table.

"I think the President is making a brave move," he said, finally. "Personally, I love taking on young, new grad students. Their fresh ideas keep me on my toes and keep me open to seeing things in new ways. I'm with Kym and Sandra."

Cecilia looked at Idris Mohammed. The black, gay man who was originally from Sudan, had been sitting quietly throughout the debate.

"What about you Idris?" she said.

"I agree somewhat with Stephen and Nasir," he replied. "I too have difficulty trusting people. But, I also try to give people a chance to prove if they are worthy of my trust."

Cecilia then looked to Danielle Chen, the young Asian-American actor, who was clearly unprepared and underdressed for the chilly, stormy weather, wearing a miniskirt and sleeveless t-shirt. She clutched her arms to her chest and clamped her legs together in a vain attempt to conserve body heat. The young woman's teeth were chattering, her body shivering, and the chilled muscles in her jaw made it a struggle to speak.

"You all know my father ... the politician," she stuttered. "If the President is anything like him ... I wouldn't trust her ... further than I could throw her ... let's give Bower's team a chance ... to earn our trust ...but keep a very close eye on them."

Danielle looked around the table at the others, her body still shaking, before her eyes finally stopped at Cecilia.

"It sounds like ... most of us are cautiously open ... to meeting with Samantha and her team," she stuttered. "Do we need to put this to a vote ... Cecilia?"

Cecilia looked around the table, polling the committee's members with her eyes. She realized that she was in the minority, and the consensus was with Danielle.

"I don't think that's necessary," she answered. "Jordan and I already released a statement to the White House ahead of the press conference, stating our preference for an in-person meeting with the president. So, I guess all we can do now is wait to see what the President has to say, and how Bryson MacDonald's going to react."

RAIN CONTINUED to splatter the windshield, as Matt Butler backed his black sedan into a parking spot to the rhythmic dance of the vehicle's wiper blades. Rain droplets continued to splatter the windshield after he turned off the ignition. He gazed through the window to his left, where a tired looking pub was wedged between a pawn shop and an Asian aesthetics establishment. Water droplets on the glass distorted the aging streetscape into a surreal kaleidoscope of muted colour, due to the day's dull grey lighting. Matt pulled up the collar on his jacket, exited the vehicle, and hurried across the street to the pub.

Inside, the English-style pub's dark, dingy interior was made even worse by narrow windows and the dark, gloomy weather outside. While the dark English-style panelling may have passed for being trendy in the early nineteen-hundreds, it could only be described as depressing by today's standards. Every surface that Matt touched felt sticky, and the dank smell of decades of stale beer managed to seep through the sickly-sweet odour of recently applied bleach.

"Jack on the rocks," Matt said to the overweight man, who appeared to be as tired and depressed as the interior of the establishment. He took a seat on a barstool while the man poured his drink.

"What a shitty day!" Matt continued.

"Looks like the worst's almost over," the bartender mumbled. "They says it's goin' to get damned hot fer a while now."

He finished pouring and slid the drink across the bar to Matt, who stood up and took it to a booth at the back of the decrepit establishment. He sought out a spot on the sticky, red vinyl upholstery that wasn't too badly cracked or scarred, and slid into the booth. As he sipped the liquor and felt its gentle burn slide past his throat, he had a clear view of the pub and its entrance, and at the handful of patrons who entered.

After about ten minutes, the door creaked open and a medium-height, slim woman with shoulder-length blond hair entered the pub and took a seat at the bar. Matt picked up his drink and moved towards the bar, where he took a seat between the woman and the entrance.

"What are you having, Elena?" he asked.

Startled, the woman turned her head in Matt's direction, then instinctively stood up to leave. Matt grabbed her by the arm firmly and pulled her back into her seat.

"Relax, Elena," he said. "I'm not here to bust you. I have a business proposition for you. More like a favour, actually. Vodka, I presume?"

He glanced at the bartender.

"Vodka for the lady. Two shots."

The woman glared angrily at Matt, her blue eyes as cold as ice.

"Vy I should trust you?" she said, with a distinct Russian accent.

"Because this isn't FBI business, Elena. You're not in any more trouble. This is a private matter, business that requires your special talents."

"Not interested, Butler," she blurted. "I not trust you! What is in it for me?"

"I'd pay you handsomely, of course," Matt answered. "But, what if I told you I have friends who could make those hacking charges of yours disappear?"

The bartender set two shots of vodka in front of Elena. She squinted at Matt, still suspicious, but starting to show some interest. Then, abruptly, she shook her head from side to side.

"No, you lie. I not believe you!"

"That's up to you. Maybe you'd rather have my friends arrange for you to be deported back to Russia. I'm sure there's plenty of people back home who'd love to settle some scores with you."

Elena's eyes opened wide, then narrowed again into that icy blue glare.

"Okay, I listen," she said grudgingly. She picked up one of the vodka shots and threw it back, followed shortly thereafter by the second.

Matt picked up his phone and brought up a video feed to show Elena.

"This is the DCMP security video feed from the encampments surrounding the White House. Let's go to the back where we can talk more discreetly." Matt turned to the bartender.

"Another shot for the lady."

After the bartender poured the shot, Matt picked it up and guided Elena to the same booth he had previously occupied in the dark corner at the back of the pub.

"I assume that hacking into this site wouldn't pose much of a problem for you?" he said.

Elena laughed.

"Of course, is child play," she replied sarcastically.

Matt reached into his pocket and pulled out a folded piece of paper with handwriting on it. He handed it to Elena.

"This is an outline of an operation that I need you to execute ASAP," he said, his voice hushed. "First, I need you to scour the video feed from this first encampment, to find a mark for the operation. Second, I'm assuming you have friends who can help you to execute the rest of the operation for my friends."

Elena studied the sheet of paper carefully for a few moments before dropping it dismissively on the table.

"Okay, so I get friends to help. Operation like this cost me big money."

"Show me a number," Matt replied. He handed her a pen and Elena picked up the piece of paper, taking a moment to think. Then she wrote down a number and handed the sheet back to Matt. He looked at her response, wrote another number below Elena's, and handed the paper back to her.

"My friends will meet your number, plus that second number, as long as you and your friends are successful. Do we have a deal?"

Elena picked up the paper, gave it a glance, and then picked up the third vodka shot and threw it back.

"Ahhh," she sighed. "I need dollars now for expenses. And hacking charges disappear too?"

Matt picked up the piece of paper, got up, and walked over to a metal waste basket in a nearby corner. He pulled a lighter from his pocket and set the sheet on fire before dropping it into the waste basket. He returned to the booth, sat down, and took an envelope of money from his pocket, sliding it across the table to Elena.

"My friends promise that the hacking charges will go away, *if* you're successful."

Elena peeked inside the envelope and seemed satisfied.

"Okay, ve have deal," she announced.

"Good! I thought you might be interested," he answered. He picked up a napkin from the table, wrote a phone number on it, and then handed it to Elena.

"Memorize this number and call me to arrange final payment once you've completed the operation," he said. "But remember, if you get caught, I don't know you and this meeting never happened. Understand?"

Elena threw her head back and laughed.

"Vhat meeting? You just some guy hitting on me in bar. I not interested."

"Good," Matt said. He took back the napkin with the phone number and rose from the table.

"Remember, I need this done quickly. Don't make me wait!" he said, his voice hushed. He shoved the napkin in his pocket, stood up, withdrew some cash from his other pocket, and dropped it on the table. Then he pulled up the collar on his jacket and exited the pub.

Elena picked up her empty glass and made her way back to the bar, where she slammed it on the counter and glared at the bartender.

"Is empty. One more for road!"

CONSTITUTION AVENUE

CHAPTER 9—ISLANDS IN THE STREAM

THE RAIN and wind had finally died down overnight. Campers at both encampments, many of them wet and shivering, crept warily from the shelter of their tents as sunshine peeked through the clouds. In the Liberty Convoy camp, Jessica Murray joined with her neighbours, who were all carrying wet sleeping bags and bundles of clothing or belongings, and were hanging them on camp chairs, tables, the security fences, or any other place they could find. After hanging a load of clothes on the security fence, Jessica took a break and pulled out her phone. Her thumbs flew over the phone's keyboard, tapping out a text message.

Hey babe, how'd the press conference go?

Great. POTUS unveiled her negotiators. Interesting group. Could be an opportunity for me TBD.

??? Tell me more?

Can't right now. Managed to get a few minutes to interview M. Chen later this morning. How bout tonite?

Should be able to get away. Same time & place?

Sounds good. See u then. Luv u!

Luv u 2, babe!

Jessica pocketed her phone and crawled back into her tent. Moments later she emerged with another arm load of soaked items. As she went back to work, managing to find a few free spaces to hang them on the security fence, she noticed a man dressed in full camo attire, carrying cases of food supplies from the convoy's refrigerated tractor-trailer unit.

What the fuck? What is he up to?

Curious, she followed the man as he carried an armload of boxes to another trailer, about twenty yards away. She watched as he handed the load to another man in the back of the second trailer, which appeared to be used as storage for dry and canned goods. She hid behind another nearby trailer. After dropping his load, the first man headed back in the direction of the refrigeration trailer. The second man partially closed the rear door of the dry goods trailer, seemingly in an effort to conceal what he was doing. Moments later, the first man reappeared, carrying another load to the dry goods trailer. He knocked on the door and the second man swung it open. Jessica caught her breath as she caught a glimpse of what he was doing.

What the ... those boxes have rifle parts and handguns in them. They're hiding guns in the food trailer!

While the first man turned around and headed back towards the refrigeration trailer, Jessica saw the second man quickly pick up a rifle that he had assembled from some of the parts. Moving swiftly, he hid the weapon carefully behind a stack of toilet paper bales.

The muscles in Jessica's jaw went tight as she clenched her teeth together. Her eyes narrowed and her forehead tightened into an angry frown.

Bryson! That fucker's been lying through his teeth to the rest of us!

After hiding the rifle, the second man quickly closed the trailer door again. Jessica rushed from her hiding spot and marched determinedly towards Bryson's command centre van. She pounded on the side of the van until the corpulent protest leader opened the rear door and stuck his head out.

"The fuck do *you* want, Jess?"

"We need to talk! Let me inside or I'll let the whole world know about what I just saw in the supply trailer!"

Bryson's eyes opened wide and he quickly opened the door wider.

"Git in here, 'fore somebody hears ya!" he muttered under his breath."

Jessica climbed into the back of the van and closed the door behind her. She found a second captain's chair beside Bryson, who was seated in his usual spot in front of the rack of police scanners. She shook her index finger at him and vented her anger.

"You lying sonofabitch!" she shouted. "You told us this was a peaceful convoy! All you wanted to do was have the President hear your concerns, you said! So what's with the guns you're hiding? What are you *really* up to?"

A sarcastic grin spread across Bryson's face.

"Don't getcher panties all in a knot. They're jus' fer insurance."

"Insurance!" Jessica countered. "For what, Bryson? In case Williams won't listen, or you don't like what she says? Then what? You gonna pull another January sixth, but march into the White House this time? You gonna take over the Presidency?"

The sarcastic look on Bryson's face melted away in the face of Jessica's anger, gradually transforming into a flustered, bewildered look.

"H-hold on, Jess. It's ... ummh ... it's not like that."

"Well then, what *is* it like!" Jessica screamed. "I didn't sign up for any of this. First you lied about wanting to take control of the streets. Now you're lying about having guns. What else are you lyin' to us about? I feel like walking outta here right now, and goin' straight to the press about those guns!"

Jessica's threat had an immediate effect. His face turned red and he glared at Jessica, his eyes full of rage.

"I'll jus' bet ya would, ya fuckin' cunt! Was probly *you* who leaked my plans to the fuckin woke bastards and ruined everythin'. Ya better think twice 'bout that. No tellin' what nasty things could happen to yer girlfriend, or boyfriend, or whatever the fuck ya call 'er."

Jessica's body went rigid from head to toe, and she had to fight the urge to launch her body at Bryson.

"Are you threatening me?"

The smirk returned to his face as Bryson felt himself getting the upper hand in the confrontation.

"Who, me? Never. I'm jus' sayin ... bad shit happens sometimes."

"Well, it works both ways, asshole! I'm not gonna say anything to anybody as long as those guns stay in that trailer," Jessica countered. "But, I *will* be watchin' you and your friends closely. So, don't let me catch you lyin' to me again. Do we have an understanding?"

"Sure, Jess, sure," he replied, still grinning and smirking insincerely. "Ya don' havta worry 'bout me. We're all on the same team here, ain't we?"

"Same team?" Jessica muttered. "Is that what you call it? Okay, we have an understanding ... for now."

Without uttering another word, Jessica opened the rear door of the van and climbed out. She shot one last glare in Bryson's direction before she slammed the door shut, turned away, and stomped back to her tent.

ANNA DAHL mopped the perspiration from her forehead as she prepared for another edition of her podcast. From the Liberty Camp's performance stage, she could see relieved protesters lining up for breakfast in the mess tent. Now faced with rapidly rising heat and humidity in the wake of the storm, they were now seeking shade and shelter from what was quickly turning into a heat event.

Anna glanced at her watch nervously, then scanned the entrances to the tent, searching for any sign of Bryson.

Where is he, anyway? We're supposed to be on the air in ten minutes?

She glanced at the front row of chairs in front of the tent's stage and noticed that a lot of campers, seeking shelter from the sun, were drifting into seats under the event stage's huge awning, to watch the live stream of her podcast while they ate breakfast. She picked up her phone, about to dial Bryson's number, when she saw the big man's body fill one of the entrances to the tent and then lumber over towards the stage. He was perspiring profusely, his cotton shirt clinging to his back and large patches of sweat forming under his armpits. He mopped his brow with the back of one of his arms.

"Shee-it," he exclaimed. "It's like a furnace out there on that assphalt."

He noticed the look of concern engraved on Anna's face.

"We justa 'bout ready to roll here?" he asked.

"We will be, just as soon as we get y'all miked up," she replied. "Cuttin' it pretty close, weren'tcha?"

"Ya worry too much, Anna," he answered, as he glanced at his watch. "We gotta coupla minutes to spare."

Anna's producer attached a battery pack to the backside of Bryson's belt and clipped a microphone to his lapel.

"Talk to me, Bryson," the woman said.

"How's this? Kin ya hear me?" he shouted.

"That's good, but you don't have to shout."

The producer held onto Bryson's arm and directed him to his seat, then turned to see Anna taking hers.

"Places everybody. One minute."

More Liberty Convoy campers drifted into seats to watch the impending show. Finally, the producer counted down from ten and gave Anna the thumbs up to begin.

"Welcome to another edition of the Anna Dahl podcast. Once again, I'm streaming live to y'all from Liberty Convoy camp, outside the grounds of the White House in Washington D.C.," she began. "And my special guest, once again, is the Liberty Convoy's lead organizer, Bryson MacDonald. Thanks for joining me again, Bryson."

"Thanks fer havin' me. It's always a pleasure."

"So, Bryson," Anna said. "The last time we spoke, y'all challenged President Williams to meet personally with your convoy's organizers. But yesterday, the President introduced a so-called objective team of experts to negotiate with y'all, and with the Unite the Left organizers, on her behalf. Given her refusal to meet personally with you, what's next for y'all an' the other organizers?"

Bryson looked up, and the first face he saw in the front row was that of Jessica Murray, her face expressionless and her eyes glued on him. He shifted nervously in his seat, then cleared his throat.

"Well, let's jus' say we had a lively meetin' in our camp, an' we seriously tossed aroun' a whole bunch'a options, includin' refusin' to meet with the President's buncha amatoors!"

"Hold that thought about the amateurs, Bryson," Anna answered. "But first, what did y'all decide in the end?"

"In the end, we figgered that she was darin' us to boycott meetin' with 'er team, jus' to make us look like we're the bad guys here. So, we 'nanamously decided to give them amatoors a chance to show their selves fer bein' jus' that—a buncha young amatoors."

He took a quick glance at Jessica, who glared at him and shook her head slowly from side to side.

"Funny y'all should call them that, Bryson," Anna continued. "This reporter burned the midnight oil last night, after yesterday's press conference, tryin' to research Ms. Bower and her team."

Anna paused and looked out over the sizeable crowd that had formed in front of the stage.

"Would y'all like to hear what I found out?"

A smattering of applause and shouts of "Yeah" and "Tell us" could be heard coming from the viewers.

"Sure would," Bryson added.

"So, let's start with Samantha Bower, shall we?" Anna said. "Far from having any credible professional credentials, she is just a lowly grad student at an obscure university in Saskatchewan, wherever that is. She seems to be studying psychology and Indian issues. And her only claim to fame appears to be a memoir she wrote about her experience as a teaching assistant. The rest of her so-called team were only students in her class."

"Ya gotta be kiddin' me!" Bryson shouted.

"No joke, everybody," Anna continued. "Even Samantha Bower's memoir is sketchy, claiming to be unaware that she's half Indian until her late twenties. Really? How do we know she's not just another person pretending to be Indian?"

"How 'bout the guy who *is* an Indian?" Bryson interjected.

Anna turned her attention back to her guest.

"Glad you asked, Bryson. Ms. Bower claims that Hunter MacMillan is her team's 'expert on Constitutional Law and Indigenous Issues.' But, my research shows that he's no expert at all! He still has another year left in law school. Better yet, his only real legal experience was getting himself arrested—not just once, but twice—for desecrating a statue in a city park! Some expert! Sounds to me that the only thing he's an expert at, is bein' a shit disturber!"

This time, Anna shifted in her seat and turned her attention from Bryson to the TV camera.

"Finally," she resumed. "There's Ms. Bower's other alleged Constitutional expert, young Mr. Patel. How can y'all call a young brown kid, who's only in his first year of a Master's program, an expert on anythin'? And then there's Ms. Teresa Fortin. Bower says she's on the team to keep the other three grounded. But, I found out that she's the only member of the team that yours truly could find who has any level of expertise in anythin'. Just watch this an' judge fer yerself."

The first frame of a YouTube video appeared on the huge screen on the stage behind Anna and Bryson. At the same time, viewers of Anna's podcast were seeing the same image on their video feed. The images of Anna and Bryson remained visible in a small box in the upper right corner of everybody's video feed. Anna nodded to her producer and the video image came to life.

In the front row, Jessica's mouth dropped open at the same time that she heard gasps coming from the crowd around her. The video was one that Terri used to advertise her exotic dance school, showing a scantily-clad Terri doing an extremely seductive pole dance. In the small box in the upper right corner of the screen, Bryson's eyes went wide open as he watched. Pulling no punches, Anna let the entire video play until the dance ended. Abruptly, the images of Anna and

Bryson filled the main screen again, and Anna turned to face Bryson, who was clapping his hands ecstatically.

"Well, how 'bout that! She's a peeler!" Bryson exploded.

"That's right, Bryson and the rest of America," Anna declared. "Terri Fortin is an expert alright—an expert in pole dancin'. I guess her job must be to entertain the guys on Bower's team. But, when I did a deeper dive, it gets even better."

Bryson was still laughing so hard, clapping his hands and slapping his knees at the same time, that he could barely speak.

"A peeler! An effin' peeler! How'n hell kin ya possibly beat that!"

"Well, what I found out is that Ms. Fortin's got herself a criminal record for solicitation *and* dealin' drugs in Canada! So, I ask y'all this question: How did Ms. Fortin even gain entry into our country, with *her* record?"

Anna expertly turned her focus back to the camera, her face now wearing a serious frown as she spoke directly to her viewers.

"Is *this* the kind of so-called experts you want *your* President to call upon to deal with a major crisis on the streets around *your* cities? I think not, America. Y'all need to get online right now an' use your socials to tell President Williams what y'all think. That y'all expect her to make *much* better choices than that!"

The partisan crowd of protesters jumped to their feet and broke into applause. At the same time, Anna stood and smiled at the crowd, applauding with them. Then she shook Bryson's hand, before turning back to the crowd and waving joyously to them.

"That's all for this edition of the Anna Dahl podcast!" she shouted. "See y'all again soon!"

Having seen enough, Jessica rose from her seat, shaking her head from side to side in disbelief as she walked from the Liberty Convoy tent. Once clear of the tent, she tapped a number on her *Favourites* list, then raised her phone to her ear.

"Hey, babe. It's me, Jess. I have some urgent information for you about Sam Bower and her team. Call me."

CONSTITUTION AVENUE

JORDAN STOOD in the hallway, outside President Williams' Camp David office, her knees still trembling with excitement after her surprise one-on-one meeting with the President. Her phone vibrated and she noticed a call coming in from Jess. She was still in a state of disbelief, and could barely contain her excitement after learning that her journalistic career was about to take a sharp turn for the better. She was dying to tell Jess, but she was sworn to secrecy until the White House made an official announcement.

Suddenly, the door to the President's office opened and Representative Michael Chen exited the room into the hallway, where Jordan was waiting. He looked around, then saw Jordan and walked towards her.

"Is this still a good time for an interview, Representative Chen?" Jordan asked.

Michael Chen stepped forward and shook Jordan's hand, his face displaying a warm, friendly smile.

"Absolutely," Ms. Marsh. "I have a few minutes I can spare."

"Thank you. If you don't mind, I have my video camera set up over here."

She guided the Congressman to a spot in front of her tripod-mounted camera and its attached spotlight, grabbed her microphone, turned on the camera and light, then took her place beside her guest.

"Congressman Chen, can you tell us what you were discussing with the President?" Jordan began.

"Of course," he replied. "It's no secret that the standoff around the White House is foremost on everybody's mind."

"Did you discuss the plan that the President revealed yesterday? And if so, what do you think?"

"Well, I think everybody in America would like to see the situation resolved as soon as possible," Chen continued. "But, on the other hand, we live in a country where we all have the right to protest and to speak freely, and we must not take those freedoms for granted.

So any solution must not interfere with those freedoms, yet must try to bring the standoff to a close peacefully, with nobody getting hurt."

"Does that mean you endorse President Williams' plan to engage Ms. Bower's Canadian negotiation team?" Jordan pressed.

Chen flashed a knowing smile at Jordan, acknowledging the cat and mouse game between journalist and interviewee.

"I think that free speech and peaceful protest are both absolutely critical for the protection of our democracy. But I acknowledge that in a democracy, there are often differences of opinions, and there needs to be dialogue between parties. So, if Ms. Bower and her team can listen to the people and open up a dialogue between the two sides, I think we should give her a chance to do so."

"What about a timeline? I know that Senator Crowley has stated quite openly that he disagrees with the President's plan, and he'd like to see the National Guard brought in to clear the streets as soon as possible. Did you and the President discuss how much time you were willing to give Ms. Bower's team?" Jordan asked, flashing Chen a knowing smile of her own.

"I think it's a bit early to start talking timelines, given that Ms. Bower's team has yet to meet with the two sides," Chen replied. "Senator Crowley and I frequently have differing opinions, but we also have things upon which we agree. We'll see what happens as this process moves along."

"One more question, if you don't mind. We all know that your daughter, Danielle, is one of the key organizers of the Unite the Left protest, and that she's currently living in their encampment. Is that having any effect on your relationship, or on how you view the standoff?"

Jordan saw a microsecond of anger flash in Chen's eyes, and it sent a brief shiver down her spine. She blinked, but when her eyes opened, Chen's eyes projected their typical political warmth.

"Like I said before, I believe that everybody in this country has the right to their opinions, and has the right to protest. That applies to my daughter, regardless whether we agree on issues or not."

Chen took a quick glance at his watch, signalling to Jordan that the interview was now over. Jordan knew she'd touched a nerve, and she didn't want to ruin any chances for future interviews.

"Thank you for your comments, Congressman," Jordan said.

Chen flashed one last warm smile at Jordan.

"Thank *you*," he replied. "I'm sure we'll have more to talk about over the coming days."

Jordan turned off her camera and light, then watched as the Congressman joined his assistant and the pair exited the building. Her phone vibrated in her pocket again. She noticed Jess's name fill the screen as she withdrew the phone, bringing her back to reality. She took a deep breath and pressed the answer button.

"Hey, Jess. What's up? We still on for tonight?"

SAM TOOK her seat around a large circular table in Camp David's Laurel Lodge conference room, along with Hunter, Terri, and Arjun. They were joined by Jordan Marsh, whom the President had asked to attend their meetings. As Sam paused to gaze around the table, and then at their famous surroundings, she couldn't help but wonder how many famous world leaders, politicians, and other dignitaries had graced this room with their presence throughout history. The reality of her situation created a powerful sense of awe that threatened to overwhelm her, so she swiftly took a deep breath to calm herself and turned her attention back to the task at hand. She took a sip of water and anchored herself by looking around the table again at her colleagues.

"By now, I think you all know Jordan Marsh," she said. "She's here at the President's request, and she has a video she'd like us to watch before we begin."

"Thanks, Sam," Jordan replied, smiling at the rest of the team. "Thanks for welcoming me into your group."

With the introductions over, Jordan's smile gradually transformed into a more somber expression; her forehead became furrowed and her eyes narrowed.

"I got a hot tip, only a little while ago, that Anna Dahl just finished her latest live-streamed podcast with Bryson MacDonald," she continued. "I thought we should all watch the recording on YouTube, so you all get a taste of what you're up against."

Jordan turned her laptop computer around for the rest of the team to view, and then started the replay of the podcast. The faces of the team members took on the same serious expression as Jordan, as they watched Anna and Bryson take turns putting down each member of Sam's team. When the video ended, Jordan closed her laptop.

"And so the misinformation and political games begin," she said, sighing. "I'm afraid you guys have no idea what you're up against, and how bad this could get."

"She's a bald-faced liar!" Terri exclaimed. "She's distorting the facts. What she said just isn't true!"

"Better get used to it, honey," Jordan shot back. "In politics, they just call it stretching the truth."

Sam caught a glance of the angry look on Hunter's face, one she remembered well from their night class experience.

"She's trying to make me look like a small-time criminal!" he bellowed. "I'm not going to let her get away with that!"

"Okay, everybody," Sam said, her voice remaining unruffled. "Let's all take a few deep breaths and calm down. If we let this type of misinformation get under our skin every time we hear it, she and Bryson will win every time."

She turned to Jordan.

"Do you know if the President has contacted Anna about her press plan yet?"

"Judging from what we've just heard," Jordan answered, "I doubt it. But I'm sure that'll happen pretty soon."

Sam turned her attention back to the rest of the team.

"In that case, we're just going to have to wait and see whether Anna agrees to the plan. If she does, it's going to be a whole lot harder for her to spread misinformation. In the meantime, let's get back to focusing on our own game plan."

She looked to Arjun, who had been listening attentively throughout the conversation.

"Take it away, Arjun."

"Thanks, Sam," he replied. He turned on a projector, which sat in the middle of the table and lit up a projection screen behind him. He then clicked the trackpad on his laptop to reveal a large spreadsheet on the big screen.

"I created this graphic while I was doing research for my thesis, so I thought I'd share it with you. It lists the types of strategies that the far left and the far right tend to use habitually when they're arguing against each other, as well as how each side reacts to each others' arguments."

He moved a pointer towards the bottom of the spreadsheet.

"Pay attention to the overriding strategy of each side," he said, before pausing to let the team take in the information.

"Damn!" Hunter exclaimed. "This is a lot more complex than I expected. "How are we going to remember it all?"

"Good question," Arjun responded. "Essentially, our strategy is that we should try to avoid falling into each side's habitual, negative responses, regardless of which side we're working with."

"Overall, it looks like the left is dedicated to trying to sway people on the right with logic, information, and education," Sam observed. "That seems reasonable. Why wouldn't we want to do that?"

"Oh," Terri blurted. "I see where Arjun's going with this. Our mission is to listen. Our job isn't to respond to what each side says about the other side, or what they want from the President. Our job is just to bring back the information to her."

"Exactly!" Arjun replied. "What will happen if, instead of listening, we try to pound away at the Liberty Convoy with science and accurate information?"

Terri snorted a sarcastic laugh.

"They'll do exactly what I'd do. They'll stop listening and close their minds down. They'll just dismiss it as being part of the giant 'woke' conspiracy!"

"Right again," Arjun said. "If you look at this next slide, you'll see that the biggest tool in our strategy to gain trust from both camps, is listening. And more importantly, listening with *empathy*! Does that sound familiar?"

Hunter smiled at Terri.

"That's exactly what Sam taught us back in our night class project," he said.

Arjun looked at Sam. The two colleagues chuckled and smiled back at Hunter and Terri.

"I'm glad you remember," Arjun replied. "But we should do more than that. The arguments from both the left and right are highly emotional. And they elicit strong emotional reactions from the other sides. So, not only should we listen to what each side *says*, it's critical that we show that we understand the *emotions* that each side is experiencing."

"And if we can do that," Sam continued, "Hopefully we'll start building some trust with each side, which will allow us to continue our mission."

Terri raised her hand to get Arjun's attention.

"Before we start, there's something I just don't understand. I see so many people around the world supporting the far right, who are mostly working-class people. The sort of person I thought would tend to lean left and place more importance on government and social services for people with lower incomes. And yet, they're turning to the traditional right wing conservative parties, the bastion of corporations and the wealthy. It seems so paradoxical. Does that make any sense?"

"On the surface, it certainly doesn't," Arjun replied. "But I'll give you an example that explains the paradox: let's look at Hitler and his rise to power. He was extremely clever, and he figured out how to 'flip the script', so to speak, by finding a way to blame hard times, or things that were upsetting the working masses, on specific groups. In Hitler's case, he blamed the far left Communists, Jewish Socialists, and even the rest of the Western world, which was brutally penalizing Germany economically for its part in the First World War. Through his incredibly emotional speeches, he managed to convince Germany's working poor that the socialist policies designed to help them, were actually *the cause* of their misery, aided and abetted by the other Western countries. His answer? To make Germany great again, by appealing emotionally to their sense of Nationalism. Does that sound familiar?"

"Shit," Hunter muttered. "That sounds like it came straight from the Donald Trump playbook!"

"Exactly!" Arjun answered.

"So our job," Sam interjected, "is to listen, to try and understand the emotions attached to the far right's grievances, but also to find a way to flip the script back the other way?"

Arjun pointed at Sam, nodding his head and smiling.

"You got it! That's precisely what we need to do."

"Any idea how we're going to be able to do that?" Sam asked.

"Not yet, but I'm open to suggestions. I think the answer will come to us along the way, as long as we continue to follow our original plan: listening to their complaints and being empathic."

Terri put up her hand again.

"Are we allowed to use our own lives as examples? To show them that we're real people, just like them, and that we understand where they're coming from?"

"Now you're getting it," Arjun answered, his face lighting up. "Absolutely! If you remember our first meeting with President Williams, she suggested that Hunter and Terri handle the meetings with the Liberty Convoy, while Sam and I deal with the Unite the Left Camp."

"I see where this is going," Jordan commented, as she nodded her head slowly up and down. "You're the team's logic and information guy, which fits perfectly with the way the left sees things. And Sam's a psychologist—a scientist—so we know that the right probably isn't going to trust her."

"While Terri and I play the ordinary, everyday working man and woman: a bit rebellious, with chips on our shoulders," Hunter continued. "We'll use our own lives as examples so the right can identify with us, and maybe even stop seeing us as outsiders. Somebody they can trust instead."

"Hunter could open up about his experiences with the military in Afghanistan and Iraq," Terri added, "while I could open up about how hard I had to work to transform myself from stripping and turning tricks, to being an entrepreneur."

"While Sam and I can emphasize our academic qualifications and our humble beginnings to the Unite the Left camp," Arjun added.

"Exactly!" Sam exclaimed. "Our job is to listen, build trust, and find out what brought each group to Washington in the first place: what they wanted to say to the President and what they wanted to hear from her in the way of promises before they went home. And hopefully, we can help them feel like they accomplished something. It's not up to us to solve any problems, that's up to the President."

"But remember, we also have a primary goal," Arjun added. "We're here to help the President end the standoff. And to do that, we need to negotiate with both sides. So, while you're listening and identifying with each group, we also need to find some areas where both camps agree. Even if it's only on a couple of issues, finding some agreement could mean the difference between ending the occupation successfully, or failing in our mission."

"So, when do we start?" Terri asked.

Sam looked across the table at Jordan.

"As soon as the President hears back from Anna Dahl, and we have a press strategy in place," Sam replied. "When do you think you can be ready, Jordan?"

"Everybody's impatient to get this process underway," she answered. "With some help from the White House, I'm ready to go tomorrow, as long as you and Arjun can be ready to meet with Unite the Left."

Jordan's phone vibrated on the table in front of her. She picked it up and noticed a text message from the White House.

"Speak of the Devil," she said aloud. "I just got this text message from Nicole.

The President will be meeting with Anna early this evening. I'll let you know the outcome as soon as the meeting is over.

"Looks like we'll know, one way or the other, real soon."

RACHEL YAWNED and rubbed the sleep from her eyes as she sat down at her Camp David desk. The bags under her eyes were telltale signs that her short sleep was restless, and she was far from being rested and refreshed this morning. She reached for her cup of coffee and took a sip, then she stared at the growing mountain of paperwork in front of her. She inhaled a long deep breath, then sighed as she exhaled.

If this is what it's always going to be like for a President, I'm not sure I'm up to this.

A knock at the office door shook Rachel out of her daze.

"Come in!" she called.

Nicole opened the door and entered the office.

"Good morning, Ma'am," she said. "Have you thought about which network, or networks, are going to be authorized to cover the meetings between Ms. Bower's team and the two camps? Both Congress and the press are growing more restless by the day. You need to show the country some progress soon on resolving this standoff."

Rachel took another deep breath and pulled herself together.

"I agree completely, Nicole, and I *have* made a decision," she replied. "But, I've decided to try a new press strategy. One that's more in tune with the times, and just *might* satisfy *both* camps."

Nicole's forehead wrinkled, her eyes narrowed, and her nose scrunched as she paused to process Rachel's puzzling response.

"New strategy?" she asked.

"Yes," Rachel confirmed. "I'd like to try something radically different—live-streaming the meetings to the nation over the internet. Anna Dahl has agreed to the format, and is quite excited about the prospect."

"Of course she's excited, Ma'am!" Nicole blurted. "It will boost the traffic on her podcast and earn her oodles of money. But, the Unite the Left camp is *never* going to go for that. You might as well have authorized Fox News to be the sole broadcaster!"

"Hear me out, Nicole," Rachel continued. "That's why I also contacted Jordan Marsh, the freelancer who's been covering the Unite the Left protest from the very beginning."

"But she doesn't have a podcast, as far as I know, does she?"

"She does now," Rachel answered. "As of late yesterday. I've asked Ms. Dahl to live-stream the proceedings from the Liberty Convoy, and Ms. Marsh to stream the Unite the Left meetings. They've both agreed to only stream the raw proceedings, and to allow the people, and all of the usual news outlets as well, to editorialize about the events as they would any other news event. I believe it's critical for the public to have access to the raw, unadulterated video and audio coverage of the meetings, so they can form their own opinions about the events, free from any network bias."

Momentarily stunned by Rachel's radical decision, Nicole's forehead furrowed again, followed by a brief flash of anger, before she quickly gathered her professional composure.

"I'm afraid that I wholeheartedly disagree with that decision, Ma'am!" Nicole said, her face taught with concern. "You hired me to be the voice of this office, and to control the White House's narrative of events. But, by making this decision, you're not letting me do my job! You're going to lose control of the narrative. It's my job to protect you, Ma'am. And I won't be able to do that if you allow Dahl and Marsh to be the ones who control and distribute this news!"

"That's just the point, Nicole. The American public is growing tired of the spin that we put on everything that comes out of this office, as well as the spin that every different news outlet puts on it."

"Well, if that's your decision, then it doesn't look like you need my services anymore," Nicole said firmly. "Should I start looking for another job?"

"Of course not. I understand your frustration, and I'm sorry you feel that way," Rachel replied. Her voice remained calm and empathic. "But I'm certain there will be plenty of opportunity for you to hold press conferences. The White House will still be expected to hold regular press briefings to comment on the proceedings of the meetings, just like every other media outlet, and every other American citizen who will have access to the video's of the meetings. If anything, I'll need you more than ever."

Nicole paused to think things over. Rachel couldn't be sure, but she thought she detected a momentary look of fear and panic in her assistant's eyes, before Nicole nimbly composed herself.

"Okay," Nicole said reluctantly. "I'm willing to try it your way. But, I'm not going to take any responsibility if this idea of yours goes sideways. Is that clear?"

Rachel nodded her head up and down in agreement.

"That's totally fair," she said. "It's my plan, and I'll take the fall if this whole process doesn't work out."

The room fell silent for a moment as both women heaved sighs of relief and the tension in the room gradually eased.

"So, what do you need me to do, Ma'am?"

"I need you to contact both Anna and Jordan, to find out if there's any equipment or personnel they need, in order to make this happen ASAP—tomorrow morning, if possible!"

Nicole's eyes opened wide, and her eyebrows raised in surprise.

"Tomorrow morning? That's awfully soon."

"You already said it yourself, Nicole," Rachel answered. "We're at day six of this standoff, and the whole country is starting to get impatient with me. They expected me to do something about this mess long before now. So, I'm trusting you to get this ball rolling. Once you've provided whatever Dahl and Marsh need, I'd like you to call a press conference to announce my press strategy, and to let the country know that Sam Bower's team will start meeting with the organizers of each camp, beginning tomorrow morning."

Rachel picked up a piece of paper, then reached across the desk and handed it to Nicole.

"Here's the contact information for Anna and Jordan, and the team's proposed schedule for the meeting times: 10 a.m. to noon each day for the Unite the Left camp and 1 to 3 p.m. each day for the Liberty Convoy meetings. Any questions?"

"No, Ma'am. I guess I'll get right on it and make it happen. Is there anything else?"

"No, just let me know when things are arranged."

Nicole stood up from the desk and nodded silently to Rachel, before exiting the room and closing the door behind her. With a sense of urgency, she rushed out of the Aspen Lodge and away from the building. Once out of sight of the building's security guards, she pulled her phone from her purse, dialled, and waited for her call to connect.

"Matt?" she said. "Listen up! I've got crazy news for you to pass along the chain to your bosses, and I don't think they're going to like it!"

CONSTITUTION AVENUE

CHAPTER 10—Q-SORT

A CLOUDLESS, hazy blue sky and brilliant morning sun, already climbing higher over the nation's Capitol, foreshadowed a hot, humid sixth day of the Washington standoff. Smoke rose from grills and griddles in both camps, along with the distinctive aroma of bacon, fried eggs, and toast, while the bouquet of freshly brewed coffee wafted out over Constitution Avenue. Country Western music from the sound system of the Liberty Convoy's performance stage, along with the aroma of breakfast food, conveyed a distorted impression to casual passersby, that the atmosphere was one of a fair or carnival.

A bright reflection flickered towards the west on Constitution Avenue and gradually became brighter. Between the flashes of light, the outlines of a line of black vehicles could barely be discerned, growing larger by the second. At a distance of about two blocks, the black outlines revealed themselves as a procession of three black Cadillac Escalades, their windows heavily tinted. Within a matter of seconds, the SUVs rolled slowly into the intersection of Constitution and Seventeenth Street, the no man's land between the Liberty Convoy and Unite the Left camps. Secret Service agents emerged from the lead and rear vehicles. Moments later, Sam and Arjun emerged from the second Escalade, where they found Senator Sandra Delgado waiting to greet them.

The carnival atmosphere evaporated quickly, as a large squad of DCMP officers, decked out in full riot gear, took up security positions around the intersection. A mob of reporters and photographers pressed forward to get sound bites or photos of the Presidential representatives, whose attire was far from what would befit an official Presidential delegation. Sam wore a pair of beige capris and a simple, loose fitting, white blouse, while Arjun sported a pair of navy cargo pants and a loose fitting, open neck polo shirt.

"Good morning, Ms. Bower," Senator Delgado shouted over the crowd noise, as Sam and Arjun emerged from the crowd. The Senator reached out to shake Sam's hand. "Welcome to our Unite the Left encampment. It's a pleasure to finally meet both of you."

"Thank you, Senator," Sam shouted in return. "We're pleased to finally meet you too. And please, call me Sam."

Sandra then extended her hand to greet Arjun.

"I'm Arjun. A pleasure to meet you, Senator."

"My pleasure as well," Delgado replied. "Call me Sandra. Would you like to follow me? I'll introduce you to the rest of the organizing team."

Sam and Arjun followed Sandra through a security entrance, with two Secret Service agents in tow. The group flashed their badges at two of the camp's volunteer security personnel. Once cleared, the team followed their host towards the mess tent, where a group of small desks had been arranged in a neat circle towards the rear of the tent. The remaining Unite the Left organizers, already seated and awaiting their guests, rose to their feet as Sandra led Sam and Arjun to two empty desks, each of which was identified only by a simple, tiny Stars and Stripes flag. Near the desks, two tripods with iPads and lighting mounted on top, were being operated by Jordan Marsh, along with another female camera operator. Sandra turned to the rest of her colleagues.

"I'd like to introduce Ms. Bower and Mr. Patel, representing President Williams."

"Thank you, Sandra," Sam replied. "Please call us Sam and Arjun. We'd like to extend greetings on behalf of President Williams. Please, be seated."

Sam paused and remained standing while Arjun and the organizers took their seats.

"As part of my Indigenous heritage," she said, "I'd like to point out the circular arrangement of our desks in this tent. In our culture, we gather in a circle to show that we are all equal, and no person is greater than any other. Before we begin, I'd also like to invite each of you to join in a sacred Smudging Ceremony, in order to cleanse our meeting space, and to allow us to pray silently and focus on our intentions for what we hope to accomplish here."

Sam picked up a shallow bowl containing sprigs of sage from the desk in front of her. She lit them carefully before walking around the circle, stopping before each organizer to wave the fragrant, sacred smoke over their torsos and heads. When she was finished, she remained standing in front of her desk and repeated the ritual on herself. She snuffed the glowing sage and set the bowl down on the desk.

"We are all gathered together on the ancestral lands of the Nacotchtank and the Piscataway People, who have lived on this land for more generations than can be counted. We pay our respects to their elders, past and present. Please take a moment to consider the many legacies of violence, displacement, migration, and settlement that bring us all together to this place today."

With the opening proceedings behind them, Sam glanced towards Arjun and gave him a nod as she took her seat. He cleared his throat and rubbed his chin in an effort to quell his anxiety.

"Thank you for agreeing to meet with us today," he began. "Sam and I would like you all to think of us as mere messengers, who are here today to listen, and to take your messages back to the President."

"We're also here to take any questions you have for the President," Sam continued. "We're *not* here to grill you or question your motives for being here. The only questions we have for you are what brought you here to Washington, and what do you want to tell President Williams? Anybody care to start?"

Cecilia Robinson raised her hand.

"I might as well start by addressing the big elephant in the room," she said. "What makes you and your team qualified to act for the President? Why you, of all people?"

Sam smiled warmly at Cecilia, then turned her attention back to the rest of the group.

"I'm glad you asked," she replied. "Because that's exactly the same question I asked the President when she first called me, so I'll try to keep it short. First, as you might have heard, it was my job a few years ago to work with Arjun and seven other university students on a challenging team project on Indigenous Reconciliation. The group was extremely polarized, and we had to learn to overcome that polarization in order to complete the project in a short period of time. We all learned a great deal from that experience, and the members of my team have all applied that learning to our subsequent academic and business pursuits.

Sam reached for a glass of water on her desk, pausing to take a swallow and to sort out her thoughts.

"As for why a group of Canadians has any business getting involved in this standoff," Sam continued. "You've got two very polarized groups in this stalemate, just like we had in our team's past Reconciliation project. We have no allegiances to your group, or to the Liberty Convoy. That's why I think we're the perfect choice for the job, and that's why I said yes to the President's request."

She turned to Arjun.

"I'll let Arjun speak for his own qualifications," she said. "Do you have anything to add?"

"Thanks, Sam," he answered. "I'd just like to add that, as a student of political science, I'm fascinated by the extreme political polarization that exists in your country, because that phenomenon is starting to spread around the globe, and it's causing increasing instability in democracies around the world. But, enough about us. What other questions do *you* have for us? And what brought you all to Washington?"

"I'll go next," Sandra Delgado called out. "I came because I'm proud that the previous Democratic Presidency led to a lot of progress in legislation that improved a wide range of human rights in this country. And I think all of us around this circle are very afraid of the late President Spencer's promises to peel back those rights, even if it meant appealing to the Supreme Court. I came to ask our new President to respect those rights that we worked so hard to improve."

"Thanks, Senator," Sam said. "Would anybody like to expand on that for the President? What rights are we talking about?"

"Yes, I am Idris Mohammed. Coming from my country in Africa, where being gay is illegal and dangerous, I thought I would be safe here in America. Now I see and hear more hatred of gay people every day. I fear for the safety of me and my friends if this becomes worse. Unless you are gay, and come from my country, your team and the President cannot truly understand what we endured. The hate language must be stopped. We only want the same rights as everybody else in America."

A man with brown skin, sitting beside Idris, raised his hand.

"My name is Nasir. The hate language is not just directed at the LGBTQ2S+ people. Political refugees like me, who seek asylum in America, should not be treated like criminals. The former President, before Spencer, understood that. He treated us with equality and respect."

"As a son of immigrants myself," Arjun replied, "I understand why that's so important to both of you. Thank you, anybody else?"

"I have another question," Cecilia called out. "I want to know where President Williams stands on voting rights for the disadvantaged, especially Blacks and Hispanics. Is she going to let the states move forward with more racist election laws? And what about the rights of disadvantaged people to be kept safe if, or when, another pandemic comes around? Will she support Public Health measures, even if they do interfere with some of peoples' usual freedoms?"

A young blonde woman in her early twenties, who had been sitting quietly beside Sandra Delgado until now, rose to her feet.

"I'm Kym Babineau," she stated. "What about gun laws? Under the Democrats, at least we were able to see some restrictions on certain types of weapons pass through Congress. I've lived through two mass shootings, one myself and the other when my sister was involved, and I don't ever want to experience that again! So, where does President Williams stand on gun control?"

"I'm so sorry for what you've had to go through," Sam answered. "And thank you for your comments. They are exactly what the President wants to hear! Anybody else have other concerns?"

As Kym took her seat again, the older gentleman beside her raised his hand.

"I'm Dudley," he said. "Under a Democratic President, I think America was finally starting to understand the severity of the current climate emergency, and the need for drastic action. But, when President Spencer took office, he made it clear that he questioned climate science. His policies would have been a disaster for this country, and for the rest of the planet. But, we've yet to hear anything from President Williams on this urgent issue. Is she at all concerned? What does she propose to do?"

A middle-aged man beside Arjun raised his hand and caught Sam's attention. She nodded for him to proceed.

"I'm Stephen. I agree with Idris and Nasir," he said. "I'm Jewish, and I'm all for freedom of the press and freedom of religion. But, we can't give people a blank cheque to say hateful, threatening things about other peoples' race, religion, or sexual orientation, or to plaster places of worship with swastikas, in the name of freedom of speech. There's got to be some reasonable limits set on those Constitutional rights."

"I hear all of you," Arjun answered. "And what I'm starting to hear is that most of you are concerned about Constitutional rights and freedoms. Is that a fair assessment?"

He and Sam looked around the room and saw everybody's head nodding up and down in agreement.

"You just hit the nail on the head, young man." Cecilia blurted. "In some cases, like the failure to pass the Equal Rights Amendment, or the need to add womens' right to choose, we need to add more rights to the Constitution. But in other cases, we've seen too many people making their own interpretations of existing freedoms, like speech and religion, to serve their own interests. The Republicans are abusing the Supreme Court's powers by appealing some of that court's previous decisions, and that shouldn't be allowed!"

"Thanks for summarizing, Cecilia," Sam replied. "You've all given us quite a list of things that you'd like to raise with the President. Any more issues you'd like to raise before we adjourn for the day?"

A young Asian woman, seated beside Stephen, raised her hand. Sam recognized her immediately as the popular young actress, Danielle Chen. She nodded for the young woman to proceed.

"Yes, there's another big one that nobody's mentioned yet: the so-called 'entitlements' that President Spencer promised to cut back drastically."

The diminutive young woman rose to her feet to continue her address to Sam and Arjun.

"The Constitution needs to entrench people's rights to have access to medical care, education, and social assistance. And most importantly, the right to earn a living wage. Does the President plan to cut back the vital social programs that the Democrats improved or proposed? And does she see how important it is for us to stand up for those rights?"

"I agree," Nasir answered. "Very few immigrants are as fortunate as Ms. Chen or her father, who have been lucky enough to achieve the American dream. Most of us live in poverty, making minimum wage or less. And many of us need to work multiple jobs, just to survive in our new country!"

"Thanks Danielle and Nasir," Sam answered. "Thank you for raising that issue, and for letting the President know that you think these programs should be fundamental Constitutional rights."

Sam took a moment to look at each member of the Unite the Left team, making eye contact and nodding her appreciation to each one of them.

"You've given us a long wish list to pass along to the President. Thank you for your frank, honest answers. I imagine that the Liberty

Convoy will also be passing along their wish list this afternoon. Once the President has had a chance to review both lists, we'll be back to meet with both camps again. Shall we call it a day?"

LATER THAT day, at the intersection of Constitution Avenue and Seventeenth Street, the faint rumble of a Harley Davidson motorcycle could be heard, drifting in gradually from the west. A small black smudge and a single headlight could be seen, growing quickly in size while the rumble of the machine escalated rapidly. In less than a minute, the sleek bike, accompanied by two black Escalades, rumbled into the intersection and stopped near the entrance to the Liberty Convoy's camp.

Two figures climbed off the Harley and removed their helmets. Hunter, attired in new blue jeans, a lime green t-shirt, and a black leather vest, removed his helmet and wiped away the sweat that had built up on his forehead on this very sunny, hot afternoon. He quickly removed his leather vest and hung it, along with his helmet, on the bike. His passenger, Terri, was casually dressed in khaki capris, brown sandals, and a loose-fitting yellow blouse. She removed her helmet, hung it on the bike, and shook out her shoulder-length blonde hair.

It took only seconds for the hungry media mob to press forward, hoping for their snapshots and soundbites, but they were thwarted by the handful of Secret Service agents who had jumped from the two Escalades and quickly surrounded the two bikers. The tight formation of Hunter, Terri, and the Secret Service agents made their way slowly towards the Liberty Camp entrance, where they were greeted by Jessica Murray. She flashed a warm smile at her two guests.

"Boozhoo! Welcome to our camp," she said. "I'm Jessica Murray, here to greet you on behalf of Bryson and the rest of the team."

"Miigwech," Hunter replied.

"It's a pleasure for us to finally meet you," Terri added.

"Same here," Jessica continued. "If you'd like to follow me, I'll take you to meet the others."

Jessica led the group through the camp's entrance gate, where they were swallowed up by a crowd of the convoy's security volunteers, and whisked away in the direction of the camp's huge mess tent and events stage.

THE SMUDGING Ceremony complete, followed by a Land Acknowledgment, Hunter and Jessica took their places behind two remaining desks within the circular arrangement on Anna Dahl's podcast set. Two camera operators, one behind the stage and the other in front, moved around the desks while Anna's producer supervised and directed them.

"The President would like to thank you for meeting with us today," Terri began. "Our only goal for today is to listen to questions you have for President Williams. We're not here to grill or interrogate you. So, just think of us as messengers. We only have two questions for you: what brought you here to Washington, and what do you want to tell the President now that you're here? Anybody care to start?"

"Yeah, I do!" Bryson MacDonald bellowed. "Pardon my French, but what the fuck does that bitch think she's doin', sendin' a petty criminal an' a druggie stripper from Canada, to listen to our demands? Is she so yeller' she won' even talk with us, face to face?"

"I understand where you're coming from, Mr. MacDonald," Hunter replied. He glanced at Terri and flashed her a quick smile.

"I thought exactly the same thing about being on a team with Terri when we first met!"

"And he pissed me off so much," Terri answered, "that we almost came to blows. I had no idea I was picking a fight with a guy who'd served in Afghanistan and Northern Iraq!"

Norm Barfield emitted a grunt and sat up straight in his seat.

"No shit?" he bellowed. "Ain't nobody told us you was a genooine hero. Thanks fer yer service, man."

Terri caught a quick glimpse of Anna, whose upper lip curled and her eyes narrowed in anger at Terri's public debunking of the podcaster's prior misinformation about Hunter.

"Yup," Terri continued. "He had every right to pop me in the face. He probably would have too, if it hadn't been for Sam Bower getting in between us. She has a gift for listening, understanding, and bringing people together, even when they have views that are very far apart, just like me and Hunter. We learned to respect her for that, and she taught us to respect each other. I guess that's why the President thought her skills would be so helpful here in Washington."

"Well, far as I'm concerned," Bryson roared, "y'all are wastin' yer time. We ain't goin' nowhere till Williams comes down off 'er high horse an' meets us here on the streets—in person!"

"Ditto that," Norm Barfield added, from the desk next to Bryson. "We're fuckin' tired o'havin' govermint take away our freedoms. Taxin'us to death an givin' folks a free ride with them there 'titlements, usin' our hard earned dollars!"

"I hear what you're saying, guys," Terri replied. "I grew up poor as a church mouse, and now I run a business, just like many of you. I work hard for my money, and I don't like paying taxes any more than you do. In fact, we pay much higher taxes back in Canada than you do down here!"

"Hell, ya gotta be kiddin'!" Sean Pritchard shouted. "Why d'ya put up with that? No fuckin' wonder you guys sent that convoy to Ottawa to protest!"

Hunter looked around the circle at some of the rest of the organizers who hadn't spoken yet.

"So, it seems pretty clear that some of you want a lot less government," Hunter summarized. "Anybody else have any messages or questions for President Williams?"

"Yeah, I do," Anna Dahl said. "Most of us are here cuz we're concerned over loss of our freedoms under the Democrats. Our freedom to move around freely, to gather without havin' to wear masks during COVID. Our freedom of speech and freedom of the press. And havin' to worry that y'all are gonna charge us with hate crimes for callin' a spade a spade."

"Not to mention the most valuable freedom of all," Pastor Kessler added. "Our freedom to gather together, an' our freedom to worship Almighty God wherever, an' however, we want, live an' in person, without having to cover our faces with masks. We don't need no public health laws. We put all of our trust and faith in God to protect us. An' we most certainly need to uphold the Constitution to end the slaughter of unborn babies! Where does our new President stand on abortion, anyway?"

"I sympathize with your concerns, Pastor," Hunter replied. "It was hard on the people in my Indigenous community back home during COVID. We missed gathering together in our sacred places and ceremonies, especially at our pow wows, during that time."

"I agree, Hunter," Jessica added. "But, as an Indigenous person, I also have other questions for the President. The Democrats barely scratched the surface of recognizing our natural Indigenous rights. Is she going to continue that path towards reconciliation in America, or is she going to go backwards?"

John Gregg, the tall, slender, quiet man from Texas sitting beside Jessica, put up his hand to speak.

"And what I wanna know is this: is Williams gonna make America great again, like President Spencer promised us? What's she gonna do to save small town USA? What's she gonna do to save our local farms an' businesses from big corporate farms an' big box stores? Is she gonna feed our families when we can't afford to stay in business anymore, an' all the family farms are gone?"

"Yeah," Sean interjected. "An' is she gonna protect our Constitutional right to carry arms to protect our livestock, an' to hunt food to put on our tables?"

"An' don't forget," Norm added. "To protect us an' our families an' schools from illegal immigrants, drug gangs, criminals an' the crazies out there. They're the ones that kills people. It ain't the guns!"

"I hear you, gentlemen," Terri answered. "I know what it was like to grow up poor, on a farm that was failing. I know what it was like to get on the school bus each morning, with nothing in my stomach. That's how I ended up running away from home, and how I ended up on the streets: stripping, doing drugs, and stealing so I could get my next hit. And believe me, I saw my share of guns on the street."

"Just tell the President," Martin Lee interjected, "We just want to be free from government. Free to follow the American dream, man. To own property and build wealth, without worrying about being taxed to death just because we're good business men or women."

"Wow," Hunter exclaimed. "You guys definitely gave us a lot of information to take back to the President. Are there any other questions, or things you want to tell her, before we leave you for today?"

"Yeah," Anna said. "Just tell her we're here to defend our Constitution and our freedoms. And we don't plan to leave until she promises to do the same."

"You can be sure we'll do just that," Terri responded. "Thanks for stating that message so clearly, Anna. I'd like to ask the group one more question, if I may. Is it just Anna? Or do all of you have concerns that the Constitution just isn't working well for you right now?"

The Liberty Convoy organizers looked around the table, then started nodding to each other.

"Damn right, woman," Bryson blared. "I couldn'a said it better ma'self!"

"If that's the case," Hunter acknowledged, "I think we can probably call it a day. The Unite the Left camp met with Sam and Arjun this morning, and I'm sure they had their own messages for President Williams to consider. Thanks for being so open and upfront with us. We look forward to meeting with you again very soon."

THE CONFERENCE room in the Laurel Lodge was becoming more like home for Sam and the team as they sat around their circular table with President Williams and Nicole, debriefing the two women on the day's meetings with the two protest camps.

"So, I think we're agreed that there weren't any real surprises in the political issues each team raised, right?" Arjun said.

"None at all," Rachel answered. "But I'm so impressed with the way each of you handled yourselves today. You did well to show understanding and empathy towards both groups. It would have been easy to fall into the trap of judging some of those comments from both sides. Especially you, Terri. The way you stood up for Hunter and discredited Anna Dahl at the same time, was nothing short of genius!"

"Thanks, Ma'am," Terri replied. "I surprised myself with that story. But I think we were *all* amazingly solid for our first day on the job."

"I agree," Sam replied. "The biggest realization for me, and I guess this shouldn't have come as a shock, is how both sides are so dedicated to defending the Constitution. And yet, their ways of interpreting Constitutional rights and freedoms is so totally opposite."

"True," Hunter commented. "An even bigger surprise for me was that both groups actually suggested that the Constitution isn't working very well for either side!"

"I didn't expect that either," Terri added. "We probably wouldn't have seen that common view if we'd had both sides in the same room at the same time. I think Rachel was right to split us into two teams, at least for now."

"Just a lucky hunch," Rachel admitted. "Nevertheless, it's definitely something we can build on. Do any of you have any ideas for how you could do that?"

The room went silent while everybody around the table processed Rachel's question. Finally, Sam broke the silence.

"My first instinct was to give each side a questionnaire, asking each individual organizer to rate the importance of each of the issues raised in the two meetings, using a traditional number scale—let's say from zero to ten."

"But we already know which issues are most important to each group, and we pretty much know how they'd rate each issue's importance," Hunter answered.

"That's right," Sam replied. "But there may be a way around that. There's a different type of questionnaire that isn't used a lot—it's called a Q-Sort, or a rank order questionnaire. We could give them a list of ten to fifteen major rights and freedoms, and get them to *rank order* the issues from most to least important."

"I don't quite follow," Rachel queried.

"I'll give you an example," Sam responded. "We know that most of the Liberty Convoy people would probably rank 'the right to bear arms' near the top in their rankings, while the Unite the Left would rank that freedom at the bottom of their preferences. Similarly, the rankings would be completely opposite for 'a woman's right to choose abortion'. But with a Q-Sort, people can't use the same number rating twice. They can't rate half the items at zero, and the other half at ten. We force them to rate every freedom on the list using the same ranking scale from 0 to 10, but only using each number once. So, when they're finished, there must be some less controversial items that will fall somewhere in the middle of the rankings for both groups. That's where we're most likely to find some areas of agreement between the two camps."

Rachel's face lit up as the significance of the concept sunk in.

"Ahhh, I like it!"

Terri's face still looked confused, and she turned her attention to Rachel.

"I like Sam's concept, Ma'am. But, I'm just a bit confused about how we'll use the information we get from the questionnaire, when we meet with the groups next time."

"That's where politics comes into play, Terri," Rachel answered. "Sam and Arjun are right. I already know the political minefields that are most dangerous for me to wade into. But this type of information would be very useful for me in shaping my legislative agenda. I need to start by promoting legislation that's less controversial: bills that I'm most likely to get bipartisan agreement on from both sides of the floor."

Arjun nodded in agreement and looked in Sam's direction.

"Exactly. But how long will it take for you to create this—what did you call it?"

"Q-Sort," Sam confirmed, "Also called a rank order survey. Normally, it can take months or years to build questionnaires properly. But, since our goal is really just to re-shape the information the two camps already gave us, I think I could throw something together in a couple of hours."

"Could you have something ready to give both sides as early as tomorrow?" Rachel asked.

"I think so," Sam answered. "I'd just need your help in setting it all up and getting the questionnaires printed."

Rachel turned to Nicole, who was busy typing notes on her laptop.

"You're a whiz at this sort of thing. Any problem with getting this done tonight?"

Rachel thought she saw a brief, ever so subtle, rolling of Nicole's eyes, but she couldn't be sure.

"I guess so," the assistant answered hesitantly. "As long as Sam knows what she wants."

"Great," Hunter exuded, turning his attention to Rachel. "Looks like we have a strategy. Do we have anything else we need to discuss?"

"I don't think so. I'd just like to thank all of you again for how you handled yourselves today. If you keep this up, you may just prove a lot of your critics wrong. Have a good evening, everybody."

Arjun, Hunter, Terri, and Rachel rose from the table and made their way out of the conference room, while Sam and Nicole remained behind in their seats.

Nicole reached for her phone and turned to Sam.

"Can you give me a few minutes, Sam? I just need to make a couple of calls."

"No problem," Sam answered. "I'll start working on the items for the Q-Sort."

Nicole rose from her seat and walked quickly from the room, then she exited the lodge and walked until she was well clear of the building. She hit the dial button on her phone and waited.

"It's me again, Matt … Just finished the meeting between Williams and Bower's team … Not good for us … Seems as though things went way too smoothly … We may have underestimated their abilities … There's not much more I *can* do without being too obvious … What about you? What's up with that plan of yours? … Well, you need to speed things up! You know they're expecting us to keep those two camps at each other's throats … I don't care how, just get it done!"

CHAPTER 11—THE SHADOW

DAY SEVEN at Camp David dawned hot, hazy, and humid for yet another day. Already bathed in sticky humidity, and with the heat of the early morning sunshine searing her back, Sam strolled along a pedestrian pathway in Camp David. She felt sweat running down her forehead towards her eye, so she lifted her ball cap and wiped her forehead with her other hand.

The fragrance of the nearby forest and the sounds of crows, cardinals, robins, finches, and woodpeckers filled the air. Sam's mind was relaxed and meandering, until she gradually settled into thinking about this morning's meeting with the Unite the Left protesters, at which point she became lost in her thoughts.

"Sam! Wait up!"

The sudden sound of Hunter's voice, coming from about ten yards behind her, startled her out of her reverie. Her body froze involuntarily for an instant while she let out a loud squawk.

"Dammit, Hunter! You scared the shit out of me!"

"I'm sorry," he said. "You looked like you were off in your own little world. Have you got a minute?"

Sam stole a quick glance at her watch.

"Ummh, yeah," she answered. "But I need to meet Arjun at the chopper pad in fifteen minutes. Rachel's flying us to the meeting by chopper today. Are you and Terri flying too?"

"Nah, we don't have to rush like you guys. We're going to take my bike again. Terri quite enjoyed the ride yesterday!"

They resumed walking together, and Hunter slipped his hand into Sam's. The warmth of his hand felt good in hers, and the close presence of her good friend felt reassuring. Apart from her Aunt Rose, he was the one person who best understood the journey she'd been on since she found out that her biological father was Indigenous, and since her dad passed away so unexpectedly.

"I just wanted to wish you guys good luck with the Q-Sort at the Unite the Left camp today," he said. "But I know you're both gonna kick ass!"

"Thanks, same to you and Terri."

Hunter stopped talking for a moment, looking away, swallowing, and generally appearing somewhat awkward and anxious.

"We've hardly had any time to talk about us, since we arrived here. It's been such a whirlwind."

"I know," Sam answered. "Who knew the team would be together again so soon, eh? And here, with the President at Camp David. I still think I'm stuck in a dream."

"Same here," Hunter said. "We've come a long way since our team building class."

"Yeah, but it's good to see you all again," Sam replied. "I miss everybody: Aunt Rose, you, and the team. It's hard being across the country from everybody."

Hunter squeezed Sam's hand lovingly.

"I've missed you too," he said. "I've been thinking. After I graduate from law school, maybe I could come to Saskatchewan to article and write the Bar Exam. There's got to be lots of opportunities to get more experience with Indigenous constitutional issues out there. I really want to be closer to you, and I don't expect you to uproot yourself to be with me. What do you think?"

Sam went silent, taken aback by Hunter's unexpected proposition that came directly out of left field. Her eyes instinctively looked away from his, not able to make contact while she processed the sudden information.

"Ummh, wow!" Sam blurted. "I really enjoy the time we spend together too, but you know I'm still dealing with my abandonment issues, and still figuring out who I am. I just don't know if I'm ready to take things to the next level yet. Can we wait a bit, maybe till you graduate? Then see what we both feel?"

Hunter stopped walking and turned to face Sam, then he held both of her hands in his. Sam tried to look away, but she couldn't avoid his penetrating gaze.

"You know I'm falling for you, and I don't have any intention of leaving you high and dry, right?" he said softly.

Sam swallowed and nodded her head up and down slowly, but she couldn't find any words. Hunter leaned in towards her and planted a gentle kiss on her lips. It caught her completely off guard. Something deep down in her mind was afraid and told her to run, but her racing heart and the fluttering sensation in her lower belly said otherwise. She gazed into his eyes, put her arms around his neck, locked her lips onto his, and her body pressed against his as they settled into a long, intense, passionate kiss. Finally, her lips left his and she released her arms from around his neck. Her face flushed, embarrassed that her body had betrayed the part of her mind that wanted her to run. The part of her psyche that was trying to protect her from potential hurt. Suddenly, yet another part of her mind remembered the time and told her to glance at her watch.

"Oh, shit! I gotta run," she blurted. "We'll talk later, okay?"

She planted another quick kiss on Hunter's cheek, turned, and ran towards the chopper pad.

Hunter stood alone on the pathway, more than a little bewildered by the confusing mixed messages that Sam had just sent his way.

"FUCK THIS bull shit!" Bryson bellowed. "How's this here list 'sposed to get that bitch to listen to what we came here to tell 'er! I ain't gonna put down *any* numbers fer some'a these statements!"

Hunter and Terri exchanged quick glances at each other, and Hunter nodded for her to field the question.

"I take it that you disagree pretty strongly with some of them. Is that right?" she asked.

"Damn rights!" Bryson shouted.

"I get it," Terri answered. "So if you don't agree with a statement, just rate it really low. Give it a rating of fourteen or fifteen. But, if you leave items blank, the President won't know *how much* you disagree."

"Terri's right, Bryson," Jessica interjected. "Everybody in this tent isn't going to think the same as you. This is a chance for each of us to have our say to the President! If you don't fill out your ballot, you don't have a right to complain!"

Bryson's pudgy face grew redder by the second as he glared at the young Indigenous woman.

"Is there anybody in this tent who *doesn't* think it's important to keep our families safe, healthy, and protected?" Jessica asked. "Anybody who *doesn't* value freedom of speech? Or freedom of conscience and religion? Or the right of every American to vote in elections?

She surveyed the remaining Liberty Convoy organizers, who looked around at each other, shaking their heads.

"Ok," Jessica continued. "Then put a number beside each statement an' tell the President *how much* you like or dislike each one. You gotta be able to figure out that you agree or disagree with some of the statements more or less than others. It ain't rocket science!"

"I still think it's a bunch of bull crap!" Bryson grumbled.

"Me too," Norm echoed.

"For God's sake," Martin Lee shouted, as he glared at Bryson and Norm and shook his head. "Would you guys quit yer bitchin' and just fill out the damned questionnaire so we can get outta here! I have other things I'd rather be doin' than sittin' here listenin' to you!"

Bryson flipped the bird in Martin's direction, then he finally picked up his pencil and turned his attention to the page in front of him, still mumbling obscenities under his breath.

"We realize it takes some thought and some time to do this exercise," Hunter said. "We appreciate your input, and we're willing to take our time to wait until all of you are finished. Everybody's opinion matters."

He looked across the circle of desks at Jessica and gave her a silent nod to thank her for her help. She returned his nod, along with a smile, then turned her attention back to her questionnaire.

"AIN'T THIS just tellin' President Williams what we already told y'all the other day?" Cecilia asked.

Arjun glanced at Sam and gave her a knowing look.

It's your questionnaire. You do the explaining.

Sam smiled back and was just opening her mouth to speak when Dudley's voice interrupted.

"No, Cecilia. I see where Sam's going with this questionnaire. It *forces* all of us, on both sides of this standoff, to express an opinion on *all* of the issues. It's become a bad habit for each and every one of us to outright reject the issues that are important to the other side. This way, it at least makes us think about each issue. Am I correct, Sam?"

"Spot on!" Sam answered. "If the other side is arguing apples and you're arguing oranges, nobody's going to get anywhere until we can all agree to at least consider that they're both fruit."

"Oh, now I get it," Danielle sighed. "The President's looking to start her agenda with the issues that aren't so divisive."

"Bingo!" Arjun exclaimed. "That's exactly right. Does that answer your question, Cecilia?"

Cecilia nodded her understanding.

"It will likely take longer than you think to finish the questionnaire," Sam added. "When you think you've got them all ranked, you may realize that you forgot to consider one of them. Or, when you look at your final list, you may want to change your ratings. That's okay, take all the time you need until you're satisfied with your rankings."

"What happens next. I mean, after we hand these in to you," Kym asked.

"Good question," Sam answered. "I'll be compiling the data after the Liberty Convoy has finished theirs. Then I'll be running it by President Williams. Based on how everybody ranked the issues, she'll give us the go ahead to start asking both camps to give us more details on how they'd like the President to address the issues where there's some agreement."

"And from there," Arjun interjected, "we can hopefully bring the two groups together to negotiate a legislative agenda that both sides can agree upon, so that we can hopefully end this standoff."

"Seems like an impossible task, if y'all ask me!" Cecilia said. "This is already day number seven, an' we're no further ahead than we were when all'a this started."

"Yes, the prospects of finding some areas of agreement do seem pretty bleak," Senator Delgado replied. She looked around the table at the glum faces of the remaining Unite the Left organizers. "But we've got to start somewhere, and this is as good a place as any!"

"COME IN!" Rachel called. The door of her Aspen Lodge office opened and Sam poked her head around the partially-opened door.

"I hope this isn't too late," Sam said apologetically.

"Of course not," Rachel answered. "By all means, come in. You've got the data tallied already?"

"I do. Sorry it took so long."

Sam opened the door, approached the desk, and handed a copy of the results to Rachel.

"I'm surprised you did it so fast. I'm sure I'll have lots of questions after I've read this through, but can you give me a quick summary right now?"

"Sure," Sam answered. She walked around to the side of the desk and pointed at the first page of the results.

"This is the list of items that I showed you yesterday, roughly ordered with far right issues at the top, and far left issues at the bottom," she said. Then she pointed to two columns of numbers beside the lists.

"These two columns show how each camp rated the different issues."

The room fell silent while Rachel reviewed and compared the two lists of numbers.

"So, it looks a lot like what we expected, right? Each side rating the others' biggest issues in the opposite direction?"

"Absolutely," Sam said. "But take a closer look at the two lists on the next page. The first clearly shows what we already know: the issues that are most contentious to both sides. But look at the second list."

"Aha!" Rachel blurted. "Just what we were hoping for!"

"That's right," Sam replied. "A list of four or five issues where there may be some common ground!"

Rachel smiled, then she removed her glasses and rubbed her tired eyes.

"Great work, Sam!"

"Is tomorrow too soon to present the results to the two camps?"

"You're kidding, right?" Rachel said, smiling. "Of course not!"

Relieved that Rachel was pleased with her work, Sam smiled and felt her accumulated muscle tension begin to relax and drain slowly from her exhausted body.

Rachel reached for her phone and dialled.

"Nicole, Rachel here. Could you inform both camps that Sam and her team will be meeting with them both tomorrow? ... Yes, at their regular times ... Thanks."

She looked up at Sam.

"It's arranged! Now we'd better get a good night's sleep, because our real work starts tomorrow!"

DAY EIGHT of the standoff dawned overcast and cooler, a welcome change from the preceding hot, humid days and the torrential rains that followed. The fragrant scent of sage wafted into the air inside the Unite the Left dining tent, as Sam completed her methodical, patient stroll around the organizers' circle of small tables. The smudging ritual complete, she took her own seat at the table, carefully setting her ceremonial shell and feather in front of her. As usual, Jordan Marsh was busy in the background, directing her video camera operators.

"Good morning, everybody," Sam began. "President Williams wishes to pass along her thanks for the information that you all provided in your questionnaires. She wants to reassure you that it's given her lots of food for thought."

Stephen exhaled a huff of frustration.

"Food for thought? How, may I ask, is that going to help send that so-called Liberty Convoy home? How does it address all of their conspiracy theories and messages of hate?"

"Fair point," Arjun answered. "Can I ask you to hold that question for a while, until Sam goes over the questionnaire results? It may help to answer that question for you."

Arjun glanced at his team leader.

"Sam, I'll turn things over to you now."

"Thanks Arjun, and thanks for your question, Stephen. Just to jog everybody's memory, here's the list of the fifteen rights or freedoms from yesterday's questionnaire."

She gestured to a screen behind her while Arjun turned on a projector, displaying an introductory title slide. With a click of the remote, Sam's first information slide appeared, revealing two lists: the average rankings of the fifteen items by both the Unite the Left and Liberty Convoy groups.

"Here's how your group and the other side ranked those fifteen rights and freedoms. Any comments? What do you see?"

Cecilia shook her head slowly, clearly frustrated by the results.

"I see what I'd expect to see," she commented. "Both sides are far apart on what they see as the most important issues: equal rights, womens' reproductive rights, the right to bear arms, and a couple of others. That ain't tellin' me anythin' I didn't already know."

"That's exactly right," Sam replied. "But let's take a closer look at the rankings in the middle of both lists. Anybody see anything interesting there?"

Kym's arm shot into the air and she pointed excitedly at the slide.

"It looks like there's a few rights and freedoms that are somewhat important to both sides. The right to keep families safe, healthy, and protected seems important to both. The same goes for freedom of speech, freedom of conscience and religion, immigration, and the right to participate in government."

"Good eye, Kym," Sam exclaimed. "That's right. But interestingly, those rights and freedoms are also contentious issues for both sides these days. Anybody care to explain that paradox?"

Sandra Delgado raised her hand.

"Yes, my experience in Colorado is that both sides simply have very different ideas about how to define those rights, and very different views about how they affect policy and legislation. Take immigration, for example. Both sides are miles apart in their views on that subject."

"Right again," Sam said, nodding her head up and down. "Both sides are interpreting those rights and freedoms through the lenses of their very polarized political beliefs. They've become so focused on how to save individual trees, that they've forgotten that they're both trying to save the same forest. Both sides completely believe that their way of saving those individual trees will save the forest."

"I appreciate your environmental metaphor, Sam," Dudley Morris chimed. "But I'm still having difficulty seeing how it applies to the current standoff. What do you think, Arjun?"

"From where I stand," Arjun replied, "I see the forest as your U.S. Constitution, and the individual trees as how each side interprets the Constitution when it comes to individual political issues. Each side finds a different way to interpret the Constitution to support their political views."

Arjun noticed Danielle Chen's arm waving at him from across the circle, and he nodded to acknowledge her.

"It seems to me that if the rights and freedoms in the Constitution can be interpreted so differently, then the Constitution itself is the big problem. It's too general and vague. Our forefathers did a shitty job, and now we're paying the price!"

Arjun and Sam looked at each other, smiled and chuckled briefly.

"A rather harsh way to put it," Arjun answered. "And essentially correct, Danielle. But if we look back at history, the original colonies were far apart on many of the same issues that we still have today. So, in order to come up with something that everybody could agree upon, they basically watered down the Constitution with a load of compromises."

"So, using Danielle's analogy, our current Constitution's like a pig barn full of shit: it's full of potential, but it stinks as it stands now!" Stephen interjected.

The entire group burst into laughter. Sam and Arjun waited until the racket died down, then Sam resumed the discussion.

"All joking and Danielle's analogy aside, the standoff you guys are involved in today is a direct consequence of those compromises," she said. "The entire model of the federal government is one big compromise, with all its checks and balances, because many of the original colonies were so afraid that a powerful federal government and President would be just as dangerous as Britain's King and parliament."

She paused briefly to look around the table at each of the organizers.

"In fact," she continued. "They couldn't even agree on the rights and freedoms in a Bill of Rights. Those weren't added until a few years later as amendments."

"Well, ain't that just great!" Cecilia muttered. "It's been decades since the Equal Rights Amendment was passed in Congress, an' we still ain't got it ratified cuz too many states still ain't got the guts or the morals to make it law! If that's the case, how are we ever gonna fix this mess we're in now?"

"That's the million dollar question, isn't it," Sam replied. "President Williams thinks that maybe it's time to stop all the partisan fighting over the individual trees. Maybe it's time to start focusing on the forest: the wider issues that both sides agree upon, like how to keep American families safe, healthy, and protected. And how to define free speech so the majority of Americans are happy with the definition, or how to guarantee freedom of conscience and religion in ways that don't infringe on the rights of others. And also, how to give every American citizen a greater voice in how they're governed. Those are probably the issues where she thinks her policies need to focus."

"Well, good luck with that, Ms. Bower," Stephen exclaimed. "Both your team and the President have your work cut out for you, if that's where you're focusing your energy."

A FEW last wisps of sage smoke hung in the air. Bryson and Norm rolled their eyes at each other as Hunter and Jessica completed their sacred smudging ceremony and took their seats. As per the agreed protocol, the proceedings were still being streamed from Anna's two video cameras that roamed near the circle of tables on the Liberty Convoy's performance stage. Hunter leaned forward and turned on a projector, which illuminated a huge screen at the rear of the stage. He tapped on the keyboard of his laptop to bring up Sam's title slide. After a few seconds he tapped again and brought up the first information slide, then he nodded to Terri.

"Thanks, Hunter," she said, then she turned her attention to the circle of convoy organizers. "I don't think any of us were surprised by the items on these lists where there's a lot of contention. Does anybody have any comments about the rights and freedoms that were most valued in both your camp *and* the Unite the Left camp?"

"Who cares 'bout them rights that're important to both?" Bryson bellowed. "We came to Washington to tell Williams 'bout them contentious ones, like our right to own guns. We came to find out what she's gonna do 'bout them!"

"I disagree, Bryson," Jessica blurted. "What could possibly be more important than keeping families safe, healthy, and protected?"

She turned to Hunter.

"Do we even have that written into the Constitution right now?"

"No, you actually don't," Hunter replied. "But a few of the items on that list are rights and freedoms that some other countries have now written into their more modern constitutions."

"So what does being safe and protected even mean in a constitution?" Jessica asked.

"Well," Hunter replied. "In most countries, I'm pretty sure that people expect their governments to provide protection from invasion by other armies, to protect them from mass shootings and other crimes, to protect them from contagious diseases, or to protect the environment they live in."

He paused to look around the table at each of the organizers. Bryson and Norm's eyes conveyed boredom while Martin Lee was engrossed with tapping away on his phone's keyboard.

"People in those countries believe that it's their right to those protections," Hunter continued. "Are those things that the rest of you are worried about? What sorts of things do *you* need protection from?"

A brief lull ensued as the organizers looked around the table at each other. Finally, John Gregg spoke up.

"Us rural folk need a lotta protection these days: from drought, storms, or floods, from the big box stores like Walmart an' Costco, or big corporate farms. An' don' forget our right to have guns to hunt fer food or to protect our livestock."

"An' we need protection from all them illegals who's takin' jobs away from all us hard-workin' Americans," Norm added.

"Hell, yeah," Sean Pritchard chimed. "An' we need the right to have 'nuff water fer irrigatin' our crops. The govermint gave us that right generations ago, an' now they're takin' it away cuz'a climate change, or so they say, which is just'a load'a horseshit, far as I'm concerned."

Terri caught Hunter's eye and he nodded back.

"The President firmly believes in keeping *all* families safe, healthy, and protected," Terri affirmed. "And she's told us that she's in favour of *any* legislation or Constitutional Amendments that will help to accomplish that!"

Pastor Kessler shook his head slowly.

"I'm sorry," he retorted, "But us believers in Christ don't need the Constitution or any government to keep our families safe! The Almighty Lord will protect his faithful believers, whether it's from plague, drought, famine, invasion by armies, or even from Satan himself!"

"Nuffa all this talk 'bout legislation an' mendments," Bryson bellowed, slamming his fist on his table. "Some of us jus' wanna defend our Constitutional right to be free an' to do what we wanna do. We don' need no govermints makin' us pay taxes an' tellin' us what to do!"

Jessica caught Hunter's attention and he nodded to give her the floor.

"Correct me if I'm wrong," she said to Hunter. "But isn't a Constitution a set of rules for how a government operates?"

"That's true," Hunter replied.

Jessica turned to Bryson and her eyes narrowed.

"So, on one hand you say you want to get rid of government, but at the same time you claim to defend the Constitution. But if you don't want government, then you don't care about having a Constitution. And without governments, who's gonna build your roads, your schools, hospitals, water treatment and sewage plants, and so on? You can't have your cake and eat it too!"

"Well, I'm with Bryson," Norm shouted. "Y'all have been conned by everythin' the govermint, the press, an' the scientists are tellin' ya! Yer all a bunch'a lazy sheep fer believin' everythin' they tell ya! We don' need no govermint! Us country folk, an' private free enterprise, kin do those things ourselves."

"That's a load'a bull, Norm!" John retorted. "You know there ain't enough of us rural folk left to pay for all those things nowadays! We need the state, an' sometime the Feds, to pay fer those services!"

"John's brought up an excellent point," Hunter added. "Did you all know that after they wrote the Constitution, Thomas Jefferson commented that he thought the document might be adequate for the country while the majority of the population was rural and mostly agricultural. But, he'd seen the huge, overcrowded cities in Europe, and he must have realized how the needs of the people, and of a Constitution, were very different when the majority of people lived in big cities. But now, here we are in that very situation, with a Constitution that's almost two hundred and fifty years out of date!"

In the background, Anna Dahl shook her head.

"I'm confused as hell, y'all!" she shouted. "Why are we gettin' so bogged down in the Constitution, when we have real issues we need the President to address? She's just avoidin' the real issues."

"I understand your frustration, Anna," Terri intervened. She pointed up at the slide on the screen. "What you guys are implying with your comments about this slide, is that because the U.S. Constitution is so vague in many ways, it causes *both* major parties to continually send new laws to the Courts to clarify whether they're Constitutional or not. And is that what you *really* want? To see the country essentially governed by the courts, instead of by you, the people?"

"The President doesn't want to see much-needed legislation get bogged down continually in the courts," Hunter added. "She wants to support laws that help keep *all* Americans protected and safe, regardless of their politics. But that's becoming increasingly difficult for *any* President to do, within the current Constitution."

"Well, if that's the case," Anna retorted, "then y'all can go back an' tell her to come here in person and tell us her plans."

Jessica waved at Hunter again to attract his attention.

"You guys are all missing the point," she said, as she looked around the circle at her convoy colleagues. "President Williams sent Bower's team here to find out what she can do for us and all Americans, instead of forcing her own opinions on the country. We all need to start thinking of this meeting as an opportunity, instead of it being something we need to fight!"

Looks of angry determination flared up on Bryson, Anna, Pastor Kessler, and Norm's faces. In contrast, the remaining organizers appeared to be mulling over Jessica's perspective.

Terri instantly discerned the dichotomy of moods and the thick tension hanging in the room. Her eyes made contact with Hunter, whose raised eyebrows indicated that he noticed the same thing. He nodded his head in agreement.

Terri turned back to the other organizers and cleared her voice to grab their attention, and to end the prolonged, awkward tension and silence.

"You've given us all a lot to think about," she said. "This might be a good time to call it a day. Hunter and I will make sure the President hears each and every one of your comments. Thank you all for your opinions, and we'll see you tomorrow."

Anna signalled her video operators to put down their cameras as the convoy organizers gradually rose to their feet and drifted away from the table. Hunter watched them retreat and then he turned to Terri.

"Good call," he said. "We weren't going to change anybody's mind today."

"For sure," Terri answered. "But hopefully we managed to plant a few seeds."

LATER THAT afternoon, Sam and the team sat in their usual circle in the Laurel Lodge, debriefing the President and Nicole on the day's meetings.

"That's about all we have to report, Ma'am," Sam summarized. "On the negative side, I think we all got a big taste of just how deeply entrenched both sides are in their politics. They're both dismissive of our attempts to divert them to the less divisive issues. But, on a more positive note, neither side told us to leave. They *did* start to open up to us a bit with their opinions. And, we did get a chance to drop a few seeds of information into the conversation, without stirring things up too much."

"I think the biggest take-away for me," Hunter continued, "at least as far as the convoy group is concerned, is that there's a clear difference of opinion that's causing some very real internal dissension within that group. We need to find ways to build on that."

"I couldn't agree more," Rachel replied. "And I can't thank each of you enough for your very thorough reports. It's fascinating, but also a bit frightening, that both sides don't have very good understandings of the Constitution that they're fighting so hard to defend. But it's promising that some people in both camps are starting to see some of its shortcomings."

Nicole took a deep breath and shook her head slowly from side to side.

"I don't know. That may be true, Ma'am. But you and I both know that making the Constitution an issue could be political suicide, especially when both sides are more focused on dealing with the most polarizing issues."

"Nicole's got a point," Arjun added. "Even if the Constitution itself is a major problem, we should bring things back to those issues where we've identified more consensus. Then, hopefully, we can link consensus on those issues to the Constitution over the longer term."

"Longer term?" Nicole blurted at Arjun. "What longer term? We've got a tense standoff on the streets of Washington that could turn into a powder keg at any moment. And the people of Washington want their city back *NOW*—not tomorrow, next week, or whatever the longer term is!"

Nicole turned to the President, her face taught and serious.

"You know that the Mayor is under intense pressure from all directions: the citizens, city council, as well as Congress and the FBI, to call in the National Guard to clean this mess up!"

"I'm well aware of that, Nicole," Rachel replied sternly. "But I think that would be a tragic mistake that could potentially make everything worse. I still have confidence in Sam's team, and I'm still committed to the process of listening and negotiation. And that's the message I need you to convey to America."

THE UNITE the Left organizers gathered around a table in their camp's mess tent, discussing the day's events, as a long line of fellow protesters filled their plates with food and searched for vacant spots to eat their evening meals. Stephen's voice rose over the din of background conversation.

"I've been talking to people in ANTIFA, and they're getting restless. They think the President should be calling up the National Guard and putting an end to the convoy protest. Enough's enough!"

"I hear you," Cecilia Robinson responded. "I'm hearing the same thing from my people at the NAACP. They don't think negotiations are going to end the convoy either. As far as they're concerned, there's only one real issue here, and that's dragging Bryson and his band of fascists off the streets one by one, if that's what it takes."

Senator Delgado pursed her lips and shook her head slowly.

"I understand your frustration, and I feel it too," she replied. "But I don't think the use of force will make anything better. If anything, the far right will see the convoy organizers as martyrs, further proof for their so-called conspiracies."

"And that's the last thing we want to see," Danielle Chen added. "Personally, I'm really impressed by Bower and her team so far. They're doing everything they can to avoid ramping up the divisions between them and us."

"I agree," Sandra said, nodding. "They're trying to bring the focus onto issues where both sides are in partial agreement. Have you noticed that they aren't trying to dismiss the right's arguments as being illogical? They're not trying to pound our version of logic and truth into their heads?"

"Sandra, you know that I'm always an advocate of diplomacy in most cases," Dudley stated. "But I fear this standoff is different. How long will the fascists stay patient? There's the rumours of guns in their camp, making it a potential powder keg. The longer this goes on, the frustration and possibility of violence are going to grow larger!"

He turned his attention across the table to Stephen.

"And getting ANTIFA involved is exactly what MacDonald and his buddies want! They're looking for any reason to pick a fight. You need to tell your friends to back off and stay patient."

Nasir glanced at his friend Idris, before adding his voice.

"I am sure Idris will agree with me that we already witnessed too much violence where we come from."

"Absolutely," Idris added. "I support the President and Ms. Bower fully in their attempt to end this peacefully."

Stephen shook his head defiantly from side to side, as frustration spread across his face.

"Fine!" he shouted. "Fall in line behind the President. But I'll be the first to say 'I told you so' if all hell breaks out on the streets again!"

"You think that isn't going to happen if your ANTIFA militants or the National Guard get involved?" Danielle retorted.

"Don't forget," Cecilia interjected, "The very reason we're here today is to clear Bryson MacDonald and his goons from the street."

"Really?" Danielle retorted. "If I remember correctly, we didn't come to Washington to confront the right at all. In your speech on the mall, before we even knew the convoy was coming, you were very clear in stating that the reason we're all here is to send *our* messages to the President. And Bower's team is helping to make that happen for us!"

"I agree," Sandra added. "That's why I came, and I'm willing to give the President and Bower's team a chance. Besides, apart from packing up and going home, what other options does this committee have right now?"

COUNTRY MUSIC from the convoy's events stage blared in the background, as Bryson and the other organizers sat around a picnic table in the mess tent, smoking weed. Bryson watched a large crowd of convoy campers who were up on their feet, dancing and singing along, then he took a long toke. As he exhaled slowly, he passed it to Norm, who did the same before inadvertently offering the weed to Pastor Kessler. Recognizing his error in judgment, he shrugged his shoulders and handed the joint to Sean Pritchard instead. Norm shouted to Bryson over the racket.

"How much longer we gonna put up with this negotiatin' horse shit, Scorps?"

Sean passed the joint along to Anna, who took a long puff before handing it back to Bryson, while she exhaled a white cloud of smoke. The organizers continued to shout at each other over the hubbub behind them, in order to make themselves heard.

"Not much longer, far as I'm concerned," Bryson bellowed. "We been here fer over a week now, an ma patience is gettin' mighty thin."

"All this talk 'bout the Constitution," Pastor Kessler shouted. "That surely ain't the reason we came here. We just wanna hear the President stand up an' defend our Constitutional freedoms!"

"So what other choices do we have?" Anna queried.

"We kin tell Williams to shove her negotiatin' committee where the sun don't shine!" Norm roared, before laughing hysterically at his own comment.

"Ya! Send the Indian an' the stripper packin' next time they come aroun'," Sean replied. "Tell em we don' wanna see em agin!"

Bryson passed the joint back to Norm, who took a long, leisurely toke, before exhaling another cloud of sweet, pungent smoke.

"I'm inclined to agree with y'all," Bryson concluded. "I think we've given Williams an' those kids from up north 'bout 'nough time. I don' know 'bout you folks, but I came here to talk to the President directly, an I ain't goin' home till I do!"

"Well, I say we give 'em more time," Jessica interjected. "Y'all say that the Constitution isn't the reason we're here. But every one of us has pointed out somethin' in the Constitution that isn't workin' for us. Maybe Bower and the President are onto somethin' that we're too blind to see."

Bryson and Norm both pursed their lips tightly, narrowed their eyes, and glared at Jessica with disdain written all over their faces.

"I'm not sure where they're headin' with this Constitution stuff," John Gregg added. "But I'm willin' to wait a bit longer to see where it goes. I know the Constitution ain't workin' fer me these days. My American dream sure 'nough didn't include workin' my ass off an' goin' broke."

He turned to address Sean directly.

"What about you, Sean? How's your dream goin' these days?"

Before Sean could answer, Bryson slammed his fist on the table.

"Gimme a fuckin' break!" he hollered. "Of course the Constitution ain't workin' fer any of us! But it ain't the Constitution's fault. It's the fuckin' Cathedral: the press, universities, an' big govermint that keep usin' the Constitution to pull the wool over everybody's eyes. So that bitch Williams an' her so-called team are jus' tryin' to distract us from the real issue. We can't trust govermint,—'specially Williams—no more! We jus' wanna exercise our Constitutional right to hold 'er 'countable, that's all!"

"Well said, Bryson!" Anna whooped.

"Fuckin' eh, Scorps!" Norm added.

Pastor Kessler raised his arms into the air in a silent call for prayer, before raising his voice over the background din.

"I think this is a good time to pray to our Almighty Lord in Heaven for His guidance an' His wisdom. Let us all join hands in prayer."

A THICK nighttime blanket of overcast, along with the distant sounds of traffic and an occasional chirping cricket, hung over the sleeping Liberty Convoy encampment. The thundering musical entertainment of day eight, from a Guns and Roses tribute band, had finally shut down one hour earlier at about 2 a.m. The only apparent movement in the camp was a lone volunteer security guard, dressed in full camo attire and wearing a sidearm, walking lazily from the mess tent, along Seventeenth Street, towards F Street. Oblivious to the distant sound of a motorcycle, the guard wandered away from the intersection towards Pennsylvania Avenue, where he turned right and continued his casual patrol.

The rumbling sound of a motorbike grew slowly in intensity as it neared F Street, then diminished when the bike slowed, as it encountered the security fence for the arm of the Liberty Convoy that stretched along F Street from Seventeenth to Eighteenth. At that point, the bike's rider, dressed entirely in black, pulled the bike off the street and parked it on the sidewalk beneath a street light. The driver removed its helmet, and gazed up at security cameras mounted on nearby office buildings. The figure then slung a backpack onto its back, looked around to make sure nobody was watching, then silently and nimbly scaled the security fence and dropped onto the pavement inside the convoy encampment.

The figure moved stealthily through the encampment, keeping low and staying in the shadows cast by semi-trailer rigs, port-a-pots, and trailers. At F Street and Seventeenth, it hung a right and move furtively towards the entertainment stage and mess tent. When the interloper reached a large dumpster and a trailer full of food stores, it stopped and crouched down. A tower of used shipping pallets stood beside the dumpster, next to the supply trailer. The intruder let its backpack slide from a shoulder, then rapidly and silently removed some items. Before long, a small flame was visible amongst the pallets and the figure moved to the dumpster, where a second flame soon appeared. The figure immediately snatched its backpack and sprinted back up Seventeenth to F Street, then back to the security fence. Within seconds, the intruder had scaled the fence and was back at the motorbike, where it took one last moment to stare up at the building-mounted security cameras, before mounting the bike. The engine rumbled to life, then the rider turned around and accelerated the bike back onto Eighteenth Street, where it roared and sped into the night.

STILL HALF asleep, Anna Dahl emerged from the port-a-pot, drying her hands on her clothing. Suddenly, a dark figure sprinted past her, heading towards F Street. Shocked and confused, her body froze and she felt her heart pounding in her chest.

"Fuck!" she squealed. "What was that!"

Before she had a chance to react, her senses detected smoke coming from behind her. She whirled around and looked towards the mess tent. At the same time, she heard a motorcycle engine roar to life behind her and disappear into the distance. Ahead of her, she saw an orange glow and smoke rising in front of a street light. Her legs came to life and she sprinted towards the mess tent. As she passed the stage and approached the tent, she caught her first glimpse of flames, leaping from the dumpster and the pile of pallets.

"Fire!" she screamed. "The dumpster's on fire!" She ran to the mess tent, where she began clanging the kitchen's raucous metal dinner triangle, while continuously screaming "Fire!"

Within seconds, figures began emerging from rigs and tents, running towards the fires with extinguishers and containers of water. Anna grabbed an extinguisher from the kitchen and joined the others in trying to beat down the flames. The first person she reached was Norm Barfield.

"The pallets!" Norm bellowed. "The flames are gonna spread to the dry goods trailer! We gotta get between 'em!"

Anna and Norm worked their way around the edge of the pallet fire with their extinguishers while the flames licked seductively at the corner of the dry goods trailer. A sudden burst of flame and heat drove the pair back, just as Bryson emerged from his nearby van. He lumbered, as fast as his corpulent body was able, towards his frantic colleagues.

"Over here, Bryson! We need help over here!" Anna shouted.

"What the fuck?" he hollered. "How'd this happen?"

"Never mind that!" Anna shouted back. "You know what y'all got hidden in the trailer. We gotta get this under control right now, unless you wanna explain to the fire department why this trailer lit up like the Fourth of July!"

Bryson shouted to six other campers who had just arrived with extinguishers from their trucks.

"You three, help us over here! The rest of you, help beat down that dumpster fire!"

Anna heard the whine of fire engine sirens in the distance, rapidly growing closer and closer. She, Norm, Bryson, and the three campers worked feverishly to beat back the licking flames from the corner of the supply trailer, which was now singed black. Their six extinguishers slowly, but steadily, overwhelmed the flames amongst the pallets.

As the fire trucks pulled into the intersection at Seventeenth and Constitution Avenue, a group of firefighters jumped from the truck and headed into the encampment. By the time they arrived at the dumpster and the pallets, only a few isolated flames and some smoke remained. Within seconds, they quenched the last of the flames. One of the firefighters turned to Anna.

"Great work, you guys! Did that trailer catch fire?"

"Nope!" Anna replied. "We managed to get here and protect it just before y'all arrived. It's just a bit singed and black."

"Any idea how this started?" a second firefighter asked.

"Not really sure," Anna answered. "I just came outta the port-a-pot over there, and a guy dressed in black ran past me like a bat outta hell, and disappeared up the street. I think I heard a motorcycle after that."

Bryson's eyes opened wide and his nostrils flared in anger.

"It's those woke ANTIFA bastards!" he bellowed. "We're done with negotiatin'. They're gonna pay fer this!"

CHAPTER 12—SPIES IN THE NIGHT

THIRTY MINUTES later, after the fire trucks had departed, Bryson, Norm, and Sean burst out of the Liberty Convoy encampment and spilled into the night in no man's land between the two camps at the intersection of Seventeenth and Constitution, followed by a mob of angry convoy protesters. The mob immediately jeered and hurled insults at the Unite the Left encampment. Many of the convoy protesters carried baseball bats, but some wore holstered sidearms.

"So ya fuckin' woke cowards wanna fight, eh?" Bryson hollered at the top of his lungs. "Well, here's a bit o' yer own medicine!"

One member of the mob lit a molotov cocktail and hurled it into the Unite the Left camp, where it burst into flames on the asphalt. Occupants of that camp ran to beat out the flames with blankets and fire extinguishers. At the same time, a mob of angry Unite the Left protesters surged out of their camp and into no man's land to confront the Liberty Convoy mob. Before long, a full-fledged street fight had broken out, with a number of participants from both camps lying on the ground, being punched, kicked, or both. A number of protesters were bleeding from the head and neck, or holding injured arms and legs after being struck by baseball bats.

Within minutes, the DCMP tactical and riot squads began arriving at the scene in armoured vehicles and waded into the fight en masse. Bryson, Norm, Sean, and many of the protesters managed to flee the scene and scurry back into the safety of their encampments. Back in the intersection, any remaining street fighters from both encampments, who hadn't yet scattered and returned to their respective camps, were rounded up efficiently and arrested. Paramedics loaded the last of the injured into ambulances, while the tactical squad and paddy wagons left the intersection as the first hints of daybreak announced the ominous beginning to day nine of the standoff.

"THE ZOOM call's set up, Ma'am," Nicole announced. "Captain Robby should be logging on any second now."

Rachel sat in front of a laptop computer at the round table in her Camp David office, with Sam, Hunter, Arjun, and Terri looking on. Nicole took her seat next to the President, using her own laptop to moderate the virtual conference call with the DCMP Captain.

"Can you hear and see me?" Robby asked.

His image and voice appeared on both Nicole's and Rachel's laptops. Sam and her team sat quietly, listening to the proceedings.

"Yes, we can," Rachel answered. "Thank you for taking the time to update me on last night's events. I know you must be incredibly busy. How's the situation right now?"

"Things are stable at the moment, Madam President," Robby replied. "But I must tell you, last night was almost our worst nightmare come true! With all those trailers blocking the side streets, the Fire Department couldn't get their equipment close. We were damned lucky the Liberty camp people caught it early! And the Mayor has my ass in a sling over this!"

"I appreciate that, Captain," Rachel responded. "Don't worry about the Mayor. I have a meeting with her next, and I'll smooth things over. Frankly, from what I've seen, I think your teams did an excellent job of responding and containing the street fighting."

"Thank you, Ma'am. But I wouldn't be so sure that the Mayor will be easy to appease. She's really pissed, and getting a lot of heat from City Council and citizens, especially the nearby businesses and tourist attractions that are taking a huge hit from the blockades on the streets around the White House. I can tell you right now that she's a hair's breadth away from calling in the DCNG to clear the streets!"

Captain Robby held up his fingers to his webcam and gestured to emphasize the tiny distance. Rachel shook her head slowly.

"I still believe that would be a grave mistake," she answered. "The street fight you had to deal with last night will seem like a school yard dust-up if the rumours are true: if Bryson and his friends have guns and decide to use them!"

Sam raised her arm to let the President know she had something to say, and Rachel gave her the go-ahead with a nod.

"Any ideas about who broke into the compound and lit the fires, Captain? We've talked to the Unite the Left organizers, and they vehemently deny that anybody left their camp prior to the fire and the street fight."

"To be honest, that's the reason why I needed to meet with you right away this morning, before the press latches onto this."

A frown spread across Rachels' face.

"Why? What's up?"

"Something else has come up that puts the Unite the Left camp's statement into question, and it has me leaning towards supporting the Mayor on this," Robby answered. The frown on Rachel's face deepened.

"And that is?"

Captain Robby paused to swallow, and then took a deep breath before continuing.

"We have security video from two buildings in the area, the FDIC and the Eisenhower Executive Buildings. They both show a person parking a motorbike, donning a backpack, scaling the security fence on F Street, and disappearing into the Convoy Camp. The person ran back a few minutes later, climbed the fence, and hightailed it outta there on the bike."

"So what are you telling me?" Rachel asked. "Is there any useful information in those security videos?"

"Yes, Ma'am. And you're not going to like this. The bike's license plate is registered to the journalist, Jordan Marsh. Her face is clearly visible after she takes off her ski mask."

The room went silent while its occupants digested the stunning revelation. Finally, Sam broke the silence.

"That's just not possible," she blurted.

"That can't be right," Arjun added. "We've gotten to know her really well over the past week. She's just not capable of doing anything like that!"

"Are you absolutely sure about this?" Rachel probed.

"Yes Ma'am. Both videos are perfectly clear and leave no doubt. I have a team headed to the Unite the Left camp right now to arrest her."

Another silence descended upon the President's table, as she and the team continued to process the startling news and its implications.

"Now I understand why you and the Mayor are so concerned," Rachel said. "Once this news breaks, things could go one of two ways. Hopefully, Bryson and his friends will praise you guys for finding the perpetrator quickly, and that will be enough to keep things calm."

"Or?" Captain Robby queried.

"It could tip them over the edge and they'll spill out onto the streets again, looking for blood. I can't let that happen, so this is what I'm willing to do, Captain. Tell the Mayor to put DCNG on standby, and make sure the media knows I'm on board as soon as possible. Hopefully, that will cause Bryson to think before he does anything rash."

"Thank you, Madam President," Robby replied. "I'll let her know right away. And I'll keep you fully up to date."

"Thank you, Captain."

The call ended as Captain Robby logged off.

"That figures!" Nicole exclaimed. "I never trusted that Marsh from the moment I met her. She'll do anything for a story!"

Sam looked around the table at her team. They still sat staring at each other with stunned dismay. Finally, Hunter turned to the President.

"So, what does that mean for us and our negotiations?"

"If we stop now," Sam added. "We'll lose any credibility we ever had, especially with the Liberty Convoy protesters. Surely you're not going to abandon the talks!"

Rachel took a few seconds to ponder the dramatic turn of events.

"I don't think we know enough yet to make a decision. Nicole, advise the two camps that I'd like them to meet with Sam and her team tomorrow. That will give us a chance to take the temperature within each camp after the news breaks. Also, advise them that both meetings won't be live-streamed, in order to allow each side to speak completely freely to the team."

"Yes, Ma'am," Nicole answered. "I'll get right on that after I take a quick break."

Rachel turned her attention back to Sam and the team.

"Okay," she said. "Let's talk about how we want to handle those two meetings. We may only have one chance to get this right and keep these talks alive!"

NICOLE SLIPPED out of the Aspen Lodge and onto the grounds of Camp David, out of earshot, where she stopped and lit a cigarette. As she took her first drag, her cell phone rang. She took a quick glance to check who was calling, then looked around to make sure nobody was close enough to hear her.

"Hey Matt," she said, her voice hushed but excited. "I can't believe our good luck. That reporter, Marsh, did us a huge favour!"

"I'd like to think it was more than just good luck," Butler answered. Nicole's forehead creased and her eyes narrowed while she processed his comment. Seconds later, her face broke out into a smile.

"Don't tell me you're behind this! This was part of what you've been planning?"

"C'mon, girl," Butler replied. "Show a little faith. Hold on a sec, I have somebody here who wants to have a word with you."

Nicole's face fell the instant that a heavily disguised voice began speaking, and an uneasy sensation spread rapidly through her body.

"Hello, Ms. Davies. We haven't spoken in person before, but I thought it was time to introduce myself. Since we're celebrating your colleague's success today, I thought this would be the ideal opportunity for me to do so."

"Hello," Nicole answered timidly. "I'm honoured that you're calling me personally. And I'm really glad to hear that you're pleased with Matt's success."

"Indeed," the mystery voice continued. "Unfortunately, we haven't seen similar success from you in managing the President. She continues to follow this foolhardy course with her so-called Canadian negotiating team. And you *did* promise to steer her in another direction, did you not?"

"I'm sorry, sir," Nicole replied, her trembling voice giving away her rising anxiety. "She's very headstrong and hard to dissuade. I'm still trying."

"Enough!" the voice bellowed. "I don't want to hear excuses Ms. Davies. I need action. When I hang up, your colleague is going to give you some specific instructions, which I expect you to follow to the letter. Do I make myself clear?"

The muscles in Nicole's face tightened and pulsated, and her eyes opened wide. The tremor in her voice worsened. She threw her cigarette to the ground and stomped it out with her shoe as fear spread through her body.

"Yes, sir! I'm at your service," she blurted.

"Good," the voice replied. "Is the President still planning on sending Ms. Bower's team back into the two protest camps?"

"Yes, sir. The plan is for them to go back tomorrow, same times as usual."

"Good. Then I'll hand you back to your colleague. And Ms. Davies ..."

"Yes?" she answered timidly.

"Do *exactly* what he says. No more trying. I want action this time, and I need to see more of your influence on the President!"

Nicole heard a click on the line.

"Matt? You still there?"

"I'm still here, Nikki. So, listen closely. Here's what we need you to do."

SAM MOPPED the perspiration from her brow, then she reached for her water bottle and took a long swallow to help rehydrate herself. The day nine humidity was building rapidly, and the forecast of a stagnant heat dome, lasting for at least the next week, was not a good omen for protesters in both camps. All of the Unite the Left camp's organizers were present for this morning's crucial meeting. But the big elephant in the room was the absence of Jordan Marsh and her crew, and Cecilia wasted no time in breaching the subject.

"Sam, maybe you can help us make sense of what's been goin' on overnight. Is it true what they're sayin' bout Jordan?"

Sam sighed and looked around the table at the expectant eyes, all focused on her and on what she was about to say.

"There's a lot of innuendo, so whether it's true or not, who knows?" she began. "What we do know, is that DCMP has security videos that appear to show Jordan climbing the fence into the Liberty Camp last night, just before a fire broke out in their trash dumpster. They've charged Jordan with arson and conspiracy to incite rioting, and her bail hearing is this morning. She sent a message to the President, denying any involvement in the incident. But what's most worrisome is that the Mayor seems to be leaning towards calling in the Guard to clean up the camps after last night's events."

"Dang!" Cecilia exclaimed. "That ain't good! There's no tellin' how Bryson an' those rednecks'll respond to that. All hell could break loose on the streets again. What do you think? And what does all this mean fer all of us?"

"Yeah, what about the negotiations?" Sandra interjected. "Does the President agree with the Mayor? Is she going to pull the plug on you and your team?"

"That depends partially on you guys," Sam answered. "But mostly, it depends on Bryson and his inner circle. The President's told the Mayor to put the DCNG on standby, just in case things blow up. But she thinks my team's role is more important than ever after last night's riot. She thinks there's an opportunity for us to bring some calm to the situation. So what do you all think?"

A hush fell over the group as everybody looked around the circle at each other. Finally, Stephen broke the awkward silence.

"If Bryson and the fascists hit the streets, National Guard or no Guard, I have it on good authority that ANTIFA will meet them face to face. We're not going to let another January sixth happen!"

"Whoa, hold on a minute!" Dudley blurted. "More violence isn't going to solve anything!"

"I agree," Kym chimed. "There's got to be a better way. The President's right. Diplomacy and negotiation, and most all, compromise, are always the best route."

Danielle Chen raised her hand and jumped into the fray, without waiting to be acknowledged.

"I can't believe, even for one moment, that Jordan is capable of what they're accusing her of doing. I've gotten to know her over the past week, and she hasn't got a violent bone in her body. It's just not her personality at all!"

She turned to Sam and Arjun with a determined look on her face.

"I think you guys are needed more now than ever!"

"What about everybody else?" Arjun asked. "Nasir? Idris?"

Idris looks to Nasir, who nodded for Idris to continue.

"You know that we both condemn violence for any reason. We both experienced far too much of that in our lifetime. We support you one hundred percent."

"If that's the case," Sandra summarized, "what's next Sam?"

Sam shrugged her shoulders, raised her eyebrows, and displayed a nervous smile.

"Well, Hunter and Terri will be meeting with the convoy this afternoon to find out what kind of mood they're in. I guess only time will tell how they'll react."

THE OPPRESSIVE afternoon heat and humidity was taking a toll on everybody around the table, including Hunter and Terri. The convoy organizers, seated in their usual circle, were already engaged in a fiery argument.

"I knew that bitch, or guy, or whatever you call him or her, couldn't be trusted!" Sean bellowed.

"Yup!" Norm chimed, "It's 'nother case o' the so-called free press attackin' us an' our right to gather an' protest!"

"Come on, guys," Jessica retorted, "What possible motive could Jordan have for setting our camp on fire? She'd have to know you'd blame it all on Unite the Left. I just can't see her resorting to sabotage or violence!"

Anna glared suspiciously in Jessica's direction.

"So why are y'all jumpin' to defend somebody y'all have only known fer a week?"

A brief flicker of fear flashed in Jessica's eyes as her brain scrambled for a plausible explanation. She quickly regained her composure, hoping nobody noticed her minor lapse.

"You're a journalist, Anna," Jessica answered. "Would *you* risk *your* reputation by engaging in a terrorist act, just to create a story? I just don't get why any journalist would do that. It doesn't make any sense."

Bryson slammed his fist on his desk and turned his anger in Hunter's direction.

"Well somebody sure as shit must'a done it! Just goes to show we can't trust anybody to respect our rights an' freedoms: that bitch of a President, the press, an' 'specially *you* guys!"

Terri, who had been following the argument the whole time, looked at Hunter, then put two fingers to her lips and stunned everybody in the room with a piercing whistle. A sudden hush descended over the circle.

"Listen, Bryson. I totally understand where you're coming from. I'd feel threatened and violated if somebody broke into my home or business and set the place on fire. I wouldn't be able to trust anybody either. But, whoever did it, they win if we let them distract you guys from what brought you here in the first place. Are you gonna let that happen?"

"She's right," Hunter chimed. "The President understands that, and she's assured us that she's still committed to listening to you, and finding out more about the issues that brought you to Washington. So, until the Jordan Marsh situation is clarified, the White House is looking for another objective voice to continue the live-streaming of our talks, in conjunction with Anna."

"Whoa!" Norm shouted. "Who said anythin' bout continuin' these here talks, right Bryson?"

"Damn right! We done decided we ain't interested in any more talks, even 'fore that bitch jumped the fence an' tried to burn us down!"

"That was not unanimous," Jessica yelled. "And you know it, Bryson!"

As the infighting between Jessica, Bryson, and Norm continued, Hunter noticed a flurry of activity in their usually unobtrusive Secret Service security detail. One agent spoke anxiously into her radio, while her male partner listened closely with a look of concern on his face. The radio call ended and the female agent moved quickly towards Hunter and Terri. She leaned down and spoke quietly, but firmly, into Hunter's ear.

"Sorry to interrupt, sir. I've just been advised that there's been a bomb threat directed at Camp David, and we're being recalled to help evacuate the facility. They've advised me that DCMP is sending a temporary detail to protect you and Terri, and they should arrive momentarily."

Deep furrows of concern appeared on Hunter's forehead.

"Doesn't that seem irregular?" he asked.

"Well, yes, but it is an emergency, sir," she replied. "Our replacements will be here in a few moments. We need to go now!"

Before Hunter could argue, the two agents whirled around and rushed out of the convoy tent into the intersection, where they jumped into their black Escalade and sped away on Constitution Avenue.

SECONDS LATER, an unmarked military vehicle pulled up into the intersection. Two burly men, dressed in camouflage fatigues and carrying sidearms on their hips, stepped out of the vehicle and made their way into the convoy's main mess tent.

The moment Hunter saw them, he knew instinctively from his military training that the men weren't from any legitimate police department. He stood up, glanced at Terri, and then addressed the organizers.

"I'm sorry to interrupt, but something weird's happening here."

He continued to watch the two intruders as they were confronted by two Liberty Convoy security volunteers and an argument ensued. All of a sudden, one of the intruders looked into the mess tent and made eye contact with Hunter. He drew his sidearm and threatened the unarmed security volunteer. As he did, Hunter grabbed Terri's arm.

"We gotta run! Is there any other way outta here?"

Jessica wheeled around to see what was happening behind her. When she saw the two burly men, both of them carrying guns now, she turned to Hunter and Terri.

"Follow me," she screamed.

Jessica ran from the tent with Hunter and Terri hot on her heels. They raced past the camp's kitchen grills, past the presentation stage, and out onto Seventeenth Street, with its maze of big rigs, trailers, and trucks of assorted sizes. Finally out of sight of the intruders for a few precious seconds, the threesome stopped to catch their breath beside the singed supply trailer and the pile of blackened pallets.

"There's weapons hidden behind the boxes in this supply trailer." Jessica whispered.

Hunter turned his head and stole a quick look behind them, but didn't see their adversaries yet. His military training and instincts kicked in again.

"Take Terri! Run and find a good place to hide if you can't find a way out!"

"What about you?" Terri whispered anxiously.

"I'll be fine! Hurry!"

Jessica grabbed Terri by the hand and dragged her away from Hunter and the trailer. The two women ran a short distance and then left the main pathway, taking cover behind truck after truck as they made their way north on Seventeenth Street.

Meanwhile, Hunter climbed nimbly into the back of the open trailer and hid behind some bales of toilet paper, just as the intruders came into view with their guns drawn. Hunter slowed his breathing, calmly watching the men through a tiny slit between the bales, as they moved cautiously towards his hiding place.

The first intruder signalled the second man to search the pile of charred pallets. When the second man gave the all-clear signal, the first man carefully approached the trailer where Hunter was hiding. He peered cautiously around the corner and into the makeshift storage site. Not seeing Hunter, he quickly pulled himself up into the trailer and surveyed the inside. He ripped open a few cases, only to find them filled with cans of baked beans, boxes of plastic cutlery and paper plates, zip ties, duct tape, and other supplies. The rear of the trailer was piled high with large bales of toilet paper, where Hunter crouched, his body coiled and ready to attack if necessary. After moving a couple of bales aside, the intruder seemed satisfied that nobody was in the trailer. He wheeled around, jumped down onto the street, and signalled his partner to resume the search. The two men moved quickly up the street, systematically searching behind and beneath each truck and trailer they came upon.

Still concealed behind the bales of toilet paper, Hunter's eyes fell on the stack of boxes containing guns and ammo, that Jessica had spotted earlier in the week.

What do we have here?

He grabbed a sidearm and a number of clips of ammo from the stash, before carefully peering out from behind the toilet paper bales, moving some aside, and cautiously making his way toward the open doors of the trailer. He slid quietly to the ground, peered around the corner of the supply trailer, and spotted his adversaries moving up the street. Using the trucks and trailers as cover, Hunter moved stealthily to catch up to them.

AS THEY approached D Street, Jessica and Terri startled a convoy truck driver who sat beside his truck on a fold-out camp stool, sipping from a can of Budweiser.

"You've gotta help us," Terri whispered, as she looked back over her shoulder. "There's two armed intruders in the camp and they're looking for us!"

The driver snapped to attention, then he rose and took a slow walk around the front of his rig and poked his head out for a peek. Seeing one of the intruders approaching, he turned and nodded to Terri. He glanced up at the trucks cab, and mouthed the words "climb in" to her. Terri and Jessica wasted no time carefully opening the cab's door and slipping into the rig's sleeper, where they hastily covered themselves with a blanket.

A moment later, the first intruder came upon the truck driver.

"You seen a couple of women, one blond, the other black hair with braids, running this way?"

"Yeah, matter o'fact I did, just a minute or two ago. Not sure why they was runnin' so fast."

"Which way'd they go?"

The trucker pointed westward, up D Street.

"That-a-way. Looked like a couple'a scared deer."

The intruder looked up at the cab and then back at the driver.

"Anybody in the cab?"

"Yessir. The wife's havin' herself a nap. Spent half the night drinkin' an' dancin' to the band, an' she's sleepin' it off."

The intruder paused and stared at the driver. After a momentary pause, apparently satisfied that the driver wasn't lying, the intruder nodded and turned to look for his partner.

"Thanks!" the intruder answered curtly, giving a quick nod to the driver.

"No worries, man," the driver said. He raised his can of Bud and saluted the intruder, who was motioning for his partner to hurry up to join him.

MEANWHILE, HUNTER managed to catch up to the intruders and concealed himself behind a trailer. He watched as they left Terri and Jessica's hiding spot behind and worked their way systematically westward on D Street. He followed the two men, maintaining a safe distance, until he came upon an unattended trailer with a cooler full of beer sitting on the street beside it. He paused for a moment to think, then grabbed a beer from the cooler and poked his head around the trailer, noting that the intruders were only about 20 yards in front of him. He ducked back behind the trailer and scampered around the other side for better cover. Then, he gripped the beer can like a grenade and whirled it through the air as far as he could throw in the direction of the intruders, before scampering under the trailer and hiding behind one if its tires.

The can exploded with a large pop, followed by a hissing noise. The two intruders jumped instantly, whirled around and stopped in their tracks. Moving cautiously, they gradually worked their way back towards Hunter, each man taking a different side of the street. As the second intruder passed him, Hunter silently leapt from behind the tire and put a choke hold on the unsuspecting man until he passed out. Moving quietly and efficiently, Hunter laid the man on the ground, hiding his body behind the tire.

Hunter peered out carefully from behind the tire and spotted the first intruder, who was still moving very slowly on the opposite side of the street, unable to see his partner. The intruder readied his gun, crossed the street cautiously, then peered around the corner of the truck. He spotted his partner's feet protruding from behind the trailer's tire and scurried towards him.

Thirty feet away, Hunter dove for cover behind another truck, but his elbow thumped on the vehicle's cab as he passed. Hearing the thud, the first intruder crouched and fired a shot beneath the trucks, in the direction of the sound. The bullet ricocheted off the undercarriage of the truck under which Hunter was hiding.

The sound of the gunshot and bullet's ricochet instantaneously caused the occupants of nearby trucks and campers to come alive. People ran in every direction, not knowing where to go for safety. Hunter put his hand on the gun he had tucked away in the small of his back, then decided against using it. Instead, he crept silently, but quickly, away from the area and back towards the intersection of Seventeenth and D Streets, where he caught a glimpse of Terri and Jessica peering through a rig's window. He got to his feet and sprinted towards the rig. As he did, he motioned for them to jump down and join him.

"Come on!" he bellowed. "We need to get out of here while we can!" As they emerged from the truck, Hunter saw the driver peering around the corner of his cab.

"Call 9-1-1! Tell them to come to the convoy camp entrance on Constitution Avenue!" He turned to Jessica and Terri.

"Follow me!"

As they ran back down Seventeenth Street towards Constitution Avenue, the first intruder knelt on the ground, attending to his partner, who was just regaining consciousness. He spoke urgently into a microphone mounted on his shoulder, and then turned to the security fence behind him. Taking a pair of wire cutters from a pouch on his belt, he proceeded to cut strands of wire on the fence. When he managed to make the opening large enough, he helped his groggy partner through the fence and out of the camp. They managed to make their way slowly to the next intersection, just as the familiar unmarked military vehicle reappeared. The uninjured intruder helped his partner into the vehicle, then jumped in after him. The vehicle did a quick u-turn, then the engine roared and the vehicle flew up Eighteenth Street, where it disappeared rapidly into the distance.

RACHEL SHOOK her head slowly from side to side in disbelief, as she sat at her Aspen Lodge desk. Her telephone felt as if it was glued to her ear, due to the flurry of emergency calls over the past two hours. Her stomach growled, but dinner was the last thing on her mind at the moment.

"Are you *absolutely* sure?" she pleaded.

"The Secret Service played me the recording of the phone call, Ma'am," Captain Robby replied. "It's pretty convincing, and it leaves little doubt."

"What about the FBI?" Rachel pressed. "What did they say?"

"They're of the same opinion, Ma'am. Butler says they've run a preliminary comparison of the recording to some available file videos, and they're convinced of the caller's identity."

Rachel wracked her brain, searching for some explanation; some way of reconciling the dissonant information she'd just heard. Finally, she sighed. She knew she had to accept that her intelligence sources were telling the truth.

"So what's next?" Rachel asked.

"Our department's passing along the findings to the DA's office. It'll be up to them to determine the charges. What you do at your end is up to you, Ma'am."

There was a knock on Rachel's door. She looked up as Nicole poked her head into the office. Rachel motioned for her assistant to come in and take a seat.

"Thanks, DeWayne," Rachel answered, a look of total dejection on her face. "I appreciate your candour. Let me know if you hear anything new."

"Of course, Ma'am. Goodbye"

Rachel set the receiver down in its cradle, sighed slowly, and sat back in her chair.

"Long afternoon," Nicole observed. "Will you be having dinner in the dining room, or shall I ask them to bring your meal to the office?"

Rachel shook her head from side to side.

"Neither right now," she answered. "I'm not hungry at the moment."

"Is anything wrong? Any word yet on who placed that call to the Secret Service?" Nicole asked.

Rachel forced herself to straighten up in her chair, and to make eye contact with her assistant.

"Why did you do it, Nicole?" she said dejectedly.

Nicole's eyes almost popped out of their sockets and her jaw dropped open wide.

"Excuse me? You think that was me? That's not possible, Ma'am. I didn't do it!"

"I trusted you. How could you do that to me?"

CHAPTER 13—BREAKDOWN

THE DAY'S events, almost losing Hunter and Terri to the rogue kidnappers, and finding out that Nicole was part of the kidnapping plot, weighed heavily on Sam. Needing some time and space to clear her mind, she slipped out of the Birch Lodge to walk around the grounds of Camp David. She welcomed the darkness that surrounded her as she slipped into the night.

After another oppressively hot and humid day, the evening air was still clammy and her clothing clung annoyingly to her skin. The sound of mosquitos buzzed frequently in her ear, and she found herself swatting continuously at the pesky creatures.

Away from the hustle and bustle of the many nearby urban areas surrounding Maryland and Camp David, the President's country retreat was amazingly quiet. Unlike the city, there was no background hum of traffic nor distant cries of sirens. The only notable sound was the chorus of chirping crickets. But the humid summer night also brought out another of Mother Nature's magical performances: a myriad of fireflies floating through the darkness, flickering on and off as they searched for a mate.

Sam stopped and laid down in the cool grass. She gazed up at the hazy sky, taking deep breaths to slow her mind and calm herself as she listened to the crickets and watched the fireflies light up, disappear, then light up again. Gradually, her eyes glazed over and she slipped into a semi-hypnotic state. She started speaking silently to her departed father.

Charlie? Are you out there? Can your spirit hear me? I think I'm losing myself and I feel so small, like I have the weight of all creation on my shoulders. Two of my best friends almost died today, because of me. I don't think I could bear losing anybody else. If you can hear me, send me a message. Please?

The sounds of the evening continued undisturbed for a few moments. Then, out of the stillness, a solitary crow cawed in the trees near Sam. She sat up and listened. A moment later, the crow cawed again, this time about a hundred yards away. She stood up and followed the sound. Then the cawing came from another one-hundred yards further along. Sam continued to follow the crow's call until she realized she was standing in front of the President's Aspen Lodge swimming pool. The pool deck and surrounding area were dark, the only eerie light coming from the pool's underwater lighting.

Is this what you're trying to tell me?

Seconds later, the crow cawed again, this time three times in a row. Sam paused for a few seconds, then looked around nervously to see if anybody might be watching. Finally, she shyly pulled her t-shirt over her head and reached around behind her back. Her unfastened bra dropped to the ground, then Sam wriggled out of her shorts and her panties all at once, leaving them in a pile on the pool deck. Feeling exposed and vulnerable, she covered her bare breasts with her arms and skipped swiftly to the pool, where she slipped into the turquoise waters. She filled her lungs and dove. Completely submerged, she swam to the far end of the pool, her slim body gliding through the water as the submerged lighting rippled and sparkled over her lithe body. Finally, as she reached the shallow end, she surfaced. Her feet touched the bottom and she gasped for breath. After taking a few more deep refreshing breaths, she dove again. This time her strokes took her down into the depths of the pool, before she swam upwards to where she had started. She breathed deeply, laid back in the water, opened her eyes, and gazed up at the sky as she floated motionlessly. The crow cawed again.

Thank you, Charlie. I think I understand. It's the water, isn't it? Water is life. It supports us and keeps us afloat.

The crow cawed once more. Now more relaxed, Sam allowed herself to giggle aloud into the silence of the evening.

And the skinny dipping. Telling me not to worry so much about what others think: to just be myself.

The crow's raucous call broke the silence three more times, then Sam heard the bird's wings flap, gradually carrying it away into the night.

It's okay to be vulnerable. I'm only human, just like everybody else. I just need to trust myself. Thanks, Charlie.

Sam swam to the pool's edge, where she pulled herself onto the pool deck, gathered her clothing, and skipped away quickly until she was once again shrouded in darkness. She dropped her clothes onto the damp grass and twirled her body round and round. Goosebumps popped out all over her bare skin as she danced, and as the water slowly evaporated. Every inch of her skin was alive and reinvigorated. After a few moments, she stopped, sighed, and bent over to pick up her clothing. She struggled to pull the damp garments over her still-damp, sticky skin, before finally walking back towards the lights of Birch Lodge and a welcome night's sleep.

THE EARLY morning sun, barely over the horizon at 6 a.m., glowed orange through thick, hazy, humid Maryland air, as the relentless heat dome continued to build over the eastern portion of the continent. Rachel was already seated at the team's round table in the Laurel Lodge when Sam was the first of the team to arrive. Sam took a seat in front of two carafes of coffee and an array of pastries and fruit.

"Good morning," Rachel said, then she flashed a smile and a sly wink at Sam.

"It was a beautiful warm evening last night, wasn't it? Did you enjoy your midnight swim?"

Sam felt her face grow hot instantly, and she turned beet red.

"Oh, my God," Sam gasped. "You saw me? I'm so sorry!"

Rachel burst into laughter, then she rested her hand on Sam's arm.

"Good Lord, don't be sorry!" she said. She smiled reassuringly at Sam, then leaned in close. "Personally, there's nothing I like better than a late night skinny dip. I wish I could get away with doing that, without it becoming a national scandal. Somebody may as well put that pool to good use. So, as long as you're here, you and your team are more than welcome to do so—after dark, of course."

At that moment, Hunter and Arjun entered the room. Rachel smiled and flashed another unobtrusive wink at Sam, before the two women greeted the new arrivals.

"Good morning, Ma'am," Hunter said, then he smiled at Sam.

"How are *you* this morning," Rachel replied. "I hope you and Terri are both recovered from yesterday's adventure."

"Thanks," Hunter answered. "I can't speak for her, but I'm good."

"Morning," Arjun mumbled. "I hope the coffee's fresh."

The last team member, Terri, appeared in the doorway and made her way to the table.

"Morning, everybody," she said. "Sorry I'm a bit late."

"Not a problem," Rachel answered. "As soon as you've all got some coffee and some food in front of you, we can get started."

Moments later, satisfied that everybody was ready, Rachel proceeded with their daily strategy session.

"If you don't mind, Hunter and Terri, I'd like to go back over some of the details of that Liberty Camp disaster yesterday."

"Of course," Hunter answered.

At that moment, Sam's cell phone vibrated on the table in front of her. She took a quick glance and frowned. A puzzled expression crossed her face as she read the cryptic note:

U dont know me but I cant reveal who I am. I know Jordan didnt set liberty fires. Somebody trying to frame her!

Sam had to resist the urge to answer the message right away, instead forcing herself to bring her mind back to the meeting.

"So, exactly what did the two Secret Service agents tell you?" Rachel inquired.

"Only that they were recalled to Camp David because of a bomb scare, and that somebody from DCMP would be there soon to replace them. Any idea yet on who called the Secret Service?"

"That's just it," Rachel answered. "They claim it was Nicole who made the call. She denies it, but they've played me the recording. It's definitely her voice!"

The jaws of Sam and her team all dropped open at once, their eyes wide with shock.

"I can't believe Nicole would be involved in something like that," Sam blurted. "And what do you make of the claim that a branch of the Brothers of Liberty were responsible for the kidnapping attempt? That's more believable for me."

"Within minutes of that claim going viral, Anna streamed an interview with Bryson," Rachel replied. "He was absolutely livid! He denied that *anybody* inside his organization had anything to do with it."

"Whether that's true or not," Terri added, "the whole incident's made him look bad, given that he insists that he's gone to great lengths to keep his protest peaceful. Not only has it damaged his credibility, but now Butler's FBI team is on his case about the gun stash that Hunter found. We've heard that Butler's with Robby and the Mayor right now, pushing for the DCNG to march in and shut down the Liberty camp."

Arjun, who had been silent up to this point, addressed the President.

"Do you believe Nicole?" he asked. "Like Sam said, it just doesn't seem like something she'd do. Why would she put her career on the line?"

"I know," Rachel concurred. "It doesn't make any sense to me either. But, the recording? I just don't know."

"This is a lot like Jordan's situation," Sam added. "We all know her, and breaking into the Liberty Camp to set fires isn't like her at all."

"Then how do we explain the security video?" Hunter asked.

A hush fell over the room for a moment while the group mulled his question. Finally, Sam broke the silence.

"There's something else I should tell you," Sam admitted. "I just got a weird text message, claiming that Jordan didn't do it—that she was framed."

Rachel's body stiffened and she sat up straight in her chair. A puzzled frown spread over her face.

"You're kidding! Do you recognize who sent it?"

"Nobody I know. But, there's something about all of this that smells rotten to me: both Jordan's video and Nicole's phone call. Anybody else feel that way?"

Rachel and the rest of the team all nodded their heads in silent agreement.

"What if we're going about this entirely the wrong way?" Sam continued. "Jordan's video and Nicole's phone call have convinced *everybody* that they're both guilty. But, what if they're telling the truth? What if they're *both* being framed by somebody?"

"Hmmm, possible false flag operations? An interesting theory," Hunter mused. "But by whom?"

"Exactly," the President blurted. "It's one thing to claim that somebody's conspiring to frame them, but we can't say that publicly without a stitch of evidence! I can't call in the FBI to investigate a hunch."

"It's an interesting theory," Arjun added. "But who would stand to benefit from seeing this standoff explode into violence? Bryson?"

"I don't think so," Terri volunteered. "We may not like his politics and his way of standing up for his rights, but he's mostly stayed true to his message of peaceful protest up until now, and he looked genuinely pissed on Anna's podcast last night."

"I agree," Sam said. "So, if both Jordan and Bryson are telling the truth, it's in somebody's interests to keep the left and the convoy fighting against each other. And it's a good bet that they don't want us to successfully negotiate an end to the standoff."

"Okay," Rachel replied. "But who?"

A long pregnant pause filled the room, until Sam finally broke the stillness once again.

"That's the million dollar question, isn't it. But maybe we don't need to figure that out, at least for now."

"Why not?" Terri mused.

"Well, I've been thinking," Sam answered. "There are countless spy novels, movies, and TV shows that hypothesize secret conspiracies by factions of the wealthy elite—capitalist conspiracies. Is it that far fetched to think that something like *The Da Vinci Code* or *Killing Eve* could be at work in this country, or around the world for that matter?"

"I don't like it," Rachel mused. "Isn't that exactly the kind of conspiracy theory that Bryson wants us to believe? Wouldn't we just be playing into his hand if we pushed something like that? And the business community in this country would think I'd lost my marbles if I even hinted at such a thing!"

The group went quiet again for a few moments until Terri broke the silence.

"I agree that we need to be very careful," she said. "But, a few of those convoy organizers might be ripe for planting that seed: people like John, Sean, Jess—maybe even Bryson and Norm—if we introduce the idea in the right way."

"Terri's got a point," Hunter added. "Most of them already think there's a big anti-freedom conspiracy out there. Maybe this is what we've been looking for. A way we can flip the script and give them somebody else to blame."

"I don't know," Rachel replied. "I just don't think I'm willing to take that risk. I'm definitely going to need some time to think it over."

SAM AND Arjun's black SUV wound its way through the streets of Washington, en route to the Unite the Left encampment. Already, they saw heat waves shimmering in the morning air above the asphalt, as the oppressive heat dome extended its grip over the entire eastern part of the continent.

"I'm not looking forward to leaving the AC in this car," Arjun commented.

"You're not kidding," Sam replied. "Spending the next hour or two under that tent is going to feel like being in a sweat lodge. And everybody's patience is getting thinner each day too."

"Do you really think they'll buy into your theory?" Arjun queried.

"We'll find out soon, but I feel like there's a good chance. The Unite the Left generally trusted Jordan and her coverage before that video went viral. I'm more worried about whether Bryson and the convoy group will buy in."

"Right, but that won't even be an issue for us if the left doesn't bite first," Arjun added.

Their SUV slowed as it neared the no man's land intersection between the two camps. Sam exited the vehicle first. She felt the heat's grip almost instantly, her lungs seemingly seizing up and trying to reject the moisture laden, super-heated atmosphere. Behind her, she heard Arjun emit a gasp as the heat struck him. She turned to him, made eye contact, and raised her eyebrows as their Secret Service escort exited the SUV ahead of them.

"Cross your fingers," she said, then they turned and followed their escort towards the crowd of onlookers and press that were already gathered at the camp's entrance. Once inside the encampment, Sam and Arjun immediately noticed a beehive of activity, as volunteers busied themselves setting up large cooling fans inside the mess tent. Other volunteers were testing portable misting units around the outside of the tent, near their events area.

The foursome made their way to the usual small circle of tables within the tent, where the group's organizers were already seated and waiting for them. This time, however, there was no video equipment in sight. Two large fans stood on either side of the circle instead, cycling back and forth slowly to help cool the participants. Arjun took his seat, but Sam remained standing in front of her table.

"Good morning, everybody. It's good to be with you again. I'm glad to see that everybody has lots of water in front of them. It looks like it's going to be another hot one."

"It's good to see you both again," Senator Delgado replied.

Nods and mumbles of agreement from around the circle greeted the pair of negotiators.

"Let's not waste any time," Sam continued. "But first, let's smudge, pray, and state our intentions for our meeting."

"A CONSPIRACY?" Stephen blurted. "You expect us to believe this *isn't* the work of MacDonald and the convoy? Come on, give us a break!"

"I'd like to believe you, Sam," Senator Delgado added. "But you need proof. Do you have any at all, even a little bit? Without that, you're going to come off as sounding just like Bryson and the conspiracy theorists."

Sam raised her eyebrows and shrugged her shoulders.

"Only that cryptic text message I read to you," she answered. "But, the President's ordered the FBI and Secret Service to examine Jordan's video and Nicole's alleged phone call more closely."

"You're sure you have no idea who sent you that message?" Dudley pressed.

"Sorry," Sam replied, shaking her head slowly from side to side as she spoke. "I wish I did."

"You know I like you, girl," Cecilia added. "But you ain't got nothin' to back y'all up!"

"Please," Arjun intervened. "Give Sam a chance and hear her out. The rest of us on the team—and the President too—were all skeptical at first, just like all of you. But we gradually realized that something about the intrusions on the Liberty Camp doesn't pass the smell test."

"I'm willing to listen," Danielle replied. "What else do we have to lose? Go ahead, Sam, convince us."

"Thanks, Danielle," Sam answered. "Everybody's jumped to the conclusion that Jordan and Bryson's Brothers of Liberty are guilty of the fires and the kidnapping attempt, respectively. But, what if they're not? Who else has a vested interest in keeping the left and the right at each others' throats?"

Sam looked around the circle at each person, letting her question hang in the air and settle in.

"The only answer I could come up with," she continued, "was that somebody, or somebodies, could be using the ongoing polarization of politics in this country to distract *everybody's* eyes away from the *real* issues. Like why the gap between rich and poor around the world keeps widening, and why increasing numbers of American families are lining up at food banks, losing their jobs, and losing their homes!"

"I think I see where you're going with this," Danielle interjected. "It's only the poor who are asking those questions, not people like me or my family who have money. It's not the big multinationals and their CEO's who keep making record profits, not to mention their obscene salaries and bonuses!"

"Exactly," Sam replied. "Do we all really believe that the wealthy elite cares which party controls the government, as long as that government doesn't interfere too much with their freedom to make insane amounts of money?"

"If we look at the history of this country," Arjun added, "who was it that really started to fight back against England in the Eighteenth century? It wasn't the poor man on the street. It was mostly the colonial merchants and businessmen who couldn't build the wealth they desired under Britain's rule. And it was those same people who didn't want to see a Constitution that created yet another strong government that could end up taxing them, just like Britain did. To them, freedom only meant one thing: the freedom to make as much money and to build as much wealth as possible, without interference from government."

"I think I get it," Kym interjected. "So the wealthy keep banging the freedom drum and selling that issue to the people, basically to keep us suspicious and discontented with government, so we won't go looking for ways to even the playing field between rich and poor?"

"Precisely," Sam proclaimed. "And the idea isn't new. Is it any coincidence that countless suspense novels, movies, and TV shows have hypothesized secret conspiracies by the wealthy elite? Like I asked the President, is it that far-fetched to think something like *The Twelve* in *Killing Eve*, or a Church and it's supporters—as in *The Da Vinci Code*—might be at work in this country, or even around the world?"

A relative silence descended over the circle as the organizers digested Sam's arguments, against the persistent background sounds of whirring fans and busy volunteers.

"I'm sorry, I'm not convinced at all," Cecilia declared, finally breaking the calm. "But, for the sake of argument, let's say our group *does* buy your theory. Just how are y'all gonna convince Bryson's crew to accept it? That's a whole other kettle o'fish."

Sam shrugged her shoulders, raised her eyebrows, and looked earnestly at Cecilia, and then at the other organizers.

"I guess we'll find out within the next hour or two," she answered. "All I can say is that trying to *convince* them will never work. Instead, all we can hope to do is plant some seeds of doubt, and then see if we can nurture them and get them to grow!"

WITH ARJUN now back at Camp David briefing the President on their morning meeting with the Unite the Left organizers, Sam and a single Secret Service escort sat in the Liberty Convoy mess tent, listening to a Lynard Skynard tribute band and keeping themselves hydrated. Finally, they heard the familiar rumble of Hunter's Harley approaching no man's land. Moments later, Hunter and Terri, accompanied by two very real and extremely serious Secret Service agents, entered the tent. As Sam stood and went to greet her colleagues, Bryson and the other Liberty Camp organizers filtered into the tent and took their places around their usual circle of tables.

Sam greeted Terri with a hug.

"Good tunes," Terri remarked, as she heard the band finish their performance. "Pretty close to the real thing."

"Yeah, not bad at all for a tribute band," Sam replied. She then embraced Hunter, who whispered into her ear.

"Things went well with Unite the Left?"

"As well as could be expected," she whispered in return. Hunter took her hand and gave it a squeeze.

"Good luck," he whispered. He released her hand and the trio made their way to the circle. Sam and Terri took their seats while Hunter remained standing.

When Bryson and the Liberty organizers saw Sam, their bored countenances lit up in surprise and they exchanged glances all around.

"Well, who da we have gracin' our presence today?" Bryson called out. "Williams must be gettin' desperate to be sendin' in a big-wig to blame us fer her team's security breach an' to threaten us!"

Anna, Norm, Sean, and Pastor Kessler smirked and chuckled at their leader's sarcastic remark.

"We're not here to threaten anyone, Bryson," Terri responded. "In fact, Sam's here for exactly the opposite reason. She firmly believes that you guys aren't responsible for the attempt to kidnap, or kill, Hunter and me."

The smirks on the organizers faces transformed into looks of curiosity at Terri's unexpected remark.

"But, before we hear what Sam has to say, I'd like to ask Hunter and Jess to lead us in smudging, prayer, and thinking on our intentions, as we've done before."

Jessica picked up a shallow bowl containing sprigs of sage from the desk in front of her, carefully lighting them as Hunter addressed the gathering.

"We are all here together in this sacred circle on the ancestral lands of the Nacotchtank and the Piscataway People, who have lived on this land for more generations than can be counted. We pay our respects to their elders, past and present. Please take a moment to consider your intentions, and to consider the many legacies of violence, displacement, migration, and settlement that bring us all together today."

Jessica made her way methodically around the circle, stopping before each organizer to wave the fragrant, sacred smoke over their torsos and heads. When she was finished, she remained standing in front of her desk. She snuffed the glowing sage and set her bowl down on the desk.

Bryson and Norm glanced at each other and rolled their eyes briefly, but they kept any sarcastic words to themselves. Jessica took her seat, and Hunter took control of the meeting.

"As Terri already stated," he said, "I don't think you're to blame for the attempted kidnapping. And neither does the President. But Sam has some ideas about who *could* possibly be responsible, and we're hoping you guys will give her a listen."

"No harm in listenin', I s'pose. Y'all okay with that?" Bryson asked.

Hunter looked around the table at the organizers, seeing mostly ambivalence on most of their faces, with the exception of Jessica.

"I'd like to hear what she has to say. What about the rest of you: Sean, Martin, John, Norm, and the Pastor?"

"Sure, why not?" Sean answered. "What've we got to lose?"

Bryson turned to Sam and gave her a condescending smile.

"Okay, dearie. Whatta ya got to say?"

Sam took a gulp of water and wiped the perspiration from her brow, then she cleared her voice.

"Thanks, everybody," she began. "Like Terri and Hunter said, I don't believe you guys had anything to do with the bomb threat on Camp David, nor with the security breach in your camp two days ago. And President Williams wants you to know that she doesn't believe it either."

"Okay, so who dunnit, then?" Norm interrupted. "Rumour on the web has it that it was that bitch, Davies—Williams' assistant."

"Obviously, Ms. Davies has denied any involvement," Sam replied, "especially in phoning the Secret Service to recall the security from this camp. But, there is some reason to believe that Ms. Davies' voice could have been faked."

The organizers all shouted in protest at once. Terri stood and raised both of her arms.

"Quiet!" she shouted. "Everybody, please calm down and hear Sam out!"

"Are y'all kiddin' me?" Anna retorted. "Williams must be pretty desperate if she's graspin' at straws like that. Y'all got any evidence?"

"Well," Sam continued. "It isn't just the kidnapping event that we're all questioning. Some other evidence has surfaced to suggest that the journalist, Jordan Marsh, may not have been responsible for breaking into your camp and setting the fires either, as earlier thought."

Shouting erupted again and a number of the organizers leapt from their seats. Jessica screamed out at the top of her lungs.

"Quiet, everybody! Just calm down and let her finish!"

The yelling faded gradually, while Sam waited patiently.

"Since both the security video of Ms. Marsh's alleged break-in, and the recording of Ms. Davies' voice in the Secret Service call, were leaked over the net, the whole world believes they were both guilty, right?"

The organizers looked around at each other and then started to nod in agreement.

"But," Sam continued, "doesn't that seem awfully coincidental? And suspicious? What if somebody out there is trying to frame *both* of them?"

Bryson let out an exasperated huff and shook his head from side to side.

"That's one wild story, dearie!" he blurted. "Y'all expect us to believe that? Who the hell would wanna fuck with us an' the progs at the same time? It don't make no sense!"

"Hold on, everybody," Jessica shouted. She waited a moment for the din to die down. "Let's assume you're right, Sam. Let's assume that there *is* some other conspiracy. You got any ideas who might wanna stir the pot and blow up this standoff?"

"I'll throw that question back to the group," Sam answered. She looked around the circle at each of the organizers. "Who do you think benefits most from constantly pitting the right against the left in this country? Who might want to distract the people from *real* issues like the widening gap in standard of living between the rich and the poor?"

Silence reigned again around the circle while the organizers gnawed on the bone that Sam had thrown to them. Finally John ventured a guess.

"The rich?" he answered meekly. "Big business? Multinational Corporations?"

"Ah, Jesus!" Norm bellowed. "Sorry Pastor, 'scuse my French. That's jus' the same old prog bullshit, blamin' the rich fer everythin'! If it weren't fer big business, there ain't no jobs an' no money tricklin' down fer everybody to live!"

"What do you say to that, John?" Terri interjected. "Are you and your family seeing any of that Big Box money in your town?"

"Hell no!" he answered, his usually meek manner giving way to anger. "They're chokin' the life outta my grocery store! An' it ain't just my store. It's the local hardware store, the bakery, the clothing stores. They're all gone now. Stores that supported families fer generations, all dried up. Ain't but precious few dollars tricklin' down in the town neither. The wages them big box stores pay, most of 'em part time, ain't nuff to live on!"

"So where's all that money going?" Hunter interjected. "Any ideas?"

"To wealthy shareholders and overpaid executives," Jessica retorted. "To offshore tax havens, so the tax burden falls more and more on poor folk who are just tryin' to scratch out a livin'!"

"Fuck this noise!" Bryson exploded. "Y'all ain't got a shred of evidence fer any o'this! There ain't no laws 'gainst makin' money in America, far's I know. It's the American dream! It's guaranteed in the Constitution!"

Sam and the team paused for a moment as Norm, Sean, Martin, and Pastor Kessler shouted their agreement with Bryson. Jessica caught Sam's eye, and Sam nodded for her to take the floor again.

"The American dream, eh?" Jessica hollered over the racket. "If all us poor people just put our minds to it and work hard enough, we can *all* be rich? How's that working out for each of you? You gettin' rich drivin' truck, Norm? I don't know about the rest of you, but I'm sure as shit not getting rich on the reservation. Look around, assholes! The American dream is a fuckin' myth, and it's gradually killing us all!"

Martin Lee, who hadn't taken his eyes off his phone for the past ten minutes, finally came to life.

"You're full of shit, Jess! I've worked my ass off at Pro Gaming. I earned seven figures last year and I'm damned proud of it. I'm proof that the American dream's real and still alive."

Jessica's head shook slowly from side to side and a look of pity crossed her face.

"I'm happy that it's worked out for you, Martin. But, don't you see? Just because one person makes it, it doesn't mean everybody can! The stats show that for every one of you who got rich from gaming, I'll show you a thousand who didn't!"

"Of course, you bitch!" he shouted. "That's life. There's always going to be winners and losers!"

"Is that what you want in this world, Martin? A handful of huge winners and the rest of the world just big losers? You are so out of touch with the reality of the rest of the world!"

"Okay, everybody!" Sam called out. "Let's all take a deep breath. I didn't come here today to argue politics. I just came to let you know that both the President and I believe you. We don't think you had anything to do with the attempted kidnapping, unlike most people on the internet, who seem to think you did. And we don't see any reason for continuing to pause our discussions about ending the standoff."

She turned and looked directly into Bryson's eyes.

"You're right, Bryson. I don't have any hard evidence of a conspiracy. But, is it any accident that books, movies, and TV shows, over many decades, keep floating variations on conspiracies of the ultra-rich? Is it too far-fetched to think that something like that could be at work in this country? That the wealthy might be working in the shadows to manipulate our democracy to their benefit? To fool us into believing that we're losing our freedom to big government?"

Sam continued to stare into Bryson's eyes, and he fidgeted anxiously under her constant gaze.

"Well, I dunno," he finally answered. "I s'pose it *could* happen, but y'all ain't got no evidence. Show me some proof an' maybe I'll believe ya."

"Fair enough," Sam replied. She looked around the circle at the rest of the group. "Anybody else have anything to add?"

Sam looked around the circle once again and saw only negative nods or shrugging shoulders. Her eyes met with Terri, and then with Hunter, who both gave her a positive nod to proceed.

"If that's the case, Hunter and Terri will be back tomorrow to continue hearing what you want to pass along to the President. Thanks for meeting with us, and for listening to what I had to say today."

RACHEL LEANED back in her chair and took a deep breath. Sam and the rest of the team waited while the President took a moment to ponder their reports of the daily proceedings. Only the gentle, steady whir of the Laurel Lodge's air conditioning in the background broke the momentary calm. Finally, Rachel took another deep breath and sat upright again.

"Well," she said, "on a positive note, the jury seems to be out on Sam's theory in both camps, and neither side said they wouldn't keep meeting with you."

"That's what we're thinking too," Sam replied. "We're cautiously optimistic at this point."

"But," Rachel countered, "on the other hand, it sounds like you almost pressed Bryson and his supporters too much. Would you agree?"

"For sure," Hunter answered. "These are deeply emotional issues in both camps. We knew that before we started. It's so easy to get sucked into debating politics and losing sight of our strategy: listening, being empathic, and letting them think they're smarter than we are."

"I noticed Sam growing more uncomfortable with the emotions that were building around the table," Terri added. "But I think she caught herself and did a great job of cooling tempers and getting back to our strategy. And Hunter and I will definitely have our work cut out for us, continuing to convince Bryson that we still believe him."

Sam turned to Rachel, shrugged her shoulders, and her eyes met with the President.

"I'd say we've sown some seeds of doubt in both camps and bought some time," she said solemnly. "But, we're going to need some serious proof, or we'll start losing our street cred on both sides. Have you heard anything yet from Captain Robby? Anything new on the Jordan video and Nicole's phone call?"

Rachel pursed her lips and shook her head from side to side.

"Nothing yet. They're having to call in some experts to examine those recordings more closely. Robby has assured me that examining their integrity is high on his list. But he was also blunt. The pressure on him and on the Mayor is building, especially from businesses, residents, and tourist attractions in and around the two camps. There's growing support for calling in The Guard, and he's not sure how long we can hold them off."

Sam shook her head slowly from side to side as she listened to the President's warning.

"I still can't believe that either Jordan or Nicole would do something so stupid to endanger their careers. I realize we haven't known them for long, but the whole thing just smells fishy."

NICOLE SAT on a barstool in the dark, dingy downtown Washington pub. With a full second glass of Cabernet in front of her, she was making small talk with the bartender, but glancing anxiously at her watch every minute or so. The alcohol was helping to keep her calm, but was also making her clearly tipsy. The bartender, a black woman about the same age as Nicole, took stalk of Nicole's expensive white suit, jewelry, and high maintenance figure, which automatically pegged her as a fish out of water in this part of town.

"Waiting for somebody?" the bartender inquired.

"Yeah," Nicole mumbled. "Am I that obvious?"

"Well, honey, let's jus' say I don't get too many girls lookin' like you, hangin' out in this fine establishment."

Nicole nodded up and down and allowed herself a chuckle. Out of the corner of her eye, she saw the front door open, letting in a bright flash of daylight. The silhouette of a man came through the door and moved towards the bar. As the door closed and Nicole's eyes readjusted to the room's dim lighting, she recognized the dark figure as that of Matt Butler, who approached the bar and took a seat beside her.

"What'll it be sir," the bartender asked.

"Got any good IPA's on tap?" Butler answered.

"Not exactly a popular choice in this neck o'the woods," she countered.

"Make it a Bud, then," Butler decided.

While the bartender carefully dispensed the foamy brew from a tap in the background, Matt turned to Nicole.

"You know we're not supposed to meet outside of work," he whispered. "Pick up your drink. We're moving to a booth."

"Here you go," the barkeep announced, as she slid his beer across the bar. Matt grabbed the beer glass and used his free hand to grasp Nicole by the elbow as he stood up. He steered her to a dark corner at the rear of the bar, where they slipped into a booth, with its decrepit and sticky red vinyl upholstery.

"So, what was so fuckin' important that you had to see me?" Matt hissed.

"You know damn well why I called you here. I don't know how you did it, but you used me! You used my voice somehow to call the Secret Service!" Nicole replied, her voice rising in volume. "Now I'm screwed. I'll never work in this town again!"

"Keep it down, Nikki! You want the whole world to hear us? You're over-reacting."

"Over-reacting?" she hissed back. "Are you effin' kidding me? I just came from meeting with Williams this morning. I'm suspended with pay, pending further investigation into that phone call they say I made!"

"So, what did you tell her?" Matt inquired.

"I told her that somebody must have faked my voice somehow, but I didn't have a clue who would want to try to frame me," she continued. "What was I going to say: that my good friend, the FBI agent, set me up? How would I prove that?"

"Don't worry so much, Nikki. This is all going to blow over. I promise."

"Why would you and your mysterious bosses think that throwing me under the bus was a good idea?"

Matt's demeanour changed abruptly. He reached across the table and grabbed Nicole by the wrists, jerking her body across the surface so that the two were face to face.

"I told you to shut up so the whole world doesn't hear you," he hissed. "Just shut the fuck up and do as you're told. Take one for the team, and I've been told to tell you that you'll be taken care of."

"What the fuck does that mean?" Nicole scoffed. "Take care of me? And what if I don't shut up?"

Matt's grip on her wrists tightened. His jaws clenched and veins in his temples became visible.

"If you know what's good for you, you'll shut up and ride this out," he threatened. "Let's just say this won't end well for you, if that's *not* the road you choose to go down."

He released his grip on her wrists and smiled. Still angry and shaking with fear, she rubbed and tried to soothe her reddened wrists.

"Be a good girl, Nikki," Matt continued. "You have no idea who you're dealing with. And don't ever call me again! We'll contact you if we need you."

Matt slid out of the booth, stood up, and dropped some bills on the table. He headed towards the exit, nodding to the bartender on his way out.

Still shaking after being manhandled, Nicole tipped up her glass and drained the remaining Cabernet. She paused for a moment in a vain attempt to gather her wits, then she lowered her head into her hands. Unable to stem the tears of frustration and hopelessness that were now streaming from her eyes, she sobbed uncontrollably.

A GRIM look of dejection etched deep, dark lines onto Rachel's forehead, along with crow's feet at the corner of her eyes and downward creases at the corners of her mouth. A knock came from the office door and she glanced at her watch.

Almost midnight. Might as well get this over with.

"Come in!" she called.

A female Marine, Nicole Davies' replacement, ushered Sam into the room.

"Ms. Bower, Ma'am," the Marine announced. "As you requested."

"Thank you," Rachel replied. "That will be all Sargent. Have a seat, Sam."

Sam noticed the stern look on the President's face immediately.

"Is anything wrong, Ma'am?" Sam asked.

"That would be an understatement," Rachel answered. "I just had a call from Cecilia Robinson. She informed me that the Unite the Left organizers have lost confidence in your negotiations—and in the White House, I might add—given the allegations against Jordan Marsh and my Chief of Staff, Nicole. They've reiterated their initial claim that they won't leave the streets until Bryson and his convoy leave."

Sam's jaw dropped open from shock and her eyes opened wide.

"Where did that come from?" Sam asked. "Unite the Left still seemed on board when we met with them this morning. I don't understand. What changed between now and then?"

"I wish I could give you an answer, Sam. I'm just as shocked as you are. I suspect that Danilenko and ANTIFA are aligning themselves with the Mayor, and with those who want to see the Guard brought in to clear the streets. But I can't be sure at this point."

"Do you think it had anything to do with my alternative conspiracy idea?" Sam offered.

"Cecilia did hint at that," Rachel answered. "Apparently there's a lot of protesters in their camp that weren't on board like their organizers: people who don't like the idea that there's another bigger conspiracy out there. They don't think you're taking The Brothers of Liberty's claims of responsibility for the attempt on Hunter and Terri seriously. They feel like you're taking Bryson's side now."

"That's bullshit, ... er, I'm sorry, Ma'am. I mean a load of crap!"

Rachel managed a weak smile at Sam.

"I know, I understand," she said. "But perceptions are everything in this business. It puts me between the proverbial rock and a hard place. I still have confidence in you and your team. But it's not just Cecilia and Unite the Left. It's public opinion. It's the Mayor and Congress too. They're all starting to lose their patience with me and the negotiation process. I'm afraid we're running out of time, Sam."

"Damn!" Sam muttered. "Just when I managed to buy some time from Bryson and his organizers. So, what does that mean for us? Are we done? Are you sending us home?"

Rachel paused to ponder Sam's question.

"No, at least not yet," Rachel answered. "We still haven't heard back from Captain Robby's investigation into the security video and Nicole's alleged phone call. I'll try to buy you at least a couple more days until that happens."

"And in the meantime?" Sam asked.

"Your entire team had better focus all your energy on Bryson and the convoy. Unite the Left won't be an issue if you can still manage to talk the convoy into going home."

"I see," Sam said, sighing. "Now that I've planted the seeds of a different conspiracy with them, it's all in Hunter and Terri's hands. All we can do is hope that they've built enough trust to keep the convoy engaged."

"It's a long shot, for sure," Rachel concluded. She glanced at her watch again. "But, it's getting late. I guess all we can do is try to get a good night's sleep, and see what tomorrow brings."

SAM STOMPED into Camp David's Birch Cabin, which she'd been sharing with Terri since their arrival, and slammed the door behind her. Seconds later, Terri's head poked out of her open bedroom door.

"What's up, Sam?" she asked. "Something wrong?"

"You could say that," Sam replied sarcastically. "We just got screwed over by Cecilia Robinson and Unite the Left!"

"Whaaaat?" Terri cried. "What the hell happened? They were still on board with the negotiations just a few hours ago."

"Seems like a lot of their protesters weren't happy campers after hearing about my alt-conspiracy diversion. They even accused us of taking Bryson's side in the dispute."

"Well, that sucks! What about us? What happens next?"

"The President's going to give us a couple of days to continue working with the Liberty camp, while she's waiting for the test results on the Jordan video and the Nicole phone tape."

"You're pretty upset. Want to sit and de-stress for a while?"

"Thanks, but no. I've gotta go for a walk to try and clear my head. I shouldn't be long."

She wheeled around and stomped from the cabin, letting the door slam behind her again. The hot, clingy evening air wrapped around her the second she stepped back into the night, providing little relief from the unrelenting daytime heat. In the sky in front of her, she noticed a hazy full moon and only a few of the sky's brightest stars that were able to penetrate the humid atmosphere. She wandered slowly along a pathway and was soon deep in thought, ruminating on the President's bad news. After a few minutes, still unable to stop obsessing, she pulled her phone from the pocket of her shorts, tapped on a contact, and listened for the call to connect. A confused voice finally answered.

"Hello?"

"Rose? ... It's me, Sam. Sorry it's so late, I need to talk."

"It's really you?" Rose asked, still a bit confused. "This *is* unexpected. Is everything okay?"

"No, not really. I just met with the President, and apparently the Unite the Left camp has lost confidence in us. Everything we've worked so hard for—it's all starting to fall apart!"

Sam's eyes turned red and she wiped a stray tear from one eye.

Finally waking up, Rose's voice now took on her usual calm, reassuring tone.

"I'm sorry to hear that, dear. But, how are *you* doing?"

"Shitty!" Sam muttered. "Everybody was right! I'm stupid and naive. I have no right being here, and I had no right to drag Hunter and the others into this. I'm doing my best to please everybody else, but I'm losing myself. It all feels so hopeless!"

The dam burst and Sam wept, her tears now flowing freely.

"Now, now, my dear," Rose said comfortingly. "Calm yourself. Take some slow, deep breaths."

Sam followed Rose's instructions by taking one slow breath after another, until the tension gradually drained from her mind and body. Her tears slowed to a trickle.

"You must have patience with yourself before you can be understanding of others," Rose said. "They will only learn or change their minds when they see the need for change for themselves."

Finally beginning to relax, Sam sniffled and allowed herself a brief chuckle.

"I know, you can't make a horse drink. But, you know me. Patience isn't my strong suit!"

Rose laughed, relieved that Sam was starting to calm down.

"I know, dear. Just try to remember that you're not responsible for the stalemate in Washington. It's been hundreds of years in the making, and you're not going to change these people overnight."

"You know me too well," Sam answered. "I just want to have a positive impact on other people."

"Tell me, dear, is the sky clear down there tonight? Can you see the full moon?"

Sam gazed up into the night sky.

"It's hazy, but I can still see it. And it's really peaceful out here in the country tonight. It kinda reminds me of my first Full Moon Ceremony at your lodge."

"You've got some sage and tobacco with you, don't you?" Rose inquired. "Why not make your own Full Moon Ceremony? Let Grandmother Moon shine her light on you and help unburden you."

Sam paused and allowed Rose's idea to sink in.

"I may just do that. Thanks Auntie, I really needed to hear your voice."

"I'm glad I could help, dear. Just one more thing. Spend more time with Hunter—smudge and pray together. It will help to keep you both grounded. Have a good night. Love you."

"Thanks, I love you too! Bye."

Sam replaced her phone in her pocket and walked back towards the Birch Cabin. Moments later, she returned, carrying her ceremonial materials. She found a grassy area beside the pathway, then she laid the items out beside her on the dewey grass. She dispensed some tobacco into an elongated porcelain tray, and then lit the tobacco with a lighter. As the first wisps of smoke wafted into the air, Sam inhaled some of the sweet, fragrant fumes. She opened her arms wide and spoke a silent prayer.

"Hear me, Grandmother Moon. I bring you this sacred gift and offering. I thank you for the gifts of Creation and everything on Turtle Island that gives us life. Please hear my intentions."

She paused to gaze up at the faint moon and stars for a few moments while the tobacco in the tray slowly burned itself out and turned into glowing orange embers, before burning itself out and turning black. She laid some sage on the tray and set it aflame, watched the sage glow and smoulder, then she picked up the tray and waved the smoke with her hand, so that it covered her torso and then her face and head.

"Grandmother Moon, shine your light on me, and help me to let go of this burden of needing to fix everybody else. Give me your guidance, and the strength to accept that others can only fix or change themselves if they see the need. It isn't my burden to bear."

As Sam finished her prayer, a dark figure appeared out of the darkness in front of her. As it drew nearer, she recognized Hunter.

"I hope I didn't scare you. Terri just told me about the Unite the Left decision. I saw your flame and heard you praying. Is it okay to join you?"

Sam smiled, happy to have somebody to help her share the evening's disappointment.

"Sure, would you like to smudge with me?" she asked.

He smiled, nodded, and sat down on the cool grass beside her. She picked up the tray and waved the ceremonial smoke over Hunter's torso, then his face, and finally his head and eyes. When she finished, she handed Hunter the tray and he did the same for her. When he finished, he extinguished the glowing sage embers and set the tray down on the damp grass. Sam laid down on her back on the grass and Hunter laid down beside her.

"It's so calm out here," Sam said softly. "It's hard to believe all the shit that's happening in those camps as we speak."

"Yeah," Hunter answered. "I suppose we could be sent home soon. It's been a crazy ten days. Let's just try to forget about it for one night, okay?"

Sam remained quiet and seemed distant for a moment or two. Then, all of a sudden, she sat up and looked at Hunter.

"Screw it all!" She shouted. "You wanna do something really crazy? C'mon!"

Before he could even answer, Sam grabbed his hand and dragged him to his feet. She ran in the direction of the Aspen Lodge and Hunter followed close behind.

"Where are we going?" he huffed.

"You'll see," she shouted. "Follow me!"

They arrived at the Presidential swimming pool, and Sam immediately started peeling off her clothes until she was stark naked. Stunned by her sudden change in behaviour, Hunter watched silently as Sam dived into the pool, then surfaced a moment later.

"What are you doing?" he said, trying not to raise his voice and attract attention. "Are you crazy? What about the President?"

"Don't worry about her. She said we could do this anytime. Besides, this is how The Creator made us, and when are we ever going to get another chance to say we skinny-dipped in the President's personal pool? C'mon, I dare you!"

Sam splashed water at Hunter and that was enough to seal the deal. He peeled his clothes off and dived in after her. He headed straight for Sam's legs, trying to pull her off balance and dunk her. She squealed joyfully just before he succeeded in dragging her under. When they surfaced, they laughed and splashed each other for a while, before Sam finally laid back in the water and allowed herself to float. She gazed up through the haze at the moon and the few visible stars. Hunter followed her lead and they floated silently for a few moments.

Sam allowed her mind to drift back to her two recent near-mystical experiences: the first by the South Saskatchewan river less than two weeks ago, and the second in the President's pool only last night. On both occasions, she felt the water caressing every square inch of her body and supporting her, as it was at this moment. She remembered the mysterious calls of the crows and the whispers of the ancestral spirits that left her feeling stronger and supported from within.

Finally, Hunter's voice broke the silence and brought her back into the moment.

"Do you feel like talking about us?" he asked.

"Sure," she answered. "I'm sorry I've been avoiding you."

"So, what's up?"

"You know I like you. I like you a whole lot," she admitted. "And sometimes I miss you and need you so much."

"But you're afraid, right? So, what is it that you're so afraid of? Are you afraid I'm going to abandon you like your dad did … and then your mom too?"

"Maybe, a bit," she answered hesitantly. "But there's something else. I just can't shake the feeling that I'm still searching for my path in life."

"And you don't know if that path includes me?" he asked.

"Something like that, I guess. I think I'm afraid to get too close in case *I* decide to leave *you*. And I don't know if I could bear doing that to you!"

Hunter nodded his head up and down slightly and paused to digest Sam's confession.

"There are no guarantees, Sam. Every relationship is a risk, and you can't reap the rewards if you don't jump into the fire and take a chance."

"I know," she replied hesitantly. "But right now, I don't have the focus or the energy to think about us. Can we talk more whenever this is over?"

She took Hunter's hand while she waited for his reply, and the couple remained side by side, floating silently on their backs in the water. After a few moments, Hunter stopped floating and stood waist-high in the rippling turquoise water.

"Okay, but you know I love you, right?"

Sam stopped floating and took to her feet, facing him and extending her arms. Their naked, vulnerable bodies came together and their lips found each other, locking into a deeply passionate embrace and kiss. After a long moment, Sam reluctantly disengaged, swam silently to the edge of the pool, and climbed out. Hunter followed closely behind. As they both struggled to pull their clothing over their drenched bodies, they both lost their balance and fell over. Their laughter filled the evening air. When they finally managed to get dressed, Sam took Hunter's hand and they walked hand-in-hand.

"I guess we'd better get back. It's going to be a short night," Sam said.

"Back to reality," Hunter added. "I wonder what it has in store for us."

"Besides chaos and uncertainty, you mean?"

"Yeah, besides that," Hunter replied.

They laughed together as they talked and continued walking into the Camp David darkness towards their respective lodgings.

CHAPTER 14—NOTHIN' BUT THE TAIL LIGHTS

SAM YAWNED and then took another sip of coffee, as she struggled to stay awake and focus on their morning strategy session. The team sat in a circle around the table, listening to the President's Zoom call with Captain Robby.

"So you're absolutely certain?" Rachel asked.

"Yes, our expert gives us a ninety-five percent probability that the person in the Liberty Camp video was Jordan Marsh, and that the video is legitimate," Robby replied.

"Not one-hundred percent?"

"No, but there's never any way to prove it with that degree of certainty. In this case, she admitted that the resolution on most of the videos isn't great. But, that's to be expected from infrared security images at night. She couldn't find anything in the metadata to indicate tampering," Robby explained.

"But it's possible that somebody with excellent technical knowledge could tamper with the metadata?"

"I suppose that's possible," Robby admitted, "but if they're that skillful, it's very difficult to detect."

"I see," Rachel said, the tone in her voice reflecting her disappointment with Robby's news. "So, where does that leave us, Captain?"

"Well, we arrested Ms. Brooks first thing this morning, and she was formally charged with arson and conspiracy to incite a riot. The judge set bail at fifty thousand, so Brooks is free until her arraignment next month."

Sam gasped and looked around the table at the rest of the team, who were looking at each other in dismay.

"I see," Rachel answered. "And what about the voice analysis of the Secret Service call?"

"Still waiting on that expert, Ma'am. He's been delayed by an unexpected health issue. He says he hopes he's better by tomorrow, and hopes to have something to report later tomorrow or the day after."

"Is that it for the bad news, Captain?" Rachel asked.

"Well, no Ma'am, I'm afraid not," he answered. "The Mayor is definitely feeling the pressure to call in the Guard. And I hear she's calling on a lot of friends in the House and the Senate to put pressure on you."

"I see," Rachel answered, her face seemingly resigned to the inevitability of calling in the DCNG. "Thanks for the heads up, but I've already heard the rumours. And Senator Crowley's already on my calendar for later today. So, if there's no more bad news, that will be all."

"Thank you, Ma'am. Good day."

Sam heard the Zoom call's hangup sound and saw Rachel close her laptop. The President raised her head to address the team.

"Well, you all heard that. Hunter and Terri, looks like you need to make the best possible use of your time today. At this point, it seems everything depends on you!"

JESSICA HID behind a supply trailer at the far end of the Liberty Camp, looking around nervously to ensure she wasn't being seen or heard. She tapped the call button on her phone, waited, and then spoke in a hushed voice.

"I just heard the news, babe. How are you holding up?"

"Nothing I can't handle. I've got a month to figure this out before they arraign me."

"You don't need to do this, Jordan," Jessica implored. "We were together that night, so you have an alibi!"

"I won't do that to you, Jess. You're the only voice of reason in that camp, and some of them actually listen to you. It's not just me who needs you there: it's the whole country that needs to hear your voice."

"But what about you, babe? I can't stand by and see what they're all doing to your reputation!"

"Don't worry about me. You know I went through worse when I came out as trans, and I'll get through this too. Just one thing, Jess, and this might seem really random. Do you ever get the feeling you're being followed?"

A flash of concern shot across Jessica's face.

"Followed? Where did that come from? Not me, but do you think *you're* being followed? Are you in any danger?"

"No, nothing like that. It's just a weird sensation. You know, like when you feel the hair standing up on the back of your neck sometimes? And there's a woman, a face I've seen a few times. It's probably nothing. Probably just coincidence and nothing to worry about."

"That doesn't sound like nothing. You've got to go to the police. You've got to tell them about us, and about that woman!" Jessica begged.

"No, Jess!" Jordan said firmly. "I won't do it. I won't expose you, and that's final! I gotta go to Camp David. I'm making one last pitch to the President about the need to protect my sources. I'll talk to you later."

The call ended. Jessica peeked around the trailer once more to make sure nobody was watching or listening, before sneaking out and making her way back towards the mess tent.

Meanwhile, ten blocks away on Constitution Avenue, in front of the Federal Courthouse, Jordan stood beside her motorcycle. She stashed her phone in her pocket, donned her helmet, and mounted the bike. Seconds later, the engine roared to life and Jordan steered the vehicle carefully out into traffic, grateful for the cooling breeze as she headed northeast for Camp David.

BRYSON LEANED back in his chair and laughed heartily, along with the other Liberty Convoy organizers, as they sat at their circle of desks on the convoy's performance stage. With the proceedings now being live-streamed again, Anna stood nearby, directing her production team.

"I told y'all so!" Bryson bellowed. "The effin progs don' have any reason fer bein' here, b'sides obstructin' our rights 'n freedoms to gather an' protest!"

"Send in the guard to round 'em all up an' arrest 'em all!" Norm chimed.

"The Dems accuse *us* o'creatin' a rebellion?" Bryson continued. "Hell, from the very beginnin' all we wanted was fer Williams to sit down an' talk with us! An' so far, no disrespect intended to y'all, we still ain't heard from 'er!"

Hunter and Terri exchanged glances, and Hunter nodded for Terri to respond.

"I hear you!" she answered. "You all know my story by now: how I grew up dirt poor and abused. I never thought anybody would listen to me either. So, the only thing I *could* do was to rebel when I was old enough: to leave home and make my own way. I think we all have a little bit of rebel in us."

She turned to Hunter.

"Even you, eh Hunter?"

He laughed and looked around the circle at the convoy organizers.

"Yeah, even me. Sometimes we should all stand up for ourselves and our beliefs, even if it means painting some statues red, like I did."

"Sometimes I wonder if we all aren't hard-wired to rebel," Jessica added. "Maybe it's Mother Nature's way of gettin' us to see new ways of doin' things. Hell, if our ancestors hadn't tried new ideas, we all might still be livin' in caves without fire."

"So far, you've all given me and Terri some examples of how your Constitution isn't working for you," Hunter said, "and the President is very interested in finding out why."

"Y'all make it sound like we ain't fer the Constitution! But we all came here to defend it!" Sean commented.

"That's what I thought too," Terri replied. "But now I'm really confused. On one hand, I hear that you all want to defend the Constitution. But, on the other, we hear you talking about times when it's not working for you. Anybody care to help me out here?"

"Well, fer one thing," Bryson answered, "We want our rights'n freedoms. We don' need govermints that do nothin' but make laws to take them rights'n freedoms away from us. Or to take all our hard-earned money fer taxes, so they kin pay lazy people to sit on their asses instead'a workin'!"

"I hear you," Hunter replied. "But, did you know that the only reason that countries, including America, create constitutions is because they realize they *need* a government to help keep people organized, and they need a set of rules for how that government operates? So, if you don't want government, there's no need for you to have a constitution to defend."

"That don't make no sense!" Norm hollered. "The Constitution's there fer us, to spell out our rights'n freedoms! We don' need no help organizin'. We kin do that fer ourselves!"

"Really?" Jessica countered. "Who's going to organize who builds towns, cities, roads, water supplies, hospitals, housing, or fire departments? Who's goin' to decide what we all use for money, or how we get food to people? And I guarantee that if you were to lose your home to wildfires or floods, you'd be the first to be standing in line, shouting for state or federal aid!"

"She's right, Norm," John added. "We can't all live off the grid an' live off the land. We gotta have *some* rules an' basic services. An' we gotta have laws an' governments to make 'em, an' fair taxes to pay fer 'em."

"If I'm hearing both sides of the argument correctly," Terri interjected, "it sounds like a constitution is a balancing act. On one hand, you all need a government to make rules to help organize society. But on the other hand, you need a constitution to make sure those rules are fair, and that they ensure you're all free to live your lives—as long as you don't break the rules or interfere with other peoples' rights and freedoms."

"Well said, Terri," Hunter added. "A constitution *is* a balancing act. If the rules get too restrictive, we lose too many freedoms and we end up with dictators, like Hitler and so many others. Or, if it goes the other way, the rules get too loose and we end up with chaos and confusion."

"Sounds to me," Jessica interjected, "like in order to make a constitution work, there needs to be a lot of compromise. Am I right?"

"Absolutely," Hunter answered.

"Well, the reason we all came here's cuz we think there's too many fuckin' rules," Bryson blurted. "There's too damn' many people tellin' us how to live our lives, an govermint's takin' away our American dream!"

"Damn right," Norm echoed. "Take gun laws, fer instance. It ain't guns kills people, it's the crazies out there that kills 'em! Tryin' to control guns ain't goin' to do anythin' till we do sumthin' bout mental health an' round up all them crazies."

"I hear what you're saying, Norm," Terri replied. "But I just wonder how we do that. Do *you* think you're qualified to say who's nuts and who isn't? Because I'm certainly not."

"Course not," Norm said. "We gotta leave that to the experts."

"Okay," Terri continued. "So who's going to be the experts? The guy at the gun registration office? Your family doctor? A psychiatrist? Just ask Sam Bower, she's a psychologist. There's no practical way, either financially or technically, to screen out or to control for everybody who's got a mental health problem, let alone try to determine which of them might take a gun and use it to kill people."

CONSTITUTION AVENUE

"Absolutely," Jessica agreed. "The people who say it's impossible to control guns, don't realize it's infinitely more difficult to predict or control what people are going to do with them. People are the wild card! And are you going to be the one who forces people to get mental health exams against their wills, adding even more government rules?"

Pastor Kessler, who had so far remained silent, stood and held up his Bible.

"Govermint, laws, an' courts is nuthin' more than men pretendin' to be God an' sittin' in judgment of others!"

He waved his Bible for all to see.

"We already have all the rules we need, right here'n the words of The Almighty! An' the only laws we need to live by are His Ten Commandments! It's only God who will judge us all in the end!"

"I get it, Pastor," Terri replied. "You believe passionately in Judgment Day, and that only God has the power to judge. Am I right?"

"Absolutely," the Pastor confirmed.

"So, I'm confused, Pastor," Jessica interjected. "If I get pregnant and decide to have an abortion, only God has the right to judge me? And you don't mind if I leave that decision between me and God?"

"That ain't what I said, young lady!" the Pastor hollered. "The Lord commanded us *all* to live by those commandments, an' he commands all his believers to make sure everybody follows his word!"

"So *now* you're saying that it's every Christian's job to sit in judgment?" Anna shouted, jumping into the fray. "You're contradicting yourself, Pastor. Which is it? Is it God's job to judge, or is it *your* job or mine? Why not just leave the abortion up to my conscience and let me deal with the consequences? I'm not forcin' *your* wife or daughter to have abortions. I just wanna leave that decision between me and God on judgment day!"

"Y'all are twistin' my words! That's Satan castin' his spell on y'all!"

"Okay, okay!" Terri intervened. "I think we're getting off track here. I hear you both, and I think you've both given us a good example of freedom of religion, and how even the most basic freedoms in our constitutions are a difficult balancing act."

"I agree," Hunter said. "But if I can, I'd like to go back to what Bryson said earlier when he said that government is taking away the American dream. Can you say more about that? Maybe give us an example?"

"Sure can!" Bryson boomed. "When I was young, we were the richest country in the world. Why? Cuz we was allowed to foller our dreams, earn a decent wage, an' spend it however we damn well pleased. But things 'ave been slidin' downhill ever since. Govermint's been takin' more an' more taxes an' makin' it harder an' harder fer a guy to get ahead."

"I understand where you're coming from, Bryson," Hunter said. "But, did you know that the Constitution's Sixteenth Amendment actually embeds the right of the U.S. Government to levy taxes to support its mandates? And because that's the case, taxes are perfectly legal and *don't* actually infringe on your Constitutional rights and freedoms."

"Hmmph," Bryson grumbled. "Who knew?"

Martin Lee, who had been totally absorbed in his phone during the conversation, lowered the phone and sat up.

"In any case, I disagree with Bryson," he said. "We're all still free to follow the American dream. Just look at me. Where else in the world would I have the opportunity to work hard, to master my trade, and be rewarded by a seven figure income? Where else can we walk into a restaurant and order whatever we want, or go into a store and buy whatever we want?"

"You are so out of touch with reality, Martin!" Jessica admonished. "Have you ever been in any of this country's urban ghettos? Or ever asked the person cooking your meals how little they get paid? Or seen how people like me live on a reservation? I've got news for you. The streets of America are *not* paved with gold, and there isn't opportunity everywhere! The gap in standard of living between rich jerks like you and the poor is growing larger every day.

And wherever the streets still seem to be paved with gold, I guarantee that they were built on the backs of this country's poor!"

"She's got a point, ya know," John continued. "Look at my hometown an' how the big box store's earnin' millions while it's squeezin' the life outta local businesses! An' what about you, Sean? How's yer ranch doin'? How's the American dream workin' out fer you these days? What about you Norm? You earnin' seven figures drivin' truck yet? All I know's that yer so-called American dream's killin' me!"

Hunter and Terri made eye contact again, and he nodded an unspoken message.

"Wow, thank you everybody for speaking so openly," Terri said earnestly. "You've helped to show how the Constitution really is a very delicate balancing act that is wide open to different interpretation by every American. I think your examples will help the President understand that you all have different valid things to say to her. But I assure you that she's dedicated to hearing you, and on trying to balance the Constitution in a way that benefits the most possible Americans. I hope we have the opportunity to meet with you again tomorrow. Thanks, once again."

"And in the meantime," Hunter added, "I'd like you all to think long and hard about what you all said here today, and how it all seems to fit with Sam Bower's thoughts from yesterday. Do you think it's possible that the world's wealthy elite are sitting back and laughing while your convoy, and Unite the Left, fight each other over our democracy and the Constitution? Because I don't see *anybody,* on either side of this dispute, pointing the finger at *them*!"

"ENOUGH'S ENOUGH, Rachel!" Senator Crowley shouted.

Emotions were heating up rapidly, and patience was wearing thin in the President's Aspen Lodge office, as the political tension rose and the air conditioning in the Aspen Lodge struggled to keep up with yet another day of stifling heat and humidity. Sam and Arjun watched as the President mopped her forehead, which was glistening with perspiration.

"Public support for you in the polls is sinking faster than the Titanic," Crowley continued. "Even worse, both Houses have lost confidence in your ability to govern. Whatever battle you're fighting, you're losing. It's time to cut your losses and do something to end this mess!"

"So, what would you have me do, Sherman? If I call in the Guard, I guarantee we'll have a situation worse than Ottawa 2022. And they didn't have firearms, as we suspect the convoy does. Let's also remember our own January sixth riot, just a few blocks from here. I *do not* want to be responsible for the resulting violence and loss of life!"

"What other options do you have, Rachel? This negotiation plan of yours is going nowhere."

"Excuse me, Ma'am," Sam interjected. "May I say something here?"

"Of course," Rachel answered.

"With all due respect, Senator, I disagree that our negotiations with the two camps are going nowhere. Both groups were just beginning to trust us when the arson and attempted kidnapping happened, and neither of those events had anything to do with what was going on in the negotiations."

"How can you be so naïve, young lady?" Crowley asked. "You're just another idealistic, young, anti-establishment radical. Do you have any proof whatsoever for this conspiracy theory of yours?"

"We're still waiting for an FBI voice analysis expert to weigh in on the alleged Nicole Davies phone call, sir," Arjun replied. "And Sam received an anonymous tip from somebody who claims they have proof that Jordan Brooks didn't break into the convoy camp. We need more time to prove that somebody else might be responsible."

The Senator turned his attention back towards the President.

"Time is a luxury you don't have, Rachel. Can we speak privately?"

Rachel nodded to Sam and Arjun, who stood up and headed for the door.

"I'll call for you if I need anything else," she said. The pair left and closed the door behind them.

"This has been going on for eleven days. The Senate and the House are giving you forty-eight hours to do something decisive, or Congress is going to ask for your resignation! You know I've always supported you, Rachel, but I can't this time. They'll settle for nothing less than giving both camps an ultimatum: twenty-four hours to start leaving the streets, or you will have no choice but to call in the DCNG!"

Rachel paused, mopped her forehead again, then exhaled slowly while she processed Crowley's dispatch from Congress.

"Okay, Sherman, you win. If nothing new comes to light in the next two days, I'll issue the ultimatum to clear the streets."

The Senator, his face now wearing a victorious smile, rose to his feet and extended his hand. Rachel stood up and accepted his handshake.

"I'm glad to see that you're finally coming to your senses, Rachel. I'll pass the word along to Congress."

The veteran Senator pivoted and made his way out of the office. As the door closed behind him, Rachel slumped back into her chair. She let out a huge sigh of frustration.

You did your best, Rachel. Just looks like it wasn't good enough.

MOMENTS LATER, Rachel was still at her desk, still wearing the same look of frustration and resignation on her face, when there was a knock on her door.

"Come in!" she called.

Rachel's new Marine assistant entered the room.

"Sorry to bother you, Ma'am. Ms. Jordan Marsh has asked to see you."

Rachel heaved another long sigh before replying to the request. "Very well, send her in."

The Marine disappeared, then ushered Jordan into the office a moment later.

"Thank you for seeing me, Madam President," Jordan said.

"What can I do for you, Ms. Marsh," Rachel answered.

"I'm begging you to believe me, Ma'am. I had nothing to do with breaking into the convoy camp and setting those fires. I was meeting with a source that night, and I believe it was my source who sent that anonymous text message to Sam on my behalf."

"I see," Rachel replied. "But your source isn't willing to come forward to the police to vouch for you?"

"No, Ma'am," Jordan admitted. "You know that protecting our sources is a pillar of my profession. If I betray that trust, nobody will ever trust me with a story again. My career will be over."

Rachel paused to mull over Jordan's plea.

"Do you think your source would make a written statement, and give us some idea of how we could verify their story?"

"I'm sorry, Ma'am. That would put my source in imminent danger of harm. I couldn't do that."

Deep furrows appeared on Rachel's glistening brow as she pondered the situation.

Is her source inside the Liberty Convoy camp?

"I think I may understand your dilemma, Ms. Marsh," Rachel hinted finally. "I really do. But, you're facing criminal charges over this, and I can't be seen to be interfering in your case. If you have proof, you need to contact Captain Robby or the DA's office, and you'll need to reveal your source to them, or take your chances with a jury. I'm afraid that will be all. Now, if you'll excuse me, I have another meeting in a few minutes. Please see yourself out."

"Yes, Ma'am, thank you for seeing me."

Dejected, Jordan turned around and exited the room into the hallway, where the Marine escorted her to the Aspen Lodge's exit. She descended the stairs and walked back towards the parking lot where she had parked her bike. She donned her helmet, mounted the bike and ignited the engine, which rumbled to life again. As she guided the bike out through the security gate, its tail light blinked erratically while it rumbled into the distance and disappeared from sight.

MATT BUTLER occupied his regular booth in the dark corner of the bar, smoking a cigarette, drinking a glass of whiskey, and listening to the ominous clanking and grinding of the building's ancient AC system. As he exhaled, the front door opened and sunlight flooded briefly into the establishment. The silhouette of a woman entered and moved towards Matt as the entrance door gradually closed. As Matt's eyes readjusted to the bar's dim lighting, he confirmed that the woman was his hired fixer, Elena. She stopped briefly while her eyes adjusted to the darkness, then she made her way towards Matt and slid into the booth, opposite him. He raised his hand and waved to the bartender.

"Vodka shot for the lady!"

The pair watched as the middle-aged black woman at the bar poured the shot and carried it to the booth. She looked at Matt's nearly empty glass.

"Another whiskey?"

"Not now," Matt answered curtly. They waited for the woman to return to the bar, where she was out of hearing range.

"Congratulations on the success of your recent jobs," Matt said quietly, raising his glass.

"Boodymz darovy," she replied, before throwing the shot back in a single gulp. "To your health, and to mine. So, vat is so urgent you need to see me again so soon?"

Matt leaned across the table to get closer to Elena, then he looked over at the bartender. Satisfied that she was busy with her work, Matt continued, his voice hushed.

"We've got a bit of a problem," he began. "My FBI bosses are bringing in a voice analysis expert to examine Nicole's phone recording. Should I be worried?"

Elena gave a non-committal shrug and pursed her lips together.

"Maybe, maybe not," she answered, her voice also hushed.

"What do you mean, maybe?" Matt hissed.

"Is never perfect in such vork. Metadata is not problem. AI not perfect, so depends on how good is your expert. Is no problem vit video we make, no?"

"Well, no," Matt admitted. "No problems with the video, at least not yet. But I can't take any chances. I need you to make sure that expert can't make it to Washington for at least two days."

"Relax Butler, my source's vork is best there is. I not vorry."

"Relax?" Matt blurted. "It's my ass that's in a sling if your work isn't the best! You wouldn't want my FBI friends to accidentally find out what you and your friends do here in America, would you?"

Elena shook her head disapprovingly.

"Be careful, Butler. Ve have good arrangement between my bosses and yours. They not be happy if you—how they say? Stir up nest of bees?"

"It's a hornet's nest, not bees."

Elena shrugged ambivalently, then slid off her seat in the booth and stood up, indicating to Matt that their discussion was over. She remained for a moment, hovering over Matt.

"Vatever," she said. "You call me again when you have big fish to cook. This not big fish. Thanks for drink."

With that, Elena wheeled around and strode confidently towards the bar's exit. Behind her, an anxious and agitated Matt waved at the bartender.

"You can bring me that whiskey now."

JORDAN'S EYES flickered open, then panic set in while her eyes searched the room and her brain tried to figure out where she was. The room was becoming light, but the sun hadn't yet breached the horizon. Seconds later, she heaved a sigh of relief as she remembered that she'd fallen asleep in the hotel room. She rolled over and saw that Jessica was still asleep beside her. She resisted the urge to run her hands over the curves of her lover's body, opting instead to let her get some more sleep.

Without warning, her phone vibrated three times on the night stand beside her. She rolled back over the other way, fumbled for the phone, then brought it closer so her bleary eyes could squint at the screen. Her eyes popped open and her jaw dropped. She sat up straight in disbelief, then read the text message again, waking up Jessica in the process.

Look at the convoy camp video again—look carefully at your tail light.

Jordan's eyes took on a faraway look as she pondered the significance of the text again. After a moment, her eyes grew wide and her face lit up.

"Fuck me!" She muttered. "How could I be so stupid!"

Still groggy, Jessica sat up and put her hand on Jordan's shoulder.

"What is it, babe?" she said, still half dazed. "Something wrong?"

Jordan thrust the phone in front of Jessica's face.

"Read this!"

Jessica's eyes scanned the text.

"What the ...?" she uttered. "Who sent this? What's your tail light got to do with anything?"

"It's my get out of jail free card, Jess!" she shouted. "It proves I didn't break into the convoy camp, and I don't need to get you involved!"

Jordan snatched her phone back from Jessica's hand and gave her a huge smack on the lips, then she jumped out of bed, grabbed her clothes, and started dressing hurriedly. She stopped, half dressed, to type out a reply to the mystery messenger.

Who r u? How do u know this?

"Hey, Jess, remember when I asked if you ever thought you were being followed?" Jordan asked.

"Yeah, why?"

"I'm almost certain now. I think somebody *has* been following us!"

Her phone vibrated again in her hand.

Not important. Just watching out 4u. Tell Williams asap!

"Holy shit!" Jordan gasped. "Why would somebody be watching and helping us!" She finished dressing hastily.

"Who's *somebody*," Jessica inquired. "And where are you going?"

"Back to Camp David! I need to see the President again! This changes everything!"

She leaned over Jessica, this time giving her a more passionate kiss.

"Gotta go, babe. I'll call you and explain more later—as much as I can, anyway!"

Jordan grabbed her helmet and rushed from the room, slamming the door behind her. Jessica rolled over, reached for her phone, and glanced at the time.

"Shit!" she yelped. "I gotta get back to the camp before somebody misses me!"

RACHEL SAT quietly on the Aspen Lodge patio, taking advantage of some morning sun before the relentless heat and humidity climbed for day twelve of the standoff. She sipped at her morning cup of coffee, reading paperwork as she prepared for the busy day ahead. Her Marine assistant exited the lodge onto the patio, clearing her voice to get the President's attention as she approached.

"Sorry to bother you so early, Ma'am, but Ms. Brooks is out front again. She's got another Marine from the security gate with her, and he says it's urgent."

Rachel's forehead wrinkled into a frown, partly at the interruption, but also partly out of curiosity.

"Show her in."

"Yes, Ma'am," the Marine replied, then she disappeared back into the lodge. Moments later, she re-emerged and ushered Jordan, followed closely by the Marine from the security gate, onto the patio.

"Ms. Brooks, I thought I made myself clear at our last meeting. What is so important that you felt the need to disturb me again?"

"You need to see this," Jordan blurted. "I received an anonymous text message this morning, and it proves my innocence!"

She handed the phone to the President, whose frown deepened as she read the message string.

"So, what's this about your tail light?" Rachel asked. "And how is it related to the security video?"

"If you'll excuse me, Ma'am," the security gate Marine interjected, "I've seen the security video, and that bike isn't Ms. Brooks' bike."

"And how do you know that?" Rachel pressed.

"Ms. Brooks' bike has a loose tail light that flickers," he continued. "The first time she came to Camp David I pointed it out to her. I just checked her bike and she still hasn't fixed it. Her tail light still flickers whenever she rides it."

Rachel sat bolt upright in her chair and she turned her attention back to Jordan.

"You still have that video on your phone?"

"Yes, Ma'am, Just a moment."

Jordan swiped and tapped her phone a few times, then handed it back to Rachel, who tapped on the video's icon and watched intently for a few seconds. All of a sudden, she gasped and her mouth dropped open.

"It's not flickering at all! But it's still *your* face ..."

Suddenly, Rachel understood. She handed the phone back to Jordan.

"Damn! Somebody's deep faked that video!"

"That's what I've been trying to tell you all along, Ma'am. And it means that Sam Bower is right. Somebody out there *is* trying to stir up trouble in *both* camps. Somebody doesn't want to see this standoff resolved peacefully!"

Rachel's head shook slowly from side to side. She pursed her lips and her facial muscles tensed as she attempted to hide her anger.

"It was a Goddamn false flag operation! And they managed to completely discredit you in the process," she added. "My deepest apologies. I hope you can forgive me."

"Thanks, I appreciate that, Ma'am. But what about Nicole? If they were able to fake my face in a video, they could just as easily have faked her voice too!"

Rachel paused, still shaking her head from side to side as she thought. At the same time, Jordan's phone vibrated again. This time, the text message was from Jessica.

Bryson & militia meeting now. Lots of anger and talk of storming other camp. TELL POTUS NOW!

"You need to see this, Ma'am!"

Jordan thrust her phone back into Rachel's hand. She glanced at the message, then looked up immediately at her new assistant.

"Get Captain Robby on the phone, right now!" she commanded. "And then the Mayor and Senator Crowley!"

MATT BUTLER'S face was as red as the ancient vinyl seats in his regular booth at the rear of the bar. Elena sat stiffly across the table, her posture and her face both rigid.

"You fucked up, Elena!" he hissed, trying hard not to draw the attention of two early patrons who were sitting at the bar. "You were supposed to make that video foolproof!"

Elena shrugged defiantly.

"I tell you my contact is skilled. Is no guarantee he is perfect!"

Butler's phone vibrated on the table, the screen showing that the call was from Senator Crowley.

"I gotta take this," he explained curtly.

"We got ourselves a problem, a big one!" Crowley shouted, his voice clearly audible even though Matt's phone was not set to speakerphone. "I just met with the President, an' she's pissed!"

"If this is about the video," Matt replied, "I'm dealing with it right now."

"Fuck the video!" Crowley bawled. "She's now convinced that the Davies phone call was a fake too, an' that is one huge concern for those above us. They just got one question for you. Is there any chance Davies can link you to the fake call?"

Matt's eyes grew wide with panic and he swallowed hard.

"Don't worry, she can't prove anything," he answered contritely.

"Don't give me that bull crap, Butler," Crowley continued. "She doesn't need to prove anything. All she needs to do is point a finger in your direction! So, I have a message for you. Do whatever you need to do to make sure that doesn't happen! Understand?"

"Yes, sir. I'll take care of it."

"Good!" Crowley snarled. "And make sure there aren't any fuckups this time!"

The phone went dead. He swallowed hard and then looked across the table at Elena.

"You just got a chance to redeem yourself. I've got another job for you."

Elena's face lit up with a satisfied, smug smile.

"You mean *vee* have chance again, no?"

THE POLITICAL tension in the Liberty Convoy camp, along with another day of back-breaking heat and humidity, was building rapidly as the sun climbed higher in the morning sky on yet another day of the heat dome. Emotional fuses, getting shorter by the day, were being tested around a picnic table in the convoy's mess tent, where Bryson and the organizers were surrounded by an unruly delegation from Bryson's own Brothers of Liberty militia. The disgruntled delegation, ten men and two women dressed in camouflage gear, and sporting sidearms and determined, angry faces, listened intently as their spokesperson directed his frustrations towards Bryson.

"We been tellin' ya all along that ANTIFA's plannin' on attackin' y'all!," he hollered. "Are you gonna just sit here an' wait fer somethin' to happen, or what?"

The radical mob raised their fists and shouted their support for their spokesman. Bryson waved a hand in the air, waiting for the group's clamouring to wane. Finally, he cleared his throat and stood to address the newcomers.

"We all suspected they might try pullin' a false flag op," he bellowed. "Those woke bastards've bin playin' us. They bin hidin' ANTIFA in that camp all along, and nobody ain't been payin' any attention!"

Both the organizers and the militia members thrust their fists into the air and shouted insults about the Unite the Left camp. Norm, Pastor Kessler, and Sean had joined the mob in their derisive jeers.

"So what're we gonna do 'bout it?" Norm yelled.

"If they wanna street fight, then we'll giv'em a street fight!" Sean added at the top of his voice.

At that moment, Jessica stood and issued an ear-splitting whistle that stunned the angry mob into silence.

"Calm down everybody!" she screamed. "Let's not get carried away!" She turned her attention towards Bryson.

"So, exactly what is this 'credible intel', and where did it come from?"

"I been scourin' the net since I started plannin' all this," he yelled back. "Everythin's been sorta quiet since we got here, but a whole lotta

CONSTITUTION AVENUE

noise started up on Signal this mornin', an' it's bin spreadin' like wildfire in the last coupla hours."

"Yeah, it's all over X an' Instagram now too. Even FOX news says it's real!" Norm bellowed.

Jessica shook her head dejectedly from side to side.

"That's nothing but a bunch of unsubstantiated rumours," she countered. "To be credible, you need some reliable sources. Lots of them. Can you even give me one name, Bryson?"

"Look bitch!" he answered, glaring angrily at Jessica for challenging him. "Da y'think I'm stupid? No whistle blower's gonna blow their identity. Da y'think they want the NSA breathin' up their asses like what happened to Asange and Snowden?"

"I knew it. You got nothing," Jess screamed back. "All you got is a bunch of anonymous sources that could be anybody! Could be some college kids with nothing better to do than pulling everybody's leg. Are you willing to start another January sixth? Maybe even getting somebody killed, or ending up in jail for insurrection and treason like a shit load of them did after January sixth?"

One of the women in the militia stepped forward and thrust her face directly in front of Jessica's.

"I believe Bryson's sources, an' we're willin' to fight fer our freedom, bitch!" she screamed. "Do y'all got the balls to do that fer yer country?"

Frustrated, Jessica paused and took a deep breath.

"Look!" she answered, lowering the volume of her voice. "I'm just sayin' that we should try to verify the rumours before we do something we all regret. That's all."

She looked around the table, and then stared directly in Bryson's direction.

"What about that FBI agent that hangs out when the President's negotiators are here. What's his name?"

"Ya mean Butler," Bryson answered. "We ain't seen 'im 'round here since b'fore them negotiations stopped. An' what's he got to do with anythin', anyway?"

He stopped in mid sentence and cocked his head to one side. "What's that sound?"

The group went silent. Almost immediately, the sound of helicopters could be heard in the distance, gradually getting louder and moving closer by the second. A moment later, they heard vehicles roar into the Constitution Avenue no man's land between the camps, and screech to a stop. Another armed militia member rushed into the mess tent, out of breath.

"It's DC riot police!" he shouted between breaths. "Lots of 'em, at both camps! Somebody found out 'bout yer meetin'."

"Fuck!" Bryson bellowed. "How'd they find out so fast!"

Jessica's phone vibrated in her pocket. In the confusion, she pulled it out to take a quick glance. Without hesitating, she emitted another ear-splitting whistle. Everybody around the table succumbed to their reflexes and jumped, then fell into stunned silence.

"Listen to this," Jessica called out. "The President's just released a video on all the social media platforms. She's called in the riot police, and she's sending her negotiators to both camps this afternoon. Says they need to brief both sides on some urgent new developments!"

CHAPTER 15—CHANGING TIDE

BOTH THE deadly afternoon heat, as well as the emotional tension in the Liberty Convoy mess tent, could be cut with a knife. Tall cooling fans had been erected around two large picnic tables that were arranged end-to-end to accommodate Sam's team and the organizers. At one end of the tables, Arjun stood beside Sam. Hunter and Terri sat on either side of Sam and Arjun, while Bryson, Norm, and the remaining Liberty Convoy organizers sat along both sides and the other end of the tables.

"Okay," Sam said. "The President and my team thank you for meeting with us on such short notice."

"Yeah, so what's so important that Williams needed y'all to see us right away?" Bryson said sarcastically. "Is she steppin' down?"

The rest of the organizers, with the exception of Jessica, broke into spontaneous laughter and directed smug smiles in the team's direction.

"No," Sam answered calmly, "it's about the break-in and the arson in your camp, and about the attempted kidnapping of my team members. We now know that somebody wanted all of you in this camp —and in the Unite the Left encampment as well—to believe that Jordan Marsh was responsible for the fires. And President Williams wants you to know that she firmly believes that nobody in this camp was behind the kidnapping plot. It's become obvious that somebody out there—outside the two camps—is trying to make the President *and both sides* in this standoff, look like chumps. So, the big question is this: who stands to benefit most from having our negotiations break down, and from a continued polarization of politics in this country?"

Only the constant whir of the large fans could be heard, as silence descended over the group and the organizers looked around the table at each other. Finally, Jessica broke the silence, directing her words at Sam.

"The other day, you suggested that if there's a conspiracy in this country, it could be the wealthy elite—corporate America," she said. "Why would they have any interest in keeping the country divided, especially if it could negatively affect American companies and the economy?"

Shaking his head, and unable to contain his frustration, Bryson banged his fist on the table.

"This here convoy ain't got nothin' to do with the economy or big business!" he shouted. "It's 'bout the politics of defendin' the Constitution an' makin' sure the govermint don't take away our rights an' freedoms!"

"Actually, Bryson," Arjun interjected, "that's a popular misconception. For America, politics has *always* had everything to do with economics, even long before the Boston Tea Party, the War of Independence, and the Constitutional Conference."

"Whatta ya mean?" Norm blurted.

"Well," Arjun continued, "When it comes to independence and freedom, there's alway been two sides that have radically different meanings for those two important words. On one side, you've had the poor working man, who just wanted to be free from the oppression of King George and the wealthy English aristocracy. They just wanted their own government: one that would treat them fairly and humanely. One that would work towards making a better life for everybody in America, especially the poor. On the other hand, you had the plantation owners and merchants, who wanted the freedom to trade and make as much money as possible, without interference from the King, or their new government.

Jessica held up her hand and Arjun nodded to acknowledge.

"So when it came to making rules for the Constitution, it was basically a fight between the rich and those who were advocating for the poor?"

"That's an oversimplification, but you've got the basic idea," Arjun answered.

"I don't understand," John added. "I always thought that if businesses flourished, the money trickled down and everybody was better off. Am I wrong?"

"In theory, it sounds logical," Arjun replied, "assuming—and that's a huge assumption—that businesses and the wealthy give back to their employees and their communities, helping to make everybody's life better. But, unfortunately, history is starting to show us that the more prosperous the corporate elite becomes, the more they justify accumulating even more wealth. So, instead of willingly giving back to employees and communities, the rich are getting richer and the poor are getting poorer, all around the globe."

"I think I heard somewhere," Jessica added, "that Capitalism is just a crazy belief that the greediest of men will somehow act for the greater good of everybody else. So, history is showing that we're crazy for still believing that?"

"That's certainly one way of saying it," Arjun answered.

"Then how did that happen?" Jessica continued.

Terri flashed Arjun a nod and a look to indicate that she had something to add. He nodded back for her to take over.

"It happened," she replied, "because the wealthy have sold us a grand illusion—the myth of the American dream—that if we all work hard enough, we can all be rich, like them! They've created a pop culture that glorifies being rich and famous, so that we'll continue to hope that we can be just like them. You only need to watch *Entertainment Tonight* or *Shark Tank*, or read *People Magazine* if you don't believe me!"

"What're y'all bitchin' about, Terri?" Anna intervened. "Y'all got yer own business, from what I hear. Y'all gotta be makin' big bucks!"

"Terri's no different than you, Sean, Bryson, Norm, or John," Hunter interjected. "She's an independent small business owner just like you guys. And I know for a fact that she isn't rich. Her business has its ups and downs, just like yours. But let me ask you guys: how's the American dream working out for all of *you* right now?"

Once again, a hush fell over the group while Hunter's question sank in. Finally, John broke the temporary quiet.

"Maybe you gotta point there," he said. "The dream sure ain't workin' fer me an' my town anymore!"

"When we started these meetings," Arjun continued, "every one of you pointed out areas where your Constitution and the American dream weren't working for you. Maybe instead of you guys blaming the left, and them blaming you, maybe you should be pointing the finger at a Constitution and a system that is such a bad compromise, that it does nothing to protect hard-working Americans like you. Maybe it's time you guys decided to work together to change the system—and the Constitution—so that they both work better for all of you!"

"Okay," Jessica blurted, "if that's the case, what are we all doin' here? Where do we go from here?"

"Well," Sam answered, "President Williams wants you to know that she's willing to listen to suggestions from both sides in this standoff for changing the system. She'd like us to continue meeting with both sides to see if we can find some common ground for making those changes. Are you guys willing to get back to the table to do that?"

Once again, the organizers looked around the table at each other, waiting for somebody to speak. Finally, it was Bryson who broke the silence.

"I'm willin' to giv'er one more shot," he said. "My business ain't makin' the big bucks either. An' I ain't got nowhere else to go, so whatta we got to lose?"

ONE HOUR later, across no man's land on Constitution Avenue, Sam, Arjun, and Jordan sat informally around a picnic table in the Unite the Left mess tent. As of yet, Jordan and her production assistants weren't live streaming this meeting, but Sam and the President both agreed that it was important for Jordan to be present, now that she was vindicated and above suspicion.

"On behalf of this committee," Cecilia said," I hope you'll accept our apology, Jordan. I'm personally ashamed that I rushed to judge you so quickly."

"Thank you, Cecilia, and the rest of you as well," Jordan answered. "Given the nature of the deep fake evidence, I probably would have done the same if I'd been in your shoes. I hope we all learned a valuable lesson about the dangers of AI, and how easily it can be misused to undermine our democracy."

"Does this mean you'll be working with Anna again to stream the meetings?" Kym asked.

"Absolutely. I've received the President's blessing to finish the job I started with Anna."

"I'm glad to hear it," Kym answered. "By the way, any idea who's behind the text messages that you and Sam received?"

"Not at all," Jordan replied, shaking her head as she spoke. "All I know is that we must have a guardian angel out there somewhere who finds it necessary to watch over us!"

"So, where does that leave us, folks?" Senator Delgado interjected. "Any signs that the Liberty Convoy is ready to pack up and go home?"

"No," Sam responded. "But the good news is that Bryson's willing to get back to the table again."

"That's a big surprise," Dudley blurted. "Why the sudden change of heart?"

"I think he's a guy who doesn't like being embarrassed by somebody else," Sam answered, "and the deep fakes, especially the attempted kidnapping, definitely made him look suspicious."

"So what do you guys think?" Arjun said. "Are you all willing to give it one more go as well?"

Sam, Arjun, and Cecilia looked around the table at the other organizers, seeing only affirmative nods from the group. Cecilia turned to Sam.

"Looks like we're all on board. When do we get back to work?"

"The sooner the better," Sam replied. "But the President has asked us to change things up a bit. Hunter and I will see you all back here tomorrow morning at ten, while Arjun and Terri will meet with the Liberty Camp at one. Thanks everybody, I think that's all for today."

As people stood up from the table and the meeting broke up, Jordan hurried over to Sam. She looked around to make sure nobody was looking directly at them.

"Can I have a word with you?" she said, her voice hushed.

"Sure," Sam replied, "What's up?"

Jordan pulled Sam aside so that they had their backs to any lingering organizers. She pulled out her phone, tapped the screen, then held it out for Sam to see.

"It's another message!"

As Sam read the message, her jaw dropped open in shock.

Keep ur eyes & ears on Butler FBI. He's not all he seems to be!

"What the ... ?" Sam muttered.

"My thoughts exactly," Jordan whispered. "If Butler or the FBI is involved in this somehow, we've got a big problem!"

JORDAN WIPED the perspiration from her forehead as she busied herself with setting up her streaming equipment to start off the thirteenth day of the standoff. The air in the Unite the Left tent was already thick with humidity, and was heating up rapidly. Jordan's tank top was already sticky and clinging to her body.

I hope we get those thunder showers this afternoon. Maybe it'll cool things off and dry things out.

Out of the corner of her eye, she noticed Sam drift into the tent, followed by Hunter and some members of the organizing committee. Just as she was about to refocus her attention to her work, Matt Butler entered the tent. The hair on the back of her neck bristled and she felt self-conscious. A stream of questions stampeded through her consciousness:

Does he know I'm watching him? What happens if he does? What do I say?

She heard Sam's voice in the background, and managed to bring her focus back on ensuring her equipment was all functioning.

"Okay, everybody! Can we come to the table to smudge and pray?"

As Sam's team and the organizers settled into their circle of seats, Jordan unexpectedly found herself standing next to Butler in the background as the proceedings got underway. Totally unprepared for the uncomfortable silence, her mouth opened and she couldn't help herself.

"Well, look what the cat dragged in!" she whispered. "Where have you been hiding lately? And more to the point, what are you up to, now that the deep fakes have been uncovered?"

Shit, Jordan! How lame was that? Way to make yourself look suspicious!

The look on Butler's face made it clear that he was not amused by her comment.

"Very funny, Marsh," he answered sarcastically. "You know the President wants me involved in the Bower team's security, alongside the Secret Service. Why would I have been here while the talks were on hold?"

Butler's response pressed a button that instantly triggered Jordan's ire, causing caution and tact to fly out the window.

"Security?" she hissed. "Wow! Great job you did keeping Hunter and Terri safe over at the Liberty Camp!"

"Fuck you," Butler retorted defensively. "You know that was a Secret Service fuck-up!"

She nodded her head in mock agreement.

"Right," she said. "See if you can find anybody who believes that!"

Butler flipped her the bird, turned, and made his way to the breakfast area to refill his coffee cup. He returned a moment later, taking up a position away from Jordan, but where he was still able to watch Sam and Hunter finish the smudging ceremony.

"I'm so glad to be with you all again," Sam began. "Because Hunter has firsthand information about the Liberty Camp's perspectives, the President has asked him to share his observations today, while Arjun visits their camp to share your perspectives with them."

"Thanks, Sam," Hunter continued. "We have a lot of contentious issues to discuss today. But as we do, let's try to remember those issues where we found common ground with the other camp: keeping American families safe, freedom of speech, freedom of Religion and Conscience, and so on."

"Thanks, Hunter," Sam replied. "That said, we may as well start off by dealing with the biggest issues. Does anybody have any ideas how we can address gun control with the Convoy crowd?"

Sam heard lots of murmurs as she watched the organizers talking with each other. Kym was the first to put up her hand.

"I'll start," she said. "As you all know, I've been personally affected by two mass shootings, and I've been travelling the country, trying to change people's minds about guns. But over time, I've come to believe that I'll never be successful with that approach, because of the existing partisan divides. So, I'd like to propose another viewpoint, one I call a *Third Road*. It's a road the looks at the issue from the perspective of Family Safety."

"I'm not sure I follow," Cecilia declared.

"I'd like to propose to the conservatives that we accept their right to own firearms, but hand the responsibility for managing guns over to the states and local governments, who are more directly responsible for local public safety. Doesn't it make more sense to manage guns in big cities differently than we would in rural areas?"

"I agree," Senator Delgado answered. "But how does that address the assault rifle issue?"

"Well, the Constitution already gives Washington control over the Armed Forces and State Militias. Why not amend the Constitution slightly to also give Washington control over military-style weapons as a whole, as part of that mandate? At the same time, amend the Second Amendment to give individual states the responsibility for laws involving all other types of firearms in their jurisdiction. That way, we're not taking away anybody's rights: we're just shifting the responsibilities to make gun laws more sensible."

"Handing over gun laws to the states seems like an awful lot for us to give up," Dudley commented. "Is there anything we could ask the right to give up in exchange?"

"It's not asking a lot if we make it sound like both sides are gaining something, instead of giving something up," Hunter replied. "In return, you could suggest something like we have in Canada: giving the states control over issues like health or education as well, but with some strings attached. For example, you could suggest that Washington have the right to set up a non-partisan Federal electoral commission so that national elections for the President, the House, and the Senate would no longer have different rules and procedures in each State. You could also suggest that Washington have the right to set country-wide standards for health and education, in order for the States to get Federal money to help fund their State health and education programs."

Danielle raised her hand, and Hunter gave her a nod.

"So, we'd offer to let the states regulate health care and education, but they'd need to abide by Federal standards for providing access to quality public education, or access to contraception or abortion?"

"Exactly," Sam answered. "But you might want to emphasize the first part, while downplaying the second."

"That makes a lot of sense," Idris volunteered. "But what about the issue of equal rights for all?"

"That brings us back to asking for another amendment," Cecilia replied. "One that's never been ratified and likely never will. This country is so divided, none of your proposed Constitutional Amendments would ever pass. And we haven't even talked about electoral reform, voter rights, or Supreme Court reform yet! How do you propose to approach Constitutional Amendments on *those* issues with the right?"

"That is the key question, isn't it!" Hunter admitted. "We think our only hope is to get Arjun and Terri to link each and every Convoy beef to weakness in the Constitution that they defend so feverishly. We need to help them see that it's so vague and compromised in so many ways, that it's not worth defending as it stands."

"What do you think the chances are of *that*!" Delgado blurted.

"Realistically," Hunter admitted, "Not too good. But if we can make their list of beefs really long, we'll ask them what Constitutional changes they would suggest instead, in order to address their issues."

"There's one other important approach," Sam added. "Terri's going to try to sell the right on the notion that it's too easy for the wealthy to control government. She'll try to get them to blame the wealthy for everything that's wrong. And wouldn't they like to change the electoral system so their voices are truly heard, and so they have more control over their destiny?"

"Well, I'll be interested to see how they respond to our suggestions, but I ain't too hopeful!" Cecilia concluded.

At that moment, Sam happened to glance at Jordan, who was staring in the direction of Matt Butler. Sam followed her eyes and saw that Butler was engaged in an animated phone conversation, and his face displayed a combination of frustration and concern. As she watched, Butler glanced briefly in Jordan's direction, then his attention turned back to his phone. Sam looked at Jordan, who shrugged her shoulders. At that moment, the sound of Hunter's voice brought Sam back into the moment.

"Sam?" he questioned. "Is that about all for today?"

"Uhh, yeah," she stammered. "I think you guys have come up with some concrete proposals for the Convoy to consider. Let's see if they propose anything to the President that might end this standoff soon—maybe even as soon as tonight. Thanks everybody, we'll be in touch to keep you up to date."

The organizers and Hunter rose to their feet and moved away from the table. Suddenly Butler rushed from the tent. Seconds later, Jordan hurried over to Sam.

"Did you see that?" Jordan asked. "Something's going on with that guy! C'mon, we can't lose him!"

She grabbed Sam by the arm. Before she knew it, Sam was running out of the tent behind Jordan. They emerged into no man's land in time to see Butler's black FBI sedan squeal its tires and race from the intersection.

"Follow me!" Jordan yelled. She rushed to her motorbike, with Sam close behind. When they reached the bike, Jordan tossed a helmet to Sam, who jumped up on the passenger seat behind the reporter as the engine rumbled to life. Before Sam knew it, the engine roared and the bike flew out of the intersection, following Butler's distant tail lights while the tail lights on Jordan's bike still flickered away.

THE HURRIED huddle between Jordan and Sam caught Hunter's attention as he rose from his seat at the meeting circle. His curiosity transformed quickly into concern as the pair rushed towards the exit of the Unite the Left Camp. Out of nowhere, a voice beside him broke his concentration.

"What's with those two?" Danielle asked. "Do you think we should follow them?"

Hunter needed no additional encouragement.

"Absolutely, let's go. We'll take my bike!"

The pair raced from the tent onto Constitution Avenue, where his powerful Harley was parked. Danielle donned the spare helmet that Hunter tossed to her, then hopped on the back of the bike behind him as the big engine thundered to life. Hunter spotted the flickering of Jordan's tail light in the distance, then he kicked the Harley into gear and shot out of the intersection, with Danielle's arms clinging tightly around his waist.

Moments later, the Harley reached a maze of roadways and ramps beside the Potomac. Hunter slowed the bike as the pair searched the maze to see Jordan's bike.

"There it is!" Danielle shouted, pointing to one of the ramps. "They're taking the bridge!'

The engine revved and the bike shot onto the ramp, heading across the Roosevelt Bridge to Virginia. Hunter and Danielle kept their eyes focused on the flickering tail light.

"They're heading south on the 110!" Danielle shouted. "Hurry, you're losing them!"

Hunter urged the big bike onward as they headed south through Arlington and towards the I-395. He managed to catch up to Jordan's bike, jockeying around semi-trailers and other slower moving traffic to maintain his proximity to the other bike. Soon they were on the I-95, still heading south. They'd been on the bike for about 30 minutes, when the city gradually thinned and they found themselves riding through pockets of green countryside, interspersed with smaller bedroom communities. Five minutes later, Danielle tapped Hunter on the shoulder.

"Are they heading to Quantico?" she shouted.

Hunter shrugged his shoulders.

A moment later, Jordan's bike slowed and exited to the right. Danielle shouted to Hunter again.

"Not Quantico! They're getting off one ramp earlier. Where the hell are they going?"

CHAPTER 16—COME TOGETHER

JORDAN AND SAM tracked Butler's black sedan along a service road that led them into an industrial park. The sedan slowed as it approached a large manufacturing complex on the edge of town, with signs that read *MC Pharma*. The facility was surrounded on three sides by forest and secured by tall fences capped with razor wire. Jordan slowed her bike and then stopped, keeping a safe distance as Butler's car stopped briefly at a security gate. After a moment, it entered the facility. As the car disappeared from sight briefly, Jordan cautiously resumed moving towards the facility, eventually stopping about fifty yards short of the security gate. Butler's car was still visible, proceeding slowly for about one hundred yards before it stopped outside of what appeared to be a giant warehouse at the south end of the facility.

"What the hell is he doing way out here?" Sam asked. "Is he meeting somebody?"

"Fucked if I know," Jordan answered. "We gotta get a closer look." She looked around and spotted an abandoned farm house on the opposite side of the road, with a woodlot that bordered on *MC Pharma*.

Just as Jordan was about to turn into the abandoned farm house's driveway, the pair heard a deep rumble coming from behind them.

"Is that thunder I hear?" Jordan asked.

Sam's voice stopped Jordan in her tracks.

"It's not thunder, it's Hunter," she said incredulously. "What's he doing here? And somebody's with him!"

A moment later, Hunter's Harley rumbled up beside them. Danielle dismounted, followed by Hunter, and the pair removed their helmets as Sam ran towards them. She threw her arms around Hunter and gave him a tight bear hug, while Danielle and Jordan stood watching the reunion.

"What are you two doing here?" Sam demanded.

"Following you guys," Hunter answered. "I'd say the bigger question is what are *you two* doing here?"

Jordan and Sam exchanged glances, unsure about how much to tell Hunter and Danielle. Jordan finally broke the silence.

"It's a long story," Jordan replied. "I got another cryptic text saying that I should keep a close eye on Butler. Sam and I noticed he was really agitated after getting a phone call during your meeting, so we decided to follow him. He just drove into that facility."

"That's no ordinary facility," Danielle blurted. The other three turned and stared at her.

"What do you mean," Sam asked.

"It belongs to my dad! It's the R&D headquarters for his drug company. *MC Pharma* ... Michael Chen. Get it? So, what's Butler doing here?"

The foursome turned to gaze at the giant facility, then Jordan replied to Danielle.

"That *is* the million dollar question, isn't it!"

HUGE COOLING fans, spaced at intervals around the meeting circle, whirred constantly in a losing effort to provide relief from the deadly heat. Arjun, Terri, and the Liberty Convoy organizers all gulped water and wiped their brows repeatedly as the afternoon wore on. But it wasn't only the weather that was heated. The debate over how to ensure the President heard their concerns, and how to possibly end the standoff, was just as passionate. It continued to drag on into the late afternoon, while distant rumbles of thunder rolled in ominously from the southwest.

"I've done a lotta thinkin' 'bout what y'all said yesterday, 'bout the American dream an' bein' duped by the rich," John mused. "It hit home fer me. The dream's dead an' people are givin' up hope in my hometown. The Constitution sure ain't workin' fer us anymore!"

"I bin thinkin' too," Sean added. "John's right, somethin's gotta change to make things better fer us workin' Americans. Could be that the Constitution *could* use some fixin'!"

"I agree," Jessica chimed. "A few of these ideas your team brought from the other camp are certainly worth discussing."

"You guys already know that I'm a small business owner just like many of you," Terri said. "As an outsider and entrepreneur, I think you're wise to start questioning whether or not your Constitution might be out of date."

"Not so fast, y'all!" Bryson bellowed. "I ain't ready to give up on the American dream yet! An' I sure as fuck don' agree with some'a these woke ideas y'all brought with ya to day!"

"I'm afraid I'm with Bryson," Anna agreed. "It's a slippery slope downhill to Communism once y'all start rollin' over fer a woke agenda."

"Easy fer you to say, Anna!" John countered. "Y'all got it made with yer fancy podcast an' all. Same thing goes fer you, Martin. Everybody in America wants to be—whatcha call it these days—an influencer, or sumthin' like that? But how many are gonna make it big like y'all. An what happens when yer fifteen minutes o'fame are over?"

"What about you, Pastor?" Arjun intervened. "We haven't heard from you for a while. What do you think of the proposed concessions and suggestions from the other camp?"

"Us Christians ain't gonna stand fer takin' away our freedom o'religion, or includin' anythin' to do with the woke, heathen agenda! I agree with Anna, it's a dangerous, slippery slope fer sure!"

Jessica's patience for tolerating the Pastor finally snapped.

"For fuck sake, Pastor!" she screamed. "You Christians aren't the only religion in America! Nobody's taking away your religious freedom. But the rest of us won't stand for you tryin' to ram *your* beliefs down our throats! I have just as much right to my beliefs as you have to yours!"

The Pastor paused and rubbed his chin while he pondered Jessica's harsh condemnation.

"Well," he replied, "long as nobody innerferes with *our* freedom o' religion, I s'pose there ain't any harm in sittin' down an considerin' some changes."

"Alright," Terri interjected. "So let's summarize those suggestions from the other camp."

Jessica was the first to raise her hand, which Terri acknowledged with a nod.

"I agree that the current Constitution puts far too much power in the hands of the President and with the states, via the Senate. We need a Constitution that truly belongs to the people, and puts the power back in our hands. And the more I learn about the Proportional Representation model of government, the more I like the idea. We need a system that encourages formation of more than two parties, that encourages compromise between political agendas, and makes every single person's vote count!"

"Well said," Arjun agreed. "Just think about it. When there's only two parties and one party wins with fifty-point-one percent of the votes, the wishes of forty-nine-point-nine percent of the people count for nothing."

"I never thought about it that way before," Anna added.

"So Jess, you're in agreement with the left's suggestions that more power should be given to the House of Representatives. But, what about their suggestions about the Supreme Court? Anybody have anything to say about that?"

"You bet!" John blurted. "We barely survived the Trump circus, with him cherry-pickin' an' takin' over control o'the Supreme Court. Much as I supported the guy, that weren't right. Ain't no elected official, not even the President, should be able to get away with committin' crimes, whether that's in the course o'their duties or not!"

"Damn right," Sean added. "If you or I do the crime, we gotta do the time! I did six months after we cranked open the floodgates on that dam back home in Oregon. Shouldn't be no differint fer the President!"

"What do you all think about how France chooses their courts," Arjun added, "where they have a large committee with representatives from the judiciary, prominent lawyers, parliament, and prominent citizens, who make the recommendations for judicial appointments as a group?"

"That sounds a lot smarter than leavin' it up to the politicians," Anna surmised.

"What about allowing plebiscites: letting the people vote on whether to accept or reject legislation that's highly controversial?" Arjun asked.

"I'm for anything that gives more power back to the people," Jessica answered.

"So, what about the left's suggested changes to division of federal and state powers?" Terri asked. "Are you guys okay with shifting responsibility for guns, healthcare, and education from the Feds to the states? And for setting up a federal election agency?"

"I'm okay with them ideas," Bryson intervened. "Makes way more sense fer states, cities, an' towns to make differint gun laws fer differint situations anyway."

"Yeah, I like those suggestions too," Jessica continued. "As long as the Feds are responsible for all military-style weapons and for arming and controlling the State Militias. And I like the idea of the Feds creating minimum standards for healthcare and public education in order for the states to qualify for federal help with funding."

"I like that the big issues, like abortion and gun control, could be handed off to the states," Anna declared. "But, by attachin' strings to federal funding, it would help to ensure that women have control over their bodies and reproductive health. I could live with that."

"Now hold on!" Pastor Kessler shouted. "Ain't nobody but God who decides who lives an' who dies! I can't stand up fer anythin' that allows killin' unborn babies!"

Jessica rolled her eyes and jumped to her feet.

"Here we go again! How many times do I need to say this: n*obody's* tellin' *you* what to believe, Pastor! Could you at least extend the same courtesy to others who believe differently?"

Arjun and Terri made eye contact, realizing this was a road they didn't want to go down again.

"Okay," Arjun intervened. "I think we've already covered that issue a number of times. We've covered a lot of ground today. Terri and I want to thank you all for expressing your opinions on these issues, and on the left's proposals for possible Constitutional changes. Is everybody comfortable with what we've discussed and decided today? Can I see a show of hands?"

Arjun and Terri looked around the room and waited, while the sound of thunder grew louder and more ominous in the background. Jessica, John, and Sean's hands went up within seconds. After a brief delay, Anna's hand went up as well. Arjun and Terri both held their breath. Finally, after a few more seconds, Bryson reluctantly followed, as did Martin Lee, who still seemed bored and ambivalent about the whole process. Surprisingly, there was only one holdout: Bryson's sidekick, Norm Barfield.

"Well," Terri said, "It looks like we have a consensus of agreement that we can take to the President. And if she agrees with the importance of the changes that both sides identified, and agrees to use that as a guide to formulating policy to address your concerns, will you consider your protest to be a success? Can I see another show of hands?"

One by one, the organizers' hands went up, and this time they all nodded their approval. Arjun and Terri looked at each other, smiled, and each gave a sigh of relief.

"Then we'll take this to the President right away," Arjun declared. "Thank you, each and every one of you, for your patience and your input. I'm sure you'll be hearing from the President very soon."

CHAPTER 17—BUSINESS AS USUAL

THE SKY above Sam, Hunter, Jordan, and Danielle grew darker by the minute and the wind was picking up, while claps and rumbles of thunder grew ever closer. The foursome huddled around Jordan's bike on the edge of the abandoned farmhouse's woodlot, adjacent to the *MC Pharma* complex. Jordan reached into one of her bike's saddlebags and extracted two pairs of binoculars and a pair of wire cutters.

"You carry those with you all the time?" Sam asked.

"Tools of the trade when your job is to investigate."

"Makes sense, so what do we do now?" Sam replied.

"I need to get into that facility to find out what Butler's up to," Jordan answered.

"Why you?" Hunter inquired.

"Last time I checked, I'm the journalist here," Jordan replied. "It's my job."

"I'm coming with you," Danielle insisted. "I need to know why Butler's come to my dad's facility."

"Okay," Jordan responded. "But we need eyes out here."

She handed a large pair of binoculars to Hunter and a smaller pair to Sam.

"You guys are our lookouts. Text us if you see security patrols or anybody else showing up. Everybody ready?"

A flash of lightning lit up the sky around them, followed by a solid clap of thunder about five seconds later. Almost immediately, the foursome felt the first few droplets of rain.

"Looks like we're going to get wet," Sam commented.

"Let's move into position in the woodlot," Jordan decided. "There may be some partial cover in there."

Jordan led the way into the woodlot. When they reached the edge, they had a clear view into the *MC Pharma* complex.

"The whole place looks awfully quiet for a weekday," Sam commented, her voice hushed. "Doesn't that seem odd?"

"Not really," Danielle answered. "All of my Dad's plants close at noon on Fridays during the summer."

"Perfect!" Jordan said quietly. "We don't need to wait until dark. Everybody knows what to do?"

Sam, Hunter, and Danielle nodded silently.

"Okay, let's go Danielle."

Jordan led the younger Chen through the few remaining trees on the outskirts of the woodlot, then the pair crawled through a stretch of tall grass to the edge of the facility's security fence. Another flash of lightning lit up the sky, followed only a couple of seconds later by a deafening crack of thunder. Jordan looked up anxiously at the threatening sky.

"Shit! That was close!" she muttered quietly, as the rain intensified. She turned her attention back to her task, using the wire cutters to start cutting open a gap in the chain link. When she was satisfied it was large enough, she grabbed the torn section and pulled it open.

"Crawl through!" she whispered, then Danielle slipped through the opening. Squatting on the inside of the fence, Danielle held the flap open long enough for Jordan to creep inside. Danielle released the flap and it settled back into place, barely noticeable to passersby. Jordan looked all around her, then pointed to a nearby garbage dumpster. Danielle nodded and Jordan sprinted to the cover of the dumpster. Seconds later, Danielle followed.

Another brilliant bolt of lightning and an almost simultaneous crash of thunder exploded near them and the sky opened, unleashing torrents of rain. After one last check for anyone who might notice them, Jordan sprinted the last twenty yards to the warehouse and pressed herself against the side of the building. Once safe, she motioned for Danielle to follow her.

"Fuck this rain!" Jordan muttered. "Let's see if there's another entrance around back. We need to get out of this weather!"

Staying close to the building, they carefully peeked around the corner, then sprinted for the rear of the building.

HUNTER AND SAM huddled under some bushes at the edge of the woodlot, watching as Jordan and Danielle slipped around the corner and disappeared from sight. The bushes only provided partial shelter from the deluge, and their wet hands were turning white from the cold as they scanned the facility for any signs of activity.

After a few moments, Sam whispered urgently.

"Look! There's a white cargo van at the gate. It's inside now, and looks like it's heading in the direction of that big warehouse. Can you make out who's in it?"

Hunter swung his binoculars towards the entrance and picked up the van, tracking the vehicle as it made its way to the warehouse, where it slowed and then parked behind Butler's sedan.

"Can't see much," he cursed. "The windows are too heavily tinted."

They watched impatiently. Finally, the driver's door opened and a burly man, dressed in navy blue pants, a blue work shirt, and a navy ball cap jumped from the van. The torrential downpour showed no signs of letting up, and he was drenched before his feet even hit the ground. Seconds later, Elena emerged from the far side of the van. The pair ran to the back end of the van and worked quickly to open its rear doors.

"I'll swear that goon looks a lot like one that came after me and Terri at the Liberty Camp!" Hunter exclaimed. "He's just not dressed in camo this time."

"And the woman?" Sam inquired.

"Never seen her before."

A second man, dressed like the first, jumped from the rear of the van, dragging a reluctant woman out after him and onto the wet asphalt. The two goons yanked her to her feet. Sam and Hunter gasped in unison as they recognized the woman's face.

"It's Nicole Davies!" Hunter whispered loudly.

"Whaaaat?" Sam blurted, her binoculars riveted on the action at the rear of the van. "What the hell do they want with her?"

Their stunned eyes followed the three newcomers as they attempted to drag Nicole, still kicking and struggling, through the downpour towards the building. It was obvious that Nicole wasn't going to make things easy for her captors. Sam's mind whirled out of control, trying to make sense of what they were witnessing.

"Do you suppose those three also had something to do with the deep fake of Nicole's voice? ... Oh, damn, does that mean Butler was involved in that too?"

"Sounds like a good bet," Hunter answered. "But why are they at one of Michael Chen's pharma plants? Surely ..."

"Holy shit!" Sam exploded. "Now there's a black limo going through the security gate, and it's heading to the warehouse too!"

Their binoculars glued on the approaching limo, they both tracked it until it pulled up behind the cargo van. The driver exited the vehicle and quickly opened an umbrella as he hurried around to the other side to open the rear door. As the passenger stepped from the limo and into the shelter of the umbrella, Sam and Hunter gasped again.

"It's Chen himself!" Hunter called out. "What the fuck is going on in there?"

At that moment, Matt Butler, accompanied by none other than Senator Sherman Crowley, emerged from the warehouse to shake Michael Chen's hand. The threesome then scurried to the main entrance and disappeared into the warehouse.

LIGHTNING CONTINUED to flash and claps of thunder exploded repeatedly as Mother Nature's pyrotechnic exhibition dominated the sky. The unrelenting deluge of rain pounded on the steel roof of the warehouse, creating a continuous roar rivalling that of Niagara Falls. Now drenched to the bone and starting to shiver, Jordan peeked around the corner of the building, then raised her voice over the din so Danielle could hear her.

"Loading docks, and it looks like one's still open. Wait while I take a look."

Jordan kept her head down and scooted along the back of the building until she reached the open loading dock. Cautiously, she took a sneak peak, then ducked back down again. She looked back at Danielle and motioned for the other woman to join her. Seconds later, looking like a drowned rat, Danielle scurried alongside the building until she was at Jordan's side.

"Looks deserted," Jordan whispered in Danielle's ear. "I'm going in. Keep an eye out, and we'll signal each other if everything's clear."

Danielle nodded, then Jordan snuck another quick peek over the edge of the loading dock. Satisfied the way was clear, she hoisted herself quickly up onto the dock. Once inside, she glanced around rapidly in all directions, then took cover behind a full shipping pallet loaded with large cardboard boxes. As she reached cover, Jordan felt her phone vibrate in her pocket. She pulled out the phone and noticed there was a message from Sam. Her eye's opened wide as she scanned the message. She peeked out from behind the pallet and saw Danielle's head poke out above the edge of the loading dock. She waved at her partner to join her behind the pallet. Within seconds, Danielle had scooted into the building and ducked in beside Jordan. Although both women were now out of the rain, the deluge sounded like a freight train inside the building as it pounded away at the warehouse's metal roof.

"Have a look at this!" Jordan whispered into Danielle's ear.

She held up her phone and showed Danielle the message. The younger Chen's eyes popped open wide when she saw her father's name.

"You sure you still wanna do this?" Jordan asked, her voice barely a whisper. "Now's the time to get out if you're not sure."

The look of shock on Danielle's face gradually transformed into one of grim determination.

"Not on your life," she hissed. "Give up on a chance to catch my Dad up to no good? I wouldn't miss this for anything!"

Jordan shrugged skeptically.

"Okay, your choice," she answered. "Let's do this. We'll leapfrog. I'll lead the way, find cover, then wave you on if it's clear. If you see me wave two hands, dive for cover. Then you do the same. Got it?"

Danielle nodded, then Jordan peeked out from behind the pallet and bolted for another nearby pallet. They alternated their movements down a long aisle, towards the front of the building. As they drew closer to the front, Jordan heard voices. She moved forward again and took cover, before sneaking a quick peek. The voices appeared to be coming from what looked like a shipping office. She waved Danielle forward, but held a finger to her lips, signalling her partner to remain quiet. They listened for a moment or two, then Danielle whispered in Jordan's ear.

"What are they saying? Can you hear them?"

Jordan shook her head, then whispered to Danielle.

"No. We need to get closer. If we cross the aisle and get behind that pallet, we can crawl along the office wall and sit right beneath its windows. But we can't make a sound!"

Danielle gave Jordan a thumbs up, then the pair scooted across the aisle until they were up against the office wall. Finally at their destination, they froze and slowed their breathing. Despite their bravery, they were ill-prepared for what they heard.

THE DELUGE of rain pounded on the warehouse roof like a marching drum band. Congressman Michael Chen sat casually on the edge of a desk, while FBI Agent Matt Butler, Senator Crowley, Elena, and her two thugs stood in a semi-circle around Nicole Davies, who was seated on a chair with her hands zip-tied. A gigantic flash of light, followed by an immediate, deafening clap of thunder, caused every person in the room to duck, yielding to their base survival instincts. When the moment of panic passed, Nicole sat up and her eyes pleaded silently with Chen. Getting nothing but an icy glare, she shifted her attention to Butler.

"These guys are making a terrible mistake. Tell them Matt! Why would anybody want to kidnap me?"

Matt shook his head sadly.

"Sorry, Nikki, but you know too much. You can connect me to the deep fake phone call."

Another huge bolt of lightning lit up the room, followed almost immediately by another ear-splitting crash of thunder that rocked the building. Everybody jerked instinctively and ducked again.

As Nicole recoiled from the lightning and thunder, the reality of her situation hit home. Her eyes went wide, her heart pounded in her chest, and every muscle in her body tensed.

"I would never implicate you! Do you think I'm that disloyal?"

She moved her eyes from Matt to Michael Chen, and then to Senator Crowley.

"Please believe me! There's somebody much higher up who was giving orders to Matt, and to me. *They're* the ones you should be after!"

Crowley shifted his eyes toward Chen, whose face broke into a sinister grin as he started laughing. Initially stunned by their response, Nicole's expression changed to one of anger as she glared at Chen.

"Oh my God!" she shouted. "It wasn't somebody at the FBI who framed me. It was you! Why?"

"Why indeed," he answered rhetorically. "Isn't it obvious? You were my access to the most powerful office on the planet, the so-called heart of global democracy. With your help, I now have influence in the White House. And, as you know, influence is power."

Out of nowhere, a cell phone rang nearby, just outside the shipping office. All heads inside the office jerked in the direction of the sound, and looks of alarm swept across the faces of Butler, Chen, Crowley, Elena, and her two thugs.

"What the ..." Matt blurted.

"Find that phone!" Chen screamed.

AS JORDAN and Danielle listened to what was going on in the office, Danielle's phone exploded with sound. Waves of shock and horror crossed both womens' faces.

"Fuck, I forgot!" Danielle gasped.

Jordan looked around frantically.

"Fast! Run! Hide behind that pallet!" she hissed, pointing to the nearest pallet.

Danielle scurried from their hiding spot and ran for the pallet, diving behind it just before Matt, Elena, and the two thugs burst through the office door and out into the warehouse. At the same time, Jordan leapt to her feet and sprinted in the opposite direction from Danielle's hiding place. She made it only a few yards before she felt a sharp sting in the middle of her back. Her legs turned into rubber and she collapsed into a heap on the concrete floor, as the taser did its job and rendered her helpless. Michael Chen emerged from the office in time to see her crumble into a heap.

"Bring her into the office," he yelled to his minions. "Tie her up!"

Danielle peeked out from behind the relative safety of her pallet and watched as the two thugs dragged Jordan into the office, followed by Matt, Elena, Chen, and Crowley.

Stupid, stupid, stupid! How the fuck did I forget to silence my phone! What's wrong with me?

She held her breath, clenched her fists and made like she wanted to pound on her own head. After a few moments, she finally managed to slow her breathing. It was no time for guilt or shame. The grave reality of her situation was sinking in and she felt herself trembling. She waited breathlessly, dreading the moment of doom when they would return for her. But after a few minutes, when nothing happened, she dared to peek out cautiously from behind the pallet. Eventually, she realized they weren't searching for her. Only then did she finally allow herself to let out a cautious sigh of relief.

Time to make up for being an ass!

She crept forward, keeping as low as possible, then she crawled slowly and methodically until she was back beneath the office windows once more.

ELENA'S THUGS dragged Jordan into the office and dumped her onto an old office chair, the arms of which helped to keep her from falling over sideways onto the floor. They rolled the chair into the middle of the room so that it was beside Nicole, who had looked on in horror as the events of the last few minutes unfolded. Another flash of lightning and a clap of thunder rocked the room again, and the drumming of rain on the roof continued relentlessly.

Jordan's eyes glared at her captors, but she was unable to speak. Smiling broadly, Michael Chen re-seated himself casually on the edge of the office desk.

"Well, well, well," he gloated. "This must be my lucky day! Fate has brought me the two people who can possibly connect Agent Butler to me, and has dropped both of you right on my doorstep."

As the effect of the electrical assault on Jordan's nervous system gradually waned, she tried to open her mouth to speak.

"Wh ... wh ... wha? ..."

"Why, you ask?" Chen answered sarcastically.

"Yes, why?" Nicole answered, on behalf of both captives. "I don't get it. Why would you want to fake attacks against *both* sides in the standoff? What do you possibly have to gain?"

"Come on, Nicole," he answered. "Think, you're a smart girl."

Nicole paused for a moment to concentrate her thoughts, trying to find an answer for her own question. Finally, a look of recognition spread across her face.

"You want the standoff to continue. You want the two sides to keep fighting against each other. But why? You're a Democrat."

Jordan managed to shift her body in the chair as she gradually regained some control of her body. She opened her mouth, trying again to speak.

"Chaos ... con-speer-see ..."

"Ah, Ms. Marsh, you're back," Chen said cheerily. "Conspiracy, you say? A conspiracy against freedom and democracy? You're close, but both you and Nicole still don't get it."

"Then perhaps you'd like to enlighten our simple minds," Nicole snapped.

The sarcasm in her remark caused the smirk to vanish from Chen's face. Instead, his eyes narrowed, his nose wrinkled, and his upper lip turned up, revealing his deep disdain for his captives.

"There is no *'Cathedral'*, as the far right would have you believe," Chen sneered. "No grand conspiracy between government, the press, and the universities. It's just a simple truth—it's called Capitalism. Those of us with the brains, the resources, and the most wealth will *always* be in control, no matter what form of government you devise!"

Jordan, now nearly completely recovered from being tasered, shook her head slowly and gave Chen a look of sadness and pity.

"You really believe that, don't you?" she replied.

"It's more than just a belief, it's reality," Chen countered. "The democracy and the freedom you fight for is merely an illusion. Most of you are too naive and stupid to govern. Capitalism is the real master! Those of us with wealth allow you to have your political parties—Democrats and Republicans—leftist or right wing. We are illusionists and masters of deflection. We don't really care which of your parties is in government. When you all become disillusioned with one party, we divert our money to support the other, to give you the illusion of change: the illusion that you have the freedom and the power to govern yourselves and to control your destiny. We don't really care who wins your elections, as long as it's not the Communists, and as long as we're allowed to keep growing our companies and our wealth. In the end, the right and left both do as we say, because they need and want our money."

"And so you perpetuate the myth of the American dream," Jordan interrupted. "The dream that anybody can be as rich as you, if they just work hard enough or want it badly enough. You rich people manipulate the press so that the public admires you, and wants to be just like you. But, the sad truth is that people like you control whom you let into your club. In reality, the percentage of us who 'make it big' is minuscule!"

"Ahh, aren't you the clever one." Chen responded, finding his sarcastic smile again. "We give you hope that you can be one of us someday. And it's amazing how people can be controlled by giving them that tiny little morsel of hope!"

DANIELLE LISTENED intently, barely taking a breath during her father's tirade. The more she heard, the more she shook her head, and the more angry her face became.

"And so Ms. Marsh and Ms. Davies, there is no grand conspiracy. It's just Capitalism, plain and simple."

"So, if there's no conspiracy," Nicole asked, "I guess that means you can let us go and let Capitalism take its course."

Danielle heard her father break into hysterical laughter.

"Nice try, young lady! I thank you for your past service to our cause. But, I'm afraid you and your journalist friend are of no further use to us." He turned to Matt and Elena.

"Agent Butler, Elena, you know what you need to do. Senator, I think we're finished here."

Having heard enough of her father's rant, Danielle scurried back to the shelter of the nearby pallet. First making sure that her phone was silenced, her thumbs then typed out an urgent message to Sam.

My Dad is wacko crazy! BOTH Nicole and Jordan are prisoners. He's leaving now but I think Butler and the woman Elena are going to kill them! HELP!

DESPITE HAVING some limited shelter from trees and bushes at the edge of the woodlot, Sam was soaked to the skin. She shivered uncontrollably and her hands were white and stiff from the cold rain. She had to give up trying to hold her binoculars still. Instead, she alternated between breathing warm air on her hands, or huddling and holding her hands under her armpits, in a desperate attempt to find some warmth for them. All of a sudden, she felt her phone vibrate in the pocket of her shorts. She struggled to force her frozen, stiff hands into the soaked and sticky pocket to retrieve the device, finally wrestling it from its sodden resting place, then swiping to open her home screen.

Danielle's urgent message leapt from the screen, causing Sam's fight or flight response to ignite instantaneously.

"Oh shit! Look at this!" she shouted over the persistent rumbles of thunder and the rain's constant drumming on the landscape. She handed the phone to Hunter.

"Whoa, that's not good!"

At that moment, Chen and Senator Crowley emerged from the warehouse and climbed into the rear of Chen's limo. Within seconds, the vehicle pulled away from the warehouse, turned around, and headed for the security gate in the distance.

"So that leaves Butler, Elena, and the two thugs in there with Nicole and Jordan," Hunter thought aloud, "and it sounds like they're running out of time!"

"That's four against two," Sam shouted. "We gotta do something, but what?"

"Four against one," Hunter barked. "You're not going anywhere near that building."

"Are you kidding me?" Sam yelled. "You're gonna pull that macho bullshit on me? We're a team, remember!"

"Don't be ridiculous. I'm trained for shit like this, and you're not!"

"Then tell me what you want me to do, so I don't get myself killed!"

Hunter shook his head in frustration.

"Christ, you're stubborn! Okay, okay, let me think."

"Hurry, they don't have much time!"

It seemed like an eternity to Sam while Hunter went silent, became distant, and processed their situation. In reality, his mind was only gone for about five seconds.

"I need to get in that warehouse somehow, so we're gonna need a diversion. Is there anything else we can use? Maybe in those saddlebags on Jordan's bike? I've got nothin' useful in mine."

They wheeled around and ran back to the parked bikes as fast as their legs would carry them. Sam flipped open one bag while Hunter opened the other. Sam pulled a couple of objects from her bag and a look of confusion crossed her face.

"Is this what I think it is?"

Hunter's eyes opened wide and his mouth dropped open in surprise.

"It's a bag of firecrackers! Who carries fireworks around on their bike?"

"Must've bought them for the Fourth of July, but never used them," Sam thought out loud.

"Lucky for us, and hopefully for her!" he answered. "Okay, listen up. This is what we're gonna do!"

MOMENTS LATER, they were back at the edge of the woodlot, with Hunter crawling through the hole that Jordan had cut in the security fence. Once through, he kept his body low and ran through the tall, wet grass towards the cover of the dumpster. Another brilliant flash of lightning erupted around them, and the nearly simultaneous crash of thunder almost brought him instinctively to his knees. The rain continued to cascade down, showing no sign of relenting.

When he regained his composure, Hunter looked around in all directions, then ran to the white cargo van and rolled beneath it for cover. When he was sure he hadn't drawn any attention, he crawled out from beneath the vehicle and opened the cover of the gas filler. He whipped a length of cloth from beneath his leather jacket, doing his best to shelter it from the rain and keep it dry, then he stuffed it down into the filler pipe. He pulled a lighter from his jacket pocket, looked around quickly one last time, then held the lighter up to the piece of cloth that dangled from the filler pipe. It lit briefly, but the flame faded quickly, the cloth already wet from the pounding rain. In desperation, he held the lighter just outside the filler pipe and touched it to the cloth. He didn't stay long enough to see if it caught, as he raced from the van as fast as he could, throwing himself to the ground beside the building's front doors and holding his hands over his head and ears.

WITH CHEN and Senator Crowley gone, Matt took charge of the two hostages.

"You heard him," he barked at Elena. "Let's get this over with."

The two thugs approached Nicole and Jordan and took up positions behind them. Nicole's eyes opened wide. Overcome by panic, she struggled frantically to free her hands and feet to no avail. In contrast, Jordan remained calm and defiant.

"Really?" she said calmly. "You're going to do this right now? Splatter our brains all over this office? I thought you'd be smarter than that."

Elena emitted an hysterical laugh.

"Nothing so cliché, darlink," she answered, with a sarcastic smile. "No one ever vill know you vas here."

Her eyes moved to the two thugs and she gave them a silent nod. Each of the burly men produced a garotte, which they whipped over Jordan's and Nicole's heads before their victims knew what was happening. They yanked back hard on the deadly wires. Their victims eyes flew open wide in panic while hideous choking sounds leaked from their windpipes.

Without warning, the room was alight with a gigantic flash, followed by a thunderous, deafening roar. The room rocked as if there was an earthquake, and a wave of searing heat tore into the room, lifting everybody in the office up into the air, and then throwing them to the floor like rag dolls.

ELENA'S TWO thugs, still dazed and confused from the explosion just outside the shipping office, dragged themselves to their feet, drew their sidearms, then stumbled towards the building's exit and out into the rain.

Hunter waited until the second thug exited, then silently assailed him from behind, putting a choke hold on him and quickly disarming him before his partner knew anything was amiss. When the other thug finally heard a slight rustle behind him, the burly man turned and spotted Hunter, but it was already too late for him. Hunter took him out with a blow to the side of the head from the first man's gun.

Moving swiftly and efficiently, Hunter grabbed the second man's gun and rushed through the warehouse's front doors.

As he entered the building, Hunter stopped and poked his head around a corner. Not seeing anybody, he moved swiftly, penetrating deeper into the building, looking for the shipping office. Suddenly, Matt Butler and Elena stumbled out of the office, still somewhat dazed, and caught Hunter out in the open.

"MacMillan? What the fuck!" Matt shouted. Both Matt and Elena raised their guns and squeezed off a couple of shots, but their reactions were too slow and their aim was off, as they hadn't yet recovered fully from the explosion. By the time they fired the shots, Hunter had dived behind a nearby pallet of five-gallon plastic pails. He peeked around the corner of the pallet, then popped his head out and fired a couple of rounds himself, causing Elena to dive behind a pallet of boxes and Butler to take cover behind a forklift.

"We've got you cornered, MacMillan," Matt shouted. "Drop the gun and come out with your hands over your head!"

"Not a chance, Butler! State police are on the way, and should be here any minute. I'm sure they'll love to find out what you've been up to!"

DESPITE BEING somewhat sheltered from the deluge, Sam was still soaked and shaking from the cold as she waited anxiously beside the rear loading dock. Her body flinched instinctively when the van exploded, but she recovered in seconds and leapt into action. Throwing a plastic shopping bag ahead of her, she swung her lithe body up onto the loading dock and took cover behind the first shipping pallet full of goods that she could find. She poked her head out and looked around, checking for any signs that she'd been detected. Then she heard the chaotic shouting from the shipping office at the other end of the building.

Seconds later, she heard gunshots ring out from the direction of the office. Checking again to ensure that the coast was clear, she scurried from hiding place to hiding place, working her way cautiously, but rapidly, towards the chaos. As she neared the commotion, she stopped and managed to wrench her phone from her soaked, sticky pocket. Her frozen thumbs struggled to tap out a message for Danielle.

We r in building & coming to help. Stay where u r if safe

Seconds later, Sam received a simple *Thumbs Up* emoji in response. She pocketed her phone, and resumed moving towards the nearest gunshot sounds. She crawled through a narrow gap between pallets until she was in the next aisle, then she stopped and took a quick peek around a pallet. She saw Butler and Elena hunkered down in their separate hiding places, firing in the direction of the pallet full of white pails, some of them now slowly draining their liquid contents onto the warehouse floor. Sam concealed herself behind her pallet again, then pulled out her phone and tapped out another message to Hunter.

I m here. Where are u?

Pinned down behind pallet of pails 20 ft from entrance. Have guns but little ammo. Need ur help.

As she read the text, Sam bit her lip, her facial muscles tensed, and she felt her heart pounding in her chest. She tapped a quick *Thumbs Up* reply, then put her phone away. She reached carefully into the plastic bag, thankful that the pounding rain on the building's steel roof easily masked the crinkling white noise coming from the bag. She pulled out a string of firecrackers and a lighter, then quickly lit the string. With the fuses lit, she threw it in the direction of Butler and Elena, then scurried quickly back between two pallets, into the relative safety of the next aisle. As the firecrackers erupted, she dived in behind another pallet of goods.

Butler and Elena ducked instinctively when the firecrackers exploded. Once the pyrotechnics burned themselves out, Elena whirled around and scanned the area, ready to fire. Not seeing anybody, she crept carefully from her hideout, methodically creeping from shipping pallet to pallet, until she found the firecracker remnants. She signalled to Butler that she was going to search for their unwanted new intruder and he confirmed with a nod.

Meanwhile, Hunter poked his head out, hoping for a chance to make a run for the front door, but Butler fired two more shots, keeping Hunter pinned. Sam scurried for shelter between another pair of pallets. She was now two aisles away from Elena, searching for Danielle. As she looked down that aisle towards the front of the building, she finally spotted the young actress cowering in her hiding place behind a pallet. Sam quickly tapped out another message on her phone.

I see u. Look up the aisle for me

Danielle glanced down at her phone. Seconds later, she raised her head and her eyes darted up and down the aisle, searching for Sam until the two made eye contact. Sam pointed to a spot above Danielle's head, where a red fire alarm box was mounted on the wall. She motioned the younger Chen to pull the alarm. Right away, Danielle nodded her understanding. She popped up, yanked on the alarm, and immediately sprinted towards a new hiding spot.

AS THE alarm sounded, Elena crawled one aisle closer and spotted Sam. She fired off a quick shot, but Sam reacted instantly and scrambled behind another pallet, this time on the building's outside aisle. But now, she realized that she was backing herself into a corner. Her mind raced, looking for a way out of her predicament. In the distance, she heard Hunter and Butler exchange a few more rounds, then she heard Butler's voice rise faintly above the drumming of rain on the roof and the wailing fire alarm.

"Come on out of there, Hunter. You know you've got nowhere to run. We've got no grudge with you. Stand up, slide me your gun, and nobody gets hurt!"

"That goes for girlfriend too!" Elena bellowed. "She stand, she go free!"

"Don't do it, Sam!" Hunter screamed. "Get out while you can!"

With her panic spiraling, Sam looked around in all directions for Danielle. When she finally spotted her in her new hiding spot, she realized that Danielle was pointing frantically to the wall above and behind Sam. She whirled around and looked up, discovering that she was hiding beneath a fire hose. She exchanged glances with Danielle, then jumped up, broke the glass, and unreeled the fire hose as fast as she could.

Meanwhile, Elena was on the move again. She crept carefully towards the front of her aisle, then rounded the corner, moving swiftly towards the end of Sam's aisle with her gun raised. She stopped, then carefully poked her head around the corner to look for Sam.

At that moment, Danielle stood up and pushed a number of large pails of chemicals off the pallet where she was hiding, a mere ten feet from Elena, who reacted immediately. She jumped out of hiding and exposed herself, firing three rounds in rapid succession in Danielle's direction.

At that precise moment, Sam opened the valve on the fire hose and directed it towards Elena. The blast of water slammed into Elena's face, ribs, and right arm, knocking her to the floor and causing her to lose her grip on her gun. Sam instantly dropped the hose and raced for the loose weapon. Momentarily stunned, Elena gathered her wits, got to her knees, and dived for the gun, crashing into Sam as they reached the weapon at the same time.

Sam tried to close her hand on the gun, but Elena grabbed her wrist and twisted. As a jolt of pain shot up her arm, Sam's other hand reached for the older woman's face and clawed desperately. Elena screamed.

"Bitch! I teach you!"

Relinquishing her grip on Sam's wrist, Elena used that hand to try prying Sam's clawing fingers away from her face. At the same time, she rolled her body, attempting to land on top of Sam and gain the upper hand.

Sam felt the mass of Elena's body rolling over her, and without thinking, she dug deep for every last ounce of strength in her younger body. Using Elena's momentum, Sam rolled with her and used her arms to push Elena upwards, causing her assailant to fly over top of Sam and the gun. Sam continued her roll and scooped up the gun, aiming it at the Russian as the other woman tried to regain her balance.

"Don't move!" Sam screamed.

"Run, Butler!" Elena bellowed. "Save yourself!"

Matt heard Elena's distant warning and wasted no time in squeezing off two more rounds of cover fire at Hunter's position, before bolting from his hiding spot and racing in the direction of the front doors. He burst out into the rain and immediately heard the sounds of sirens in the north, coming towards the office park on the service road. He raced to his black sedan, fired up the engine, and hit the gas. The tires spun wildly, spewing mist and starting to smoke as they tried to find a grip on the slippery asphalt. Suddenly, the tires found traction and the car bolted for the security gate, blasting through the exit barrier, then disappearing west into the neighbouring industrial park.

Inside the warehouse, the noise from the deluge of rain was gradually decreasing, as the worst of the storm moved slowly eastward. Hunter shouted over the racket of the fire alarm.

"Sam, where are you!"

"Over here, far aisle. Help!"

Hunter ran in the direction of Sam's voice. As he neared the far aisle, he spotted Elena lying on the concrete floor on her back, with Sam hovering over her, pointing a gun at her prisoner.

"Danielle's been shot!" Sam shouted.

The young woman, stunned and in shock, staggered from behind a pallet, holding a shoulder which had taken one of the shots Elena fired in her direction.

"Keep your eye on Elena, while I check Danielle!" Hunter called out. "Help's almost here!"

"There's a first aid kit on the wall by the fire alarm!" Sam yelled.

With sirens blaring, two fire trucks slid to a stop on the wet pavement in front of the warehouse. Teams of firefighters jumped from both vehicles and raced inside the building.

As Hunter heard the firefighters enter the warehouse, he rushed to the first aid kit. He ripped open a bandage and applied it to Danielle's wound, stemming the blood flow while the voices of the firefighters drew closer.

"You were lucky, Danielle," Hunter said softly, trying to calm the panicking young woman. "The bullet only grazed the muscle in your shoulder, and you're going to be okay. Just take some slow breaths."

A lead firefighter arrived at the scene. Seeing Sam hovering over Elena and pointing the gun, he spoke tersely into a microphone mounted on his chest.

"Dispatch, we've got a weapons situation inside a warehouse at *MC Pharma*. It's under control, but we need police and an ambulance on scene ASAP. What's the ETA for the police?" His radio squawked an almost unintelligible reply.

"Police are already on their way, and an ambulance has been dispatched," the firefighter relayed to Hunter and Sam. "Shouldn't be more than a few minutes."

Two other firefighters arrived and spied the alarm that Danielle had activated, while two others spotted the fire hose on the ground and attended to that. Other members of the crew searched the building for any signs of fire. Suddenly, Sam remembered Jordan and Nicole and panic spread over her face. She turned to the lead firefighter.

"Oh, my God! Jordan and Nicole! Did you find two hostages in the office?"

"Calm down, ma'am," he answered. "We found them: they're badly shaken, but safe."

Hearing those words, the reality of their ordeal finally hit home for Sam. Tears filled her eyes and her body trembled. Her arms reached for Hunter, and the pair fell into a deep embrace as he wrapped his arms around her.

"Thank God!" Sam sobbed. A moment later, she released her hold on Hunter and looked back at the firefighters. "Can we see them?"

"We're just checking them over first to make sure they're not injured. So, while we're doing that, would you guys like to tell me exactly what the hell's been going on here?"

CHAPTER 18—NEW BEGINNING

FLANKED BY the Stars and Stripes on one side and the Presidential banner on the other, and much relieved to be back in the White House after the afternoon's hectic events at the *MC Pharma* plant in Virginia, Rachel ensconced herself behind the Oval Office's Resolute Desk. She took a final quick glance at the royal blue suit that she'd chosen for the occasion, flicked off a stray fleck of dust from her lapel, then refocused her eyes back on the network producer, just as the woman counted down the final seconds silently with her fingers, then pointed at Rachel.

"Good evening my fellow Americans. I've decided to speak to our nation tonight in light of today's rapidly moving events, both inside the two protest encampments on the streets surrounding the White House, and in a pharmaceuticals plant across the river in Virginia."

She reached for a glass of water and took a sip, purposely slowing the pace of her speech, then she made eye contact with the camera once again.

"First," she continued. "I want to talk about the standoff that has occupied the streets around the White House for the past thirteen days. As you know, I've had a negotiating team working with the Unite the Left and Liberty Convoy camps, listening on my behalf to the concerns of both groups of protesters, as they both exercised their Constitutional rights to freedom of speech. And tonight, I want to assure both camps that I *have* listened to the concerns that you expressed, and I *have* heard you!

Noticing the red light illuminate on a second camera, Rachel turned her head to face it.

"When Thomas Jefferson first saw our Constitution, he commented that he thought it would serve the original thirteen Colonies of our young nation well, but he feared it would be inadequate once American cities became more dominant, as they were in Europe at that time. And Jefferson had no idea that there would be as many as fifty states in the country. Today, his prophecy appears to have been fulfilled, and his concerns have proven to be valid, especially over the past few days of negotiations in this standoff. It has become abundantly clear that there is a common thread of discontent in *both* camps, and indeed on both sides of the political spectrum in this country. Both sides feel that many aspects of our beloved Constitution, which is now more than two-hundred-and-fifty years old, are not working well for Americans in fifty unique states in the twenty-first century. Both sides agree that our democracy needs to be revitalized and placed back more directly into the hands of the people. And both sides also agree that the division of power between our state and federal governments needs to be redefined and clarified, in order to remain relevant in today's world. We must learn to think about our current Constitution as if it were a stately old eighteenth century mansion: it has good old bones, but it is in dire need of restoration.

"For example, this current standoff on the streets of our Capitol has shown us that we need to redefine the meaning of 'peaceful protest' more precisely. We need to clarify it such that our freedom to gather, to speak, to protest peacefully, and then to go home at the end of the day without fear of reprisal, does not cross the line into passive resistance, political blackmail, infringing upon the rights of many others, or breaking reasonable and necessary laws. We all need to understand and acknowledge that difference, so that the type of standoff we've experienced over the past thirteen days, never impinges upon, or cripples the rights of our neighbours and fellow citizens again.

Rachel took a deep breath, then she moved her hands together and clasped them, resting them on the desk in front of her. She looked back at the first camera.

"It goes without saying that both sides will have some different ideas for how to address those changes, but the goodwill shown by the Unite the Left and Liberty Convoy camps over the past few days has shown that they have some common areas of agreement, as well as an emerging spirit of compromise that bodes well for the future."

She paused again and took another sip of water.

"Next, I want the citizens of Washington D.C., and all of my fellow Americans, to know that I spoke personally with both sides in the current standoff late this afternoon. I am happy to announce that both sides agreed to break camp and clear the streets, which they are commencing as I speak. I want to thank both groups, as well as the citizens and leaders of Washington, for their patience during these last thirteen trying days."

Rachel turned to the second camera again.

"The current process for amending the Constitution is arduous and impractical at a time when the country is so polarized in its views. Consequently, and in order to listen to the concerns of all Americans, I would like to announce that my first priority as your new President, will be to convene a modern-day Constitutional Convention within the coming year, in order to completely overhaul, or rebuild if necessary, our Constitution and the structure of our Democracy for the next two-hundred-and-fifty years. Our country is at a crossroads. If we cling to the past and our current Constitution, which has been our anchor since independence, our democracy is likely to sink like an anchor. But if we embrace the need for change in our Constitution, and if we truly embrace the basic democratic idea that our competing political parties accept one another as legitimate rivals, we have the opportunity to reinvigorate our democracy and to give our country a new lifeboat that can weather the unknown storms of the future. We owe this to ourselves, as well as to our children and grandchildren. It is my hope that we can return to our roots and hold my proposed Constitutional Convention in Philadelphia, the birthplace of our current Constitution."

She took a final sip of water, then looked earnestly into the TV camera.

"Finally, I want to give a huge vote of thanks, on behalf of all Americans, to Samantha Bower and the rest of her negotiating team from Canada, for their patience, their objectivity, and their dedication to listening to both sides in this dispute. Without them, I firmly believe that we would not have achieved the breakthrough that we obtained from these negotiations. With regard to the events that took place this afternoon in Virginia, I can only tell you that Sam and some team members were instrumental in notifying police and fire officials of an incident at a large pharmaceutical plant, that we suspect has some bearing on the two false flag terrorist operations that were conducted during the past few days in the Liberty Convoy camp. Those operations appear to have been designed to extend and inflame the standoff between the two camps. Because that event is part of an ongoing police investigation, I am not at liberty to tell you anything more. What I can assure you, however, is that Sam Bower and her team are not persons of police interest in that event.

Rachel turned back to the main camera one last time.

"Because I want my proposed Constitutional Convention to move forward as fast as possible, I hope to talk to you again in about one month to provide you with more details. Until then, God Bless America. Thank you, and goodnight."

The producer's hand signalled the end of the broadcast and the red light on the TV camera was extinguished. Rachel exhaled and allowed her body to relax. A crew member stepped in and helped her remove her microphone, after which Rachel pushed back her chair, stood up, and straightened out her suit. She made her way to the far side of the office, from where Sam, Hunter, Arjun, Terri, and Jordan had watched the address. Standing beside them was a pale and anxious-looking Nicole Davies, whom Rachel had reinstated as her Chief of Staff only two hours earlier.

"Well done, Ma'am," Nicole commented. "I think there's a lot of doubters out there who are willing to give you a chance now."

"Thanks, Nicole," Rachel replied. "Let's hope you're right."

"It's you I need to thank," Nicole countered. "You didn't need to give my job back to me after the way I undermined you recently. I can't believe I was so naïve in trusting Matt so blindly. He had me convinced that the FBI had security concerns about you. I've learned a huge life lesson."

"We all make mistakes," Rachel answered, as she smiled and placed her hand lightly on Nicole's shoulder. "You've been through a terrible ordeal, and I want to make sure you take the time you need to work through it. I'll manage until you're ready to come back to work."

"Thanks, Ma'am, I appreciate it. I've already talked with Sam about her experiences with PTSD, and she stressed the importance of getting proper treatment right away. So, hopefully, I'll be back at work before you know it."

Rachel turned to Sam, the rest of the team, and Jordan.

"I meant what I said in my speech. I can't thank all of you enough for what you've accomplished, not just during the negotiations, but for risking your lives today to save Nicole. And especially for exposing a potential conspiracy against my Presidency, the nation, and our democracy. I just wish I knew who sent me *The Night Class*, so I could thank them as well."

"You're welcome, Ma'am, from all of us," Sam answered. "But I think we all owe a big debt to whomever it was who sent those anonymous texts to me and Jordan. I wonder if it *was* the same person who sent you my book? Anyway, without those hints, we never would have exposed the deep fakes and the false flag operations. Jordan and Nicole would still be facing criminal charges, and the two camps would still be on the streets and at each others' throats."

"I can't stop thinking about those messages either," Jordan added. "Do I remember seeing anybody suspicious along the way? Maybe a young woman on the mall, and then again when the two crowds of protesters collided on Constitution Avenue. But, I just can't be sure. At any rate, it's eerie knowing that somebody out there might still be watching us!"

"If you don't mind me changing the subject, Madame President," Hunter interjected, "What's going to happen with Agent Butler? And especially to Congressman Chen and Senator Crowley?"

Rachel looked around to make sure the TV crew was busy, then she leaned in close to the group, her voice hushed.

"The testimonies from you, Sam, Jordan, and Danielle Chen, paint a pretty grim picture for all three of them, and I thank you for all you've done," Rachel replied. She gave an anxious glance over her shoulder once again before continuing.

"But I'll need a lot more evidence before I can call in the DOJ to press charges against people in their positions. If there *is* a conspiracy of some sort going on, you can understand that I'll need to proceed with the utmost caution."

Another quick glance reassured Rachel that nobody was listening in on their conversation. She continued in her hushed voice.

"Who knows how deep Chen's tentacles reach into the FBI, or elsewhere in government! Butler's in the wind now, and who knows where he'll end up—somewhere else in the world with a new identity, or maybe even floating in the Potomac. Let's just say I've got a few people I think I can still trust in the NSA and Homeland Security, and leave it at that."

"Mum's the word, Ma'am, but you can bet I'll be keeping a close eye on him now!" Jordan promised.

Rachel's forehead and eyebrows wrinkled, conveying deep concern.

"Please be extremely careful! You and Nicole are loose ends that people like Chen like to eliminate. Too many journalists, like you, have died around the globe recently, trying to expose corruption."

"We'll be careful," Jordan replied. "But remember, he's got to be careful now too, given that we've exposed him for what he really is."

The last of the TV crew left the office, leaving Rachel and her guests alone. With the need for privacy now gone, Rachel straightened up and felt free to speak at her normal volume.

"Jordan, would you like to take some photos of me, Nicole, and Sam's team before they leave?"

"Of course. How about in front of your desk?"

"That would be perfect," Rachel replied.

Jordan arranged the team in a line in front of the Resolute Desk, with Rachel and Nicole in the middle, and the Oval Office window and the two flags framing the background, before taking a number of shots with her DSLR camera. With today's storm having left the region a few hours before, brilliant beams of scarlet and orange sunlight glowed around a few assorted clouds in the western sky behind them, providing the perfect backdrop for the photos and the end of a most eventful day.

CHAPTER 19—GEORGIAN BAY

TWO WEEKS later, the sound of Hunter's Harley echoed through the dense forest of cedar, birch, maple, and pine, as it rumbled and bounced along the gravel road, leaving a trail of dust behind it. Sam clung to Hunter as he navigated around sizeable potholes. The sun was just disappearing behind the tree line as the road widened into a parking lot outside an imposing two-storey log structure, that overlooked Georgian Bay in Northern Ontario.

As they stopped and dismounted, a final small cloud of dust caught up to Sam and Hunter and gradually settled over them. They stretched their limbs and looked around at the thick woodland that surrounded them. At the same time, they inhaled the fresh, fragrant air of the forest, still lush and green at the peak of summer. The sun was sinking lower over the water in the northwest, and they heard gentle waves washing lazily onto a small pebbly beach. The sound of loons drifted over the water, and the chirping of the evening's first crickets and a chorus of croaking frogs wafted from the forest.

Sam and Hunter took each other by the hand and made their way towards the lodge. As they approached, a middle-aged Indigenous woman emerged and hurried down the steps, then ran towards the couple.

"Boozhoo, I'm so glad you're finally here!" Rose called out excitedly.

She and Sam greeted each other with a long embrace, rocking back and forth in each others' arms.

"I'm so happy to see you! I missed you so much!" Sam replied. "And my butt's sure glad to be here too. It's definitely not used to riding that far!"

Rose released her grip on Sam, then she reached for Hunter and wrapped her arms around him.

"Thank you for coming," she said into his ear, before the pair released each other. "This is your first time at the lodge, isn't it?"

"That's right," he answered. "When I came up for Sam's Dad's funeral, I only saw the community centre. It's so peaceful and beautiful here. I see why it's so special and so healing for Sam, and for everybody else who comes here to heal."

"You got here just in time to watch the sunset," Rose said. "Follow me."

She led the way to the beach while Sam and Hunter followed, hand-in-hand. When they neared the water, they stopped on the beach, where a number of large logs had been arranged in a half-moon pattern around a fire pit.

"I'll start a fire," Hunter offered, as Rose and Sam sat beside each other on one of the logs. "It'll help keep the mosquitos down."

The two women watched, their arms wrapped around each other's waist, as Hunter gathered the necessary grasses and kindling, lit a small flame, added some smaller sticks, and let the flames grow. He then walked over to a nearby woodpile for some larger logs. Rose squeezed Sam's hand.

"I'm so proud of you and your friends!" she said. "And I'm so grateful you're all safe. You're famous now!"

"Thanks," Sam answered, her face blushing self-consciously. "It's weird. People recognize us wherever we go now. I still can't believe it all happened."

"You were all over the news here. The whole country is proud of you too!"

Rose took a moment to gaze at her favourite niece.

"You look healthy. How is your anxiety, especially after what happened in Virginia?"

"Amazingly, once we started meeting with the protesters, my initial jitters settled down. The four of us believed in each other, and we believed in our plan. That helped a lot. But, I admit, there *were* times when I lost my self-confidence. That's when I realized I needed to talk to you, or to Hunter, to get me back on track again."

Hunter had the fire growing in height and intensity. He added one last length of firewood to the flames, then stepped back to admire his work. At the same time, Rose reached into a bag and produced some sage and a large shell.

"Shall we smudge?"

"Sure," Sam answered.

"We'd love to," Hunter added.

Rose held out a sprig of sage towards the fire, until a glowing orange ember eventually appeared. She placed it on the shell and stood in front of the young couple.

"Let us thank The Creator for taking care of Sam, Hunter, and their friends while they were away. And thanks also for bringing Sam and Hunter to this peaceful, healing space."

Rose carefully waved her hand and wisps of smoke flowed over Sam's torso, face, and head. She repeated the procedure for Hunter before completing the ritual on herself. Finally, she snuffed the smouldering sage and set it aside.

"So, what are your plans," she continued, "now that the excitement is over?"

"We just want to get back to living our lives again," Hunter replied. He looked at Sam and smiled at her. She returned the smile and took his hand.

"We've talked a lot since we left Washington," Sam added. "We've decided we want to give it a shot at being together."

Rose raised her eyebrows, nodded approvingly, and smiled.

"I'm happy for both of you!" she gushed, taking Sam's hand and reaching across Sam to take Hunter's with her other hand. They sat watching the flames dance in front of them. The sun finally slipped below the horizon, and the blue sky above them took on a darker, navy hue. Venus flickered in the west and the evening's first stars twinkled overhead.

"Tell me all about it," Rose asked. "It's a big step for you, Sam. You seem so much more confident now—about Hunter, I mean. What's changed for you?"

"Well, Hunter's graduating soon, and I asked him to move to Saskatoon so we can live together."

"I found a law firm in the city that's excited about having me," Hunter added. "Their firm's been looking for somebody who wants to specialize in Indigenous issues."

"And I think I've gotten over a lot of my fears, especially while we were in Washington." Sam continued. "Remember after I found out that Dad was Indigenous? When I told you that I felt like I was starting to see the world through two sets of eyes?"

"Of course," Rose said. "I remember it like it was yesterday."

"Well, now I think those two sets of eyes have merged and become integrated. I feel whole: like I'm seeing the world fully in three dimensions, and like I truly belong here in the world now. I'm more confident and less anxious, especially about being rejected or abandoned. That part of me seems much more distant now, like it was somebody else."

Hunter chuckled and smiled at Sam.

"When you were our night class instructor, you were so anxious that it seemed like you were even afraid of your own shadow!"

"I think I was," Sam answered, before laughing along with Hunter. "Literally, I had the worst possible imposter syndrome back then. But our experience in Washington last month taught me that I'm not an imposter anymore. I feel validated. I fully believe now that I can make a difference wherever I go, or whatever I do!"

"Why do you think President Williams contacted you?" Rose asked. "What did she see in you after reading *The Night Class* that caused her to believe in you?"

"She told me that she saw me as a real 'fish out of water' as she read the book, and that she identified with me because she felt the same," Sam replied. "I can see that now: being a black woman in a traditionally white male job—one that she never really expected to find herself in—second-guessing whether or not she had the ability to do it."

"The world sometimes works in weird and wonderful ways," Hunter commented.

Only a faint hint of the setting sun remained detectible on the northwestern horizon. The overhead sky was now black, and the Milky Way was visible through the pristine northern atmosphere. The threesome fell silent for a moment while they gazed and took in the majestic sight. Rose squeezed Sam's hand again.

"Your father would be so proud of you, if only he was still here! I'm sure his spirit, and those of our ancestors, are looking down on you right now."

A tear escaped from Rose's eye, and Sam's eyes watered as well. Sam took Hunter's hand in hers, so that she was now holding hands with both Hunter and Rose.

"If all goes well," Sam said, "I'll be able to defend my thesis next spring. But I learned something about myself in Washington. After I graduate, I want to switch my focus to Community Psychology: applying psychological knowledge to help resolve important social issues and to help communities of people. I see clearly now that I'm a social activist at heart. And I'm unbelievably lucky that a phone call from the President of the United States helped me to see that, and to see where I want my future to take me."

"It's getting chilly," Rose observed. "I'll get some blankets to cover our legs."

"I'll help," Sam added.

They got up and went to a large storage box beside the woodpile, from which Rose extracted three handcrafted blankets adorned with Indigenous designs, handing two of them to Sam. They took them back to their log and settled back in beside Hunter, with their legs now protected from the evening chill. The trio paused for a few moments, enjoying the sound of the crackling fire, the chirping of crickets, and the near-magical vista in the celestial sky above them.

"It warms my heart to see that both of you are discovering your life paths," Rose said, sighing.

"Who knows where the journey's going to take us," Hunter added, squeezing Sam's hand.

"Who knows," Sam echoed. "But I'm glad I'll have you two by my side along the way."

CONSTITUTION AVENUE

EPILOGUE—COMPLICATED SHADOWS

ATTIRED IN running gear, the young olive-skinned woman with short black hair jogged effortlessly up the stairs of her uptown D.C. Airbnb rental. She ascended two flights as if she had springs in her legs, despite the significant weight of her backpack, which was stuffed with books, her iPhone, and her laptop computer. Puffing only slightly when she reached the third floor, she slowed to scan the entire corridor. Satisfied that she hadn't been followed or observed, she approached her apartment door and inserted her key in the lock.

Once inside the small bachelor suite, she turned on the lights and allowed the backpack to slide from her shoulders, before slinging it onto a couch that also served as her foldout bed. Finally, she walked over to the TV, switched on CNN, and went to the fridge for a cold bottle of Perrier. After taking a long, satisfying swig of the sparkling water, she reached into the freezer and extracted a box containing a small frozen dinner, which went straightaway into a small microwave. While she waited for the meal to heat, she took the bottle of Perrier and allowed herself to drop onto the couch.

Her eyes roamed the small apartment. Although the building had a heritage designation, the apartments were all recently renovated to maintain their original character, but with up-to-date kitchens, appliances, and individual air conditioning units. The faint odour of sawdust and new construction still lingered in the space, and she considered herself lucky to be its first post-renovation tenant.

"Thank God I had AC during that heat dome back in July," she said to herself. "It would have been like an oven in here without it!"

In the background, the sound of President Rachel Williams' voice drifted from the TV, bringing the young woman out of her brief reverie.

... and although the two major parties, as well as many of the states, are still far apart on the makeup of a Constitutional Convention, and on the rules for choosing delegates, I'm still confident that we can reach an acceptable compromise in the next couple of months ...

"I gotta remember that my goal wasn't for Williams to try amending or rebuilding the Constitution," she said to herself. "I only needed her to bring Sam and her team to Washington so they could meet each other and work together—and be credible. That was an important part of the plan. But, the key part was saving Jordan and Nicole for the next phase. I made just enough of a difference, but not too much. That would've been too dangerous."

A gurgling in her stomach brought her back to the present. She walked back to the dinette, sat down, and tested her food's temperature before starting to eat in earnest. But her brain continued to roam while she wolfed down her dinner. In her mind, she revisited the wealth of recent news events from around the world that she'd studied, as well as all of the historical research she'd gathered over the past three months, especially those critical documents in the Smithsonian and other museums in Washington, Virginia, and Philadelphia.

"If I'm going to have any chance of succeeding in the long run," she continued, "It's going to come down to the fine details ... the devil's always in those damned details! I've accomplished all I can here in Washington, so time to move forward into phase two."

She finished off the last of her small meal, along with the rest of the Perrier, then she went to the fridge again. Apart from three more bottles of Perrier, half a container of almond milk, and one lone apple, she'd virtually used up the fridge's contents in anticipation of moving on. She removed the apple, washed it, took a bite, and then returned to the couch, where she opened her backpack and cleaned out its contents: the laptop, her phone, and a half-dozen books, including her copies of Sam Bower's *The Night Class* and Thomas Paine's *The Age of Reason*.

She paused and picked up her dog-eared copy of *The Age of Reason*, Thomas Paine's thesis on religion, and opened it to its Table of Contents.

"Thomas, you thought you could get people to see through their superstitions by appealing to logic and reason," she said to herself. "And we're still making the same mistake today. Mankind's thinking has been, and always will be, ruled by their emotional attachment to their existing beliefs. You thought it was your logic that helped the Colonies see the need for independence, but it was really the frustrations and the emotions of the day that gave the independence movement its momentum."

She flipped the book back onto the couch.

"So this time around, we're not going to make the same mistake," she said. "We're going to do something that scares the bejesus out of humanity—something that terrifies them into seeing reason and the need to let go of their self-destructive ways."

She sat down and made herself comfortable in a lotus position on the couch, then opened her laptop, booted it up, and proceeded to research air fares and train schedules for Italy. Within minutes, she'd managed to book a flight from Washington to Rome for the next day, along with some rail tickets from Rome to Cinque Terre, on Italy's west coast, and a bed and breakfast room in Manarola. That done, she turned her attention to confirming the dates for the upcoming UN Climate Change Conference in Barcelona. Finally, she booked an Airbnb in Barcelona for the duration of the conference. With those tasks completed, she shut down the laptop and connected it to its charger. She leaned back against the couch and munched on her apple while she ran through her mental checklist one last time.

I don't think I've missed anything. Just need to go to the safe deposit box for my passport and some cash. And my other phone. I've got to guard it with my life. If I lose *it*, along with all my research and videos, I'm finished—and so is everybody else on the planet!

* * *

ABOUT THE AUTHOR

David Alex Jones is a retired Clinical Psychologist who lives in Ontario, Canada. In his writing, he has combined his understanding of human identity and personality, his passion for helping victims of trauma, abuse, and Post-traumatic Stress Disorder, and his love of reading fiction, to create a unique brand of psychological suspense and political commentary. His writing is rich in complex characters and controversial social issues, resulting in an abundance of internal and interpersonal conflict, dysfunction, and tension. Dave enjoys spending time with his wife and grandchildren, as well as enjoying travel, photography, and brewing craft-beer that pairs perfectly with reading a great book. He also admits to being a reality TV geek, especially when it comes to watching "Survivor", "The Mole", or "The Traitors!"

DAVID ALEX JONES

DON'T MISS OUT

Visit David Alex Jones' website, where you can sign up to receive emails whenever he publishes a new book. There's no sign-up charge and no obligation.

http://www.davidalexjones.com

SNEAK PEEK

Did you enjoy *Constitution Avenue*? Then you should read
The Night Class by David Alex Jones

THE NIGHT CLASS is a coming of age drama, the story of Samantha (Sam) Bower, a young university teaching assistant, who is studying hard to make a career for herself as a psychologist, while also struggling to overcome the trauma of a childhood of abuse and abandonment, and navigating a journey of self-discovery. The main story is set within the current social context of recent Residential School revelations and Canada's need for addressing Truth and Reconciliation with its Indigenous Peoples. The secondary story is a love/hate relationship between two of the story's main characters: Hunter, a young Indigenous student, and Terri, a middle-age Caucasian woman who has returned to university as an adult student.

Read more at DavidAlexJones.com.

DAVID ALEX JONES

ALSO BY DAVID ALEX JONES

The Survivor Trilogy

Walls (Book One)
Faces (Book Two)
Spirits (Book Three)
Angela's Eyes (Prequel)

The Survivor Trilogy (eBook Collection)

Standalone

The Night Class

Watch for more at DavidAlexJones.com.